THE SEA MARK

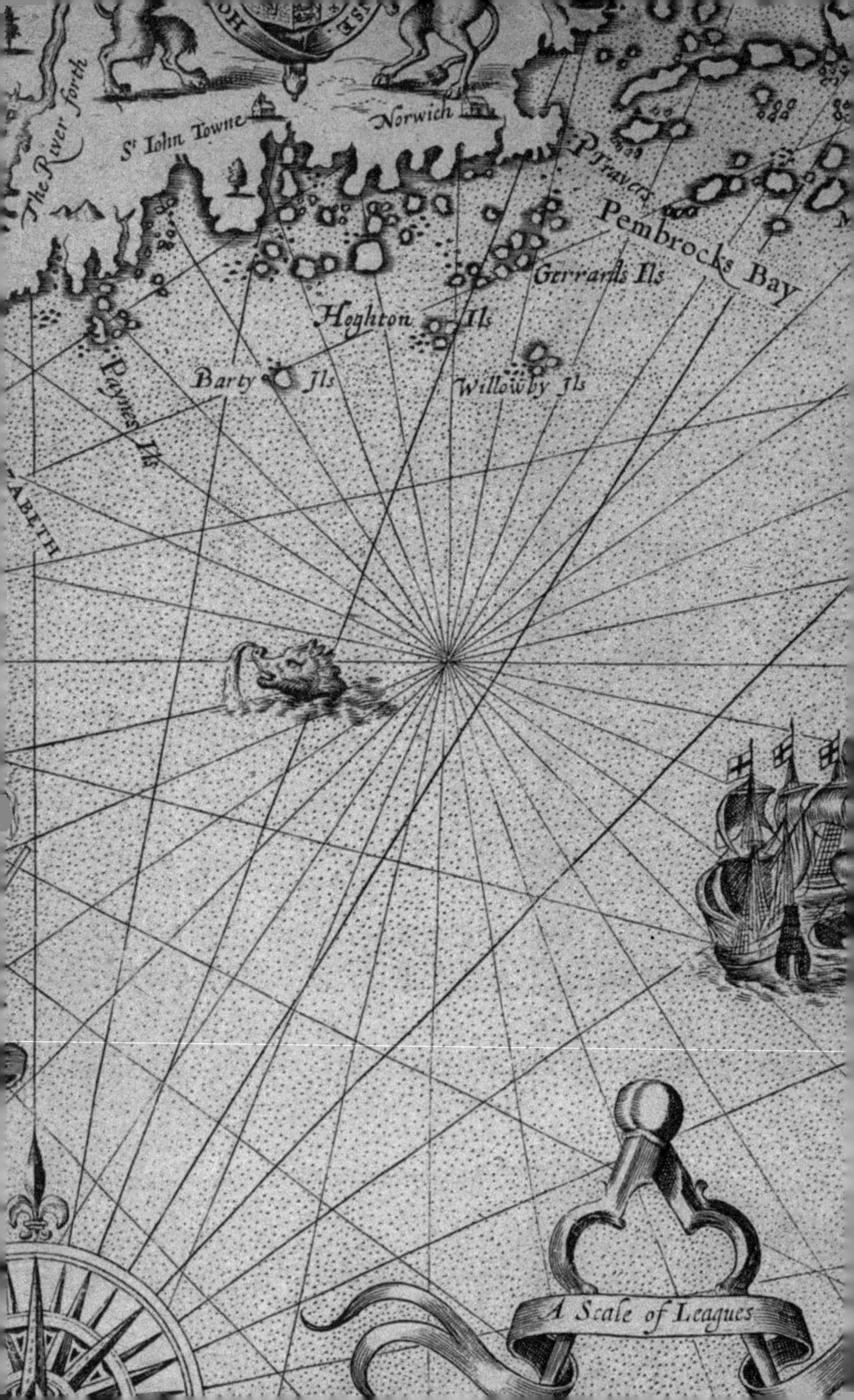

The River forth
St Iohn Towne
Norwich
P. Travers
Pembrocks Bay
Gerrards Ils
Hoghton Ils
Barty Jls
Willowby Jls
Paynes Ils
A Scale of Leagues

RUSSELL M. LAWSON

The SEA MARK

CAPTAIN JOHN SMITH'S VOYAGE TO NEW ENGLAND

University Press of New England ✤ Hanover and London

University Press of New England
www.upne.com

Manufactured in the United States of America
Designed by Mindy Basinger Hill
Typeset in Adobe Caslon Pro

Library of Congress Cataloging-in-Publication Data

Lawson, Russell M., 1957–
The sea mark: Captain John Smith's voyage to New England / Russell M. Lawson.
pages cm
ISBN 978-1-61168-516-9 (cloth: alk. paper) — ISBN 978-1-61168-717-0 (ebook)
1. Smith, John, 1580–1631—Travels—New England.
2. New England—Discovery and exploration. 3. New England—Description and travel.
I. Title. II. Title: Captain John Smith's voyage to New England.
III. Title: Description of New England, or, Observations and discoveries in the north of America in the year of Our Lord 1614.
F7.L43 2015
973.21092—dc23 2014034436

5 4 3 2 1

FRONTISPIECE: The coast of Maine, from John Smith's *Map of New England*, published in 1616. American Memory, Library of Congress.

THIS BOOK IS DEDICATED

TO THE MEMORY OF

Charles Edwin Clark

The New England cod was the premier fish, the harvest of which John Smith hoped would provide a foundation for a fishing colony in New England. NOAA Historic Fisheries Collection.

The Images of

great things are best

discerned, contracted

into small glasses.

✣ ✣ ✣

JOHN SMITH, *Advertisements for the unexperienced Planters of New-England*, 1631

CONTENTS

PREFACE

Captain John Smith, the English explorer and colonizer, is one of the most famous of early Americans. His relationship with the Indian princess Pocahontas has become legendary, propelling Smith forward in time into biographies and histories, novels and children's books, films, musicals, music theater, and art, much of which is fabulous and fictional. During the late twentieth and early twenty-first centuries, Hollywood epics of his purported romance with Pocahontas, and celebrations and historical re-creations during the commemoration of Jamestown's four-hundredth anniversary in 2007, added to the popular fame of this Englishman who spent less than three years in America, who never returned after 1614, and who has been dead and buried in England for 384 years. Why the continuing fascination with this man? Mostly it is because of Smith himself, who wrote nine books over the course of his life, in most of which the author is himself the central focus: his aims, exploits, courage, sufferings, misrepresentations by enemies, successes, and significance. Smith was, like many Jacobean soldiers and adventurers, very full of himself, and he had the wherewithal to write thousands of words of self-promotion and self-defense and go through the trouble of publishing and marketing his books.

I first became interested in Smith's life and work when I lived along the New England coast during the 1980s. I read Smith's works and began the process, in my mind, of re-creating the places he had been, which I supplemented by visiting many of those places in Maine, New Hampshire, and Massachusetts. Smith's books impressed me not so much with his arrogance and bragging as with his ability to describe America and his forthrightness. At the time, mid-1980s, I planned a book to re-create Smith's voyage and retell the story of his 1614 journey to New England. I put it off for a while, however, as it would require a technique of historical investigation and writing for which I was not quite ready. Smith, unlike Champlain and other notable explorers, did not provide a journal of his voyage—his journey and experiences are buried in works of promotional literature in which he focused on his aims and fame, and that of his country, England. To re-create such a journey would require not only research and study but intuition and empathy as well, which come with experience. Meanwhile I was at work on a Ph.D. in history at the University of New Hampshire, where I developed an initial approach to the type of history I had in mind, calling it *humanist history*.

Humanist history, as its name suggests, derived from my reading of the works of Renaissance humanist writers and thinkers, particularly Michel de Montaigne, the sixteenth-century French essayist. Montaigne's *Essays* revealed to me the true nature of historical writing: it involves the subject (self) interacting with the object (another human), bridging time between the present and the past by means of a dialogue initiated by the subject, who brings it self-consciously to the object. Montaigne did this with many people of the past, especially the ancient Greeks and Romans: Socrates, Epaminondas, Plutarch, Seneca, Cicero, Caesar, and others. Montaigne inspired me to engage in humanist history, that is, to develop a dialogue with a variety of past people, the results of some of which is published, though much is not. My first book—*The American Plutarch: Jeremy Belknap and the Historian's Dialogue with the Past*, established the technique for myself, which led to other books and other dialogues: *Passaconaway's Realm: Captain John Evans and the Exploration of Mount Washington*; *The Land Between the Rivers: Thomas Nuttall's Ascent of the Arkansas, 1819*; and *Frontier Naturalist: Jean Louis Berlandier and the Exploration of Northern Mexico and Texas*. *The Sea Mark: Captain John Smith's Journey to New England* is my newest bridging of time and place by means of the historian's dialogue with the past.

The key to recovering a past life is to become fully acquainted with the object of one's inquiry. In the case of Smith, since manuscript letters, diaries, or personal memorandums do not exist to provide us with an intimate look into his life, the historian is left with published works, in which Smith consciously sought to present a public image to English readers. Although published works are typically less revealing than private works, Smith was exceptionally frank and revealing in his books. The notion, common during the late nineteenth century, that Smith wrote fabulous accounts of his adventures has been overturned in the wake of Bradford Smith's *Captain John Smith* (1953), which includes an appendix by the Hungarian scholar Laura Polanyi Striker, and the work of Philip Barbour—*The Three Worlds of Captain John Smith* (1964) and his three-volume edition of *The Complete Works of Captain John Smith* (1986). These scholars showed beyond a doubt that Smith was not a liar—indeed, quite the contrary: sometimes he was too honest for his own good. The reader readily sees this quality of Smith's writing in his first work, published without his knowledge in 1608 in London, *A True Relation of such occurrences and accidents of noate as hath hapned in Virginia since the first planting of that Collony, which is now resident in the South part thereof, till the last returne from thence. A True Relation*, commonly called *News from Virginia*, provides an extensive, exciting account of the founding of the colony at Jamestown and the first two years of privation, exploration, and conflict. Smith revealed himself to be an excellent historical narrator of events; he was very matter-of-fact, honest to man and God, truthful of what the English did, unafraid to criticize leaders of the colony. He portrayed English and Indians engaging each other, fighting, deceiving, and struggling over the land. Smith's narrative is very descriptive of the landscape of the James River Valley and Chesapeake region, of Indian settlements, behavior, and customs. Smith described in detail his capture during the late fall and early winter of 1607–1608, and his interaction with Opechancanough and Powhatan: his recollection of his captivity, the people, places, landscape, and rivers he traversed and experienced, is remarkable, and shows the mind of a scientist who can recall with precision what he has observed. Smith, perhaps because of his journeys throughout Europe, was a quick student of languages and communicated with ease with his captors.[1]

Smith's subsequent works read very much the same. Smith was quick-witted, and he enjoyed humorous plays on words and, at times, soaring flights of rhetoric, but rarely at the expense of truth. *A Map of Virginia. With a Description of the Covntrey, the Commodities, People, Government and Religion*, published in 1612, describes the language, cul-

John Smith's drawings and notes taken during his voyages throughout the James River and Chesapeake regions in 1607 and 1608 became the bases for this engraved map, published with his *General History of Virginia/discovered and discribed by Captayn John Smith, 1606; graven by William Hole.* [London; 1624]. American Memory, Library of Congress.

ture, customs, society, and beliefs of the indigenous people as well as the natural productions and history of the James River and Chesapeake Bay. The book is more extensive in scope than *News from Virginia*, written by an intelligent observer and ad hoc scientist seeking knowledge about the human and natural history of America.[2]

In 1616 Smith published his first book describing the land he christened New England, based on a six-month voyage during the spring and summer of 1614. Smith confessed in the dedication of his book "to the Right Worshipfull Adventurers for the Countrey of New England in the Cities of London, Bristow, Exceter, Plimouth, Dartmouth, Bastable, Totneys, etc and in all other Cities and Ports, in the Kingdome of England" that "it were more proper for mee, To be doing what I say, then writing what I knowe." But happenstance had prevented his ultimate objective, the founding of a colony in New England. He felt compelled, as a result, "to expose my imbecillitie to contempt, by the testimonie of these rude lines," *A Description of New England: or the Observations, and discoueries, of Captain Iohn Smith (Admirall of that Country) in the North of America, in the year of our Lord 1614: with the successe of sixe Ships, that went the next yeare 1615; and the accidents befell him among the French men of warre: With the proofe of the present benefit this Countrey affoords: whither this present yeare, 1616, eight voluntary Ships are gone to make further tyrall.* The object of Smith's *Description of New England* was to find supporters for his ongoing plan to establish a fishing colony in America. As a result the account of his journey takes second place to the description of the land, coast, people, and natural productions, and the reasons by which a colony could be established.[3]

Smith followed up the *Description of New England* four years later in 1620 with another account of New England, *New Englands Trials*, to which two years later he added much more detail in a 1622 edition. *New Englands Trials* has much of the same information as *Description of New England* about Smith and his 1614 journey to New England, couched in an apologetic treatise through which he hoped to achieve the backing to found his long-desired fishing colony. "Thus betwixt the spur of Desire, and the bridle of Reason I am neare ridden to death in a ring of despaire; the raines are in your hands, therefore I entreate you to ease mee."[4]

Smith's pleas for sponsors went unheeded, however, so he turned increasingly to ink and quill to accomplish his aims, which were becoming more altruistic by necessity and inaction. In 1624 Smith published *The generall History of Virginia, the Somer Isles, and New England, with the names of the Aduenturers, and their aduentures. Also a Catalogue of their names who were the first Treasurers heere, and planters and Gouernours there; and how they have yeerely succeeded, from their first beginning 1584, to this present 1623, with the proceedings of these seuerall Colonies, and the accidents that befell them in all their iourneys and discoueries, with the Mappes and descriptions of those countries, commodities, people, gouernment, customes, and Religion yet knowne, for the generall good of all them who belong to those Plantations and all their posterities. Discouered, obserued, or collected by Captaine In. Smith sometime Gouernour of Virginia, and Admirall of New England.* The long and convoluted title reflects an extensive, often disorganized book, which is nevertheless Smith's greatest work in ambition and scope. Smith divided the *General History* into multiple sections outlining the English voyages of discovery during the reign of Elizabeth I; the history of Virginia from the founding of Jamestown to 1623, after the colony was almost destroyed by an Indian attack; the history of Bermuda, what had been called the Summer (or Somer) Isles; and *The General Historie of New-England*, consisting of parts of the *Description of New England* and *New Englands Trials*.[5]

During his last years Smith warmed to the task of writing about himself, other explorers, England, and the sea in general. In 1626 he published *An Accidence or The Path-way to Experience. Necessary for all Young Sea-men, or those that are desirous to goe to Sea, briefly shewing the Phrases, Offices, and Words of Command, Belonging to the Building, Ridging, and Sayling, a Man of Warre; And how to manage a Fight at Sea*, followed a year later by *A Sea Grammar, with the Plaine Exposition of Smiths Accidence for young Sea-men, enlarged.* These often confusing accounts of daily life aboard an English ship had little direct autobiographical information, unlike Smith's other works. Edward Arber, who published a full edition of Smith's works in 1884, wrote of the *Accidence* that it was a "new departure in [English] Literature, being the first printed book on seamanship, naval gunnery, and of nautical terms; and was besides written by an Army Captain." Smith's *Sea Grammar* continued his "new departure." Smith had taken to the sea, and wished to make his name as an authority on its human and natural history, and its conquest by England, resulting in an English empire in America.[6]

To these ends, expanding his fame and England's power, Smith published, in 1630, his autobiography, *The True Travels, Adventures and Observations of Captaine Iohn Smith, In Europe, Asia, Affrica, and America, from Anno Domini 1593 to 1629*. Smith provided, in an extensive subtitle, a full summary of what the book contained: "His Accidents and Sea-fights in the Straights; his Service and Stratagems of warre in *Hungaria*, *Transilvania*, *Wallachia*, and *Moldavia*, against the *Turks*, and *Tartars*; his three single combats betwixt the *Christian* Armie and the *Turkes*. After how he was taken prisoner by the *Turks*, sold for a Slave, sent into *Tartaria*; his description of the *Tartars*, their strange manners and customes of Religions, Diets, Buildings, Warres, Feasts, Ceremonies, and Living; how hee slew the Bashaw of *Nalbrits* in *Cambia*, and escaped from the *Turkes* and *Tartars*. Together with a continuation of his generall History of *Virginia, Summer-Iles, New England*, and their proceedings, since 1624. to this present 1629; as also of the new Plantations of the great river of the *Amazons*, the *Iles* of *St. Christopher*, *Mevis*, and *Barbados* in the *West Indies*." Even as Smith entered his fiftieth year, he was still asking for patronage to return again to America to make England's colonies economically and politically invincible. But he was left to lament his misfortune: "Those Countries Captaine Smith oft times used to call his children that never had mother; and well he might, for few fathers ever payed dearer for so little content."[7]

Smith's final book, published the year of his death, 1631, was *Advertisements for the unexperienced Planters of New-England, or any where. Or the Path-way to experience to erect a Plantation*. Smith referred to the *Advertisements* (as well as his other writings) as "memorandums" and "an Apology," words that succinctly sum up the true nature of his literary work. Smith's memorandums, though published, frequently appear as notes to himself and others written hastily on the way to a larger purpose, some final, unrealized goal. He believed that the hastiness, the lack of completeness, the as-yet-to-be-realized nature of his work and life deserved an apology to others, to self, to God.[8]

In the essay *Of Books*, Michel de Montaigne wrote that the best histories are those in which the historian provides firsthand accounts of past events, unadorned with needless interpretative digressions and opinionated commentary.[9] If Smith had left behind a straightforward account of his journey to New England, then perhaps it would trump the present book. But Smith did not; rather, he buried his New England experience in half a dozen books that require careful analysis as well as an intuitive dialogue to re-create the history I relate here in *The Sea Mark*.

This book is dedicated to the memory of Charles E. Clark (1929–2013). It was under his tutelage that I first began to conceive of a book on John Smith. Professor Clark introduced me to the Massachusetts Historical Society, and since then, repeated visits to the Society have helped me amass much direct and indirect data with which to understand John Smith. The staffs and resources of other repositories of knowledge have helped as well: University of New Hampshire, University of Oklahoma, Oklahoma State University, Oklahoma School of Science and Mathematics, Bacone College, Brock University. The administration of Bacone College has supported my research and writing endeavors over the past decade and a half. My initial ideas for Smith's role as *commissioner* developed during my time as a Fulbright Scholar, beginning in 2010 when I was Visiting Fulbright Research Chair in Transnational Studies at Brock University in St. Catharines, Ontario. A research grant from the Historical Society of the Episcopal Church also helped to crystallize my thinking. I wish to thank Stephen P. Hull of the University Press of New England for his help and insights. As always, I would like to thank my family for their support, and particularly my wife Linda Phillips Lawson.

THE SEA MARK

ONE

The Sea Mark

It was a pleasant late summer day, the gentle zephyr coming off the water smelling fresh and the few clouds lazily wafting by. The sun's heat upon the cold water created a haze that settled upon the sea, obscuring the distant shore. Nathaniel Hawthorne was in the second week of a visit to the Isles of Shoals, eight small islands off the coast of Maine and New Hampshire that in 1852 were becoming a place for tourists and vacationers and the curious. Hawthorne was fresh from writing a biography of his friend Franklin Pierce, the Democratic nominee for president; Pierce was to join Hawthorne at the Isles of Shoals for a brief time to enjoy the atmosphere of the sea. The islands were jagged rocks seemingly thrust from the ocean floor in the distant past. Few plants grew on the rocks, which were regularly skimmed by the ocean winds. The largest island, Appledore, had a hotel run by the former lighthouse keeper Thomas Laighton. His daughter, Celia Laighton Thaxter, and her husband, Levi Thaxter, lived on the island, as did a few fishermen and their families. Upon Hawthorne's arrival on August 30, 1852, Levi Thaxter adopted him as a friend and the two men spent a fortnight exploring Appledore as well as some of the other islands—Star, White, Londoner's, Smuttynose. Remarkable characters, past and present, fascinated Hawthorne, as did ghosts, of which the Isles of Shoals had plenty. Remains of the human and natural past surrounded the islanders, and Hawthorne.

After dinner on the first day, Thaxter and Hawthorne strolled about Appledore. They came to "a monument of rude stones, on the highest point of the island, said to have been erected by Captain John Smith before the settlement at Plymouth." The monument intrigued Hawthorne, who investigated it further on another hot, still day, a little over a week

This photograph of Hawthorne was taken a few years after his visit to the Isles of Shoals in 1852. American Memory, Library of Congress.

Appledore is the largest of the islands that make up the Isles of Shoals off the coast of Maine and New Hampshire. American Memory, Library of Congress.

later. From the cairn, all the islands, the surrounding sea, and headlands on shore were visible. "Smith's monument is about seven feet high," he wrote in his journal, "and probably ten or twelve in diameter at its base." Laighton informed him that locals knew it had existed for aeons; Hawthorne thought Smith himself had built it, being "more likely [to] have been erected by one who supposed himself the first discoverer of the island than by anybody afterwards for mere amusement." Even so, there was no way to be sure; but "the tradition is just as good as truth."[1]

There could be no better epitaph for John Smith than Hawthorne's passing comment. What is fact and what is fiction in John Smith's life has been debated for four hundred years. A trained soldier and ad hoc sailor, a self-taught man with little schooling, nevertheless Smith wrote nine books between 1608 and 1631. He wove the themes of his books—adventure, action, warfare, colonization, conquest, suffering, and eventual success—into a self-aggrandizing narrative in which he bragged of his exploits, lamented his sacrifices, portrayed himself as a selfless soldier for England and God, and unrelentingly argued that the future of England's wealth and power depended upon the work of one man—Captain John Smith. Even among the other braggarts of Jacobean England, Smith's immodest tales of his own heroics raised eyebrows, elicited jealousy, and won him enemies. Smith, in many of his later works, such as *The General History of Virginia* (1624), *The True Travels, Adventures and Observations of Captaine Iohn Smith* (1630), and *Advertisements for the unexperienced Planters of New-England, or any where* (1631), wrote elaborate self-defenses, disclaimers, and apologies for his actions and proposals. Some of his stories—such as his successive victory over three Turkish warriors, whom he beheaded, over three days in 1602, and his rescue from certain death by the Indian princess Pocahontas in 1607—appeared so amazing, so romantic, as to invite incredulity. As a result, since John Smith's death in 1631, some people have lauded him as the savior of Virginia, the greatest founder of the English colonies in America, while others have seen him as a liar whose significance is questionable in light of the truth.

One of the former was a missionary of the Society for Propagating the Gospel, George Beebe, who served the fishermen at the Isles of Shoals as a preacher, physician, and teacher during the 1850s and 1860s. Beebe, believing that Smith's stone monument on Appledore was an insufficient tribute to the discoverer of the Isles of Shoals, solicited the help of another clergyman, the Unitarian Daniel Austin of Kittery, Maine, who unlike Beebe had the funds to match Beebe's energy; the two men collaborated to erect a monument to Smith on Star Island in 1864 to commemorate the 250th anniversary of Smith's voyage. Little is known today about Beebe and Austin, and one can only guess at their motives for such an ambitious project as to decorate a desolate island with a large inscribed pillar made of granite, adorned on the top with stone carvings of the heads of three Turkish warriors. From its granite base the pillar rose seven feet; those few who dared the winds and waves and desolation of Star Island to make the visit could read inscriptions that encapsulated the life of John Smith.[2]

Inscribed "on the first side" of the pillar was the following:

> John Smith was born at Willoughby, Lincolnshire, England, in 1579, and died in London, in 1631, aged 52. He was "Governor of Virginia," and subsequently "Admiral of New England." The Isles, properly called "Smith's Isles," were discovered by him in April, 1614, while with 8 others in an open boat he was exploring the coast from Penobscot to Cape Cod.[3]

The visitor, looking beyond the pillar to the sea, waves churning and dashing against the rocks of Star Island, might wonder of the courage of such a man, who sailed the shoal-ridden waters in an open boat, unprotected from the elements of the cold Atlantic. He was a long way from home, Lincolnshire on England's northeast coast, where George and Alice Smith, small tenant-farmers, baptized their son John into the Church of England and provided a rudimentary grammar school education. Smith's real learning came not from books, rather the world; George and Alice raised John to believe that fortune was out of reach to those without the courage and will to make themselves more than their birthright. Smith learned how to learn quickly; to teach himself to fight and survive; to think on his feet and to act quickly; to gain the upper hand on a sluggish foe; to be relentless in advocating himself and his interests; to leave little to chance and only reluctantly to yield to the will of God.

The pillar, which stood at the southern extreme of Star Island, recorded the odd fact that the farm boy became in time one of the founders of the Jamestown colony in Virginia. Visitors, looking in their mind's eye south past White Island, past Cape Ann and Cape Cod, beyond the hundreds of miles to Virginia's coast and the James River, might have questioned how one man in such a brief lifetime of fifty-one years could embrace two different worlds, those of Virginia and New England, serving as governor of one and admiral of the other. Smith's time in America, however brief, involved exploring, conquering, and colonizing—Virginia from 1607 to 1609, and New England in 1614. He came to the former as part of the London Company, investors and adventurers who sought to make an easy profit in Virginia by mining for gold and finding a passage to the Orient while relying upon the native inhabitants for food. Smith, who lived at a time when social ranks separated the betters from their inferiors, sought to impose his opinions and will upon such persons of rank as Edward Maria

Wingfield, a soldier during the Elizabethan years who helped to found the company and who served for a time as president (or governor) of the colony. Imprisoned aboard ship for insubordination, Smith won release, then renown upon the arrival of the colonists to the inhospitable James River. Smith was most adept among the colonists at negotiating with the natives for food, and showed himself a match for Wahunsenacawh, whom Smith called simply Powhatan, the wily and resourceful leader of the Algonquian Powhatan Indians of the James River Valley. As men of rank around him lost heart or died, Smith rose to be president of the colony, organizing the defenses of the fort at Jamestown, forcing the hungry soldiers to work, providing sufficient food to guarantee survival. Smith, a man possessed with restless energy, was the most able explorer among the Jamestown colonists, rowing and sailing a small shallop throughout the Chesapeake Bay and its tributaries, mapping the landscape, meeting with the local Algonquian tribes, learning their customs and language. Chance rather than choice forced his return to England: in 1609 he was horribly burned by gunpowder. He departed for England leaving the colony with sufficient order to survive.

Not only a governor but an admiral as well: Smith was not born a mariner, rather a soldier, but his many adventures taught him the ways of the sea, and he became an outspoken proponent of establishing fishing colonies on America's northeast coast; his activities exploring, writing, planning, and promoting the maritime power of England compelled adventurers with the Plymouth Company of western England to grant Smith the title Admiral of New England. The title meant little in terms of power and wealth, and Smith's attempts to lead expeditions to New England largely failed. But he became the most energetic supporter of the colonization of New England, a man of vision who inspired others, such as the Pilgrims of Plymouth and the Puritans of Massachusetts, to establish their colonies in 1620 and 1630.

Inscribed "on the second side" of the pillar was the following:

> Capt. John Smith was one of "nature's noblemen." In his generosity toward the public he almost forgot himself. Those who knew him best loved him most, and say of him: "In all his proceedings he made virtue his first guide, and experience his second. Despising baseness, sloth, pride, and indignity,

> more than any dangers, he would never allow more for himself than for his soldiers, and to no dangers would he expose them which he would not share himself. He would never see any in want of what he had, or could get for them; he would rather want than borrow, or starve than not pay; he loved action more than words, and hated covetousness and falsehood more than death. His adventures were for their lives and his loss was their death."

Daniel Austin, who chose to remain anonymous on the pillar, though known as the "Erector," and George Beebe, who called himself "Supervisor," selected for the second side a long quote from Smith's second publication, the 1612 *Map of Virginia*, which, like the much more extensive *General History of Virginia*, includes long sections written by others; in this case the quote transcribed onto the pillar came from two of his comrades at Jamestown, William Phettiplace (Fettiplace) and Richard Pots (Potts), who were lamenting Smith's injury that forced his return to England in 1609. Smith, like many of the greatest commanders in history, including Julius Caesar, to whom Smith was often compared, refused to take advantage of the subordination of his men, sharing with them the work, suffering, and danger; he dealt with all, soldiers as well as Indians, forthrightly, without deception; and he put the success of the settlement and the protection of his men above his own comfort and safety. The accounts of the soldiers in *Map of Virginia* reveal that although Smith arrived at the James River under suspicion, "yet so wel he demeaned himselfe in this busines, as all the company did see his innocencie, and his adversaries malice. . . . Many vntruthes were alleaged against him; but being so apparently disproved begat a general hatred in the h[e]arts of the company against such vnjust commanders." After the challenging summer months of 1607, and the deaths of many, the men and leaders were driven to such despair as to give ad hoc command to Smith, "who, by his owne example, good words, and faire promises, set some to mow, others to binde thatch; some to build houses, others to thatch them; himselfe alwaies bearing the greatest taske for his own share: so that, in short time, he provided most of them lodgings, neglecting any for himselfe."[4]

Hereafter, during the fall of 1607, Smith explored the region, trading successfully with the native inhabitants for corn; his success resulted in several attempts by his detractors to flee and abandon the colony, which

Smith prevented. Searching for food by canoe with two men, he was in December captured and brought to Powhatan. "Many strange triumphes and coniurations [conjurations] they made of him: yet hee so demeaned himselfe amongst them, as he not only diverted them from surprising the Fort; but procure[d] his owne liberty, and got himselfe and his company such estimation among them, that those Salvages admired him as a demi-God." As a result the Indians provided the English with food, and at the same time, January 1608, a ship arrived from England with supplies and men. Smith was chief diplomat as well, bringing the English captain Christopher Newport to the Indian town of Werowocomoco to meet with Powhatan, and preventing "ambuscadoes" and other mischief from the Indians with firm dealing and unrelenting, though not always deadly, force. Even so, the winter was deadly to the colonists, notwithstanding Smith's efforts to feed them and prevent so much energy and toil being put forth to find nonexistent gold.[5]

During the summer of 1608, Smith commanded a shallop and at least a dozen men to explore Chesapeake Bay. He journeyed twice, from June to July and July to September, exploring the eastern and western shores of the bay. On the first voyage he sailed far up the Potomac River, and ascended the Patapsco and Nanticoke rivers as well. On his second voyage he reached the northern head of the Chesapeake and the mouth of the Susquehanna River, where he and his crew met the local Susquehanna people, and explored other major tributaries of the Chesapeake, such as the Rappahannock, Patuxent, and Plankatank rivers. He made contact with many tribes, became friends and trading partners with some, and fought with others. He and his men suffered from lack of food and water and from the storms of the Chesapeake; Smith also almost died after being stung by a stingray. According to *Map of Virginia*, Smith constantly had to rally his men as they headed into the unknown. They discovered no workable mines, and no route to the Pacific Ocean, rather a plentiful land and warlike people, to whom the English attempted to impart their Christian faith by words and actions.[6]

Inscribed "on the third side" of the pillar was the following:

> In reward of his valor, the Prince of Transylvania presented to Capt. John Smith his picture, set in gold, gave him 300 ducats, and granted him a coat

of arms, having three Turks' heads in a shield with the motto: "Vincere est Vivere." In 1627 he says: "I have spent 5 years and more than 500 pounds in the service of Virginia and New Hampshire, but in neither have I one foot of land nor the very house I built with my own hands, and am compelled to see those countries shared before me among those who know them only by my descriptions." Consideration of the interesting facts of his life has led to the erection of this monument.[7]

This inscription on side three includes a free rendering of passages from book 4 of Smith's *General History of Virginia*. Smith used the *General History*, his longest and most ambitious work, for self-vindication, to solicit reward for his sacrifices, to guarantee that his work on behalf of England and America would be remembered, to promote what he believed to be England's true interest, the establishment of overseas colonies, to contribute toward the Christianizing of the American Indians, and to provide a complete natural and human history of the English exploration of America. As in *Map of Virginia*, Smith intermixed, often indiscriminately, his own narrative with that of others. The *General History*, however, is much grander in scale, encompassing more time, more people, more lands. Smith considered himself the protégé of Thomas Hariot, the mathematician and scientist who in 1585 had accompanied the Grenville voyage, sponsored by Walter Raleigh, to Roanoke Island, off the coast of North Carolina. Hariot wrote *A Briefe and True Report of the New Found Land of Virginia, of the Commodities and of the Nature and Manners of the Naturall Inhabitants: Discouered bÿ the English Colony there seated by Sir Richard Greinuile Knight In the yeere 1585*. Smith's *General History* and other works were successful attempts to imitate Hariot's scientific, ethnological study of the Roanoke Indians and their lands. Hariot, though not a priest, conversed with the native Algonquians about their religious beliefs and tried to impart his knowledge of Anglicanism in turn. Christianity and the Bible fascinated them: "Manie times and in euery towne where I came," Hariot wrote, "according as I was able, I made declaration of the contentes of the Bible; that therein was set foorth the true and onelie GOD, and his mightie woorkes, that therein was contayned the true doctrine of saluation through Christ, which manie particularities of Miracles and chiefe poyntes of religion, as I was able then to vtter, and thought fitte for the time. And although I told them the booke materially & of itself was not of anie such vertue, as I thought they did conceiue, but onely the doctrine therein contained; yet would many be glad to touch it, to embrace it, to kisse it, to hold it to their brests and heades, and stroke ouer all their bodie with it; to shew their hungrie desire of that knowledge which was spoken of."[8]

Likewise Smith, not a priest but one of "nature's noblemen" (in the words of the inscription side two), believed that he owed the indigenous people of America much more than the sword. The *General History*, Smith wrote in the opening lines of his book, "humbly sheweth the truth; that our most royall King James hath place and opportunitie to inlarge his ancient Dominions without wronging any; (which is a condition most agreeable to his most just and pious resolutions:) and the Prince his Highness may see where to plant new Colonies. The gaining Provinces addeth to the Kings Crown: but the reducing Heathen people to civilitie and true Religion, bringeth honour to the King of Heaven."[9]

Smith believed that he was not only a conqueror and a colonizer but a commissioner as well: a conqueror who would "reduce heathen people," a colonizer who would "plant new colonies," and a commissioner who would "bringeth honour to the King of Heaven." Conquest, colonization, and commission, he argued, were "just and pious" works that, rather than "wronging any," would bring "civilitie and true Religion." Smith argued, in short, that the work of conquest and colonization was the work of the Great Commission, which was the commandment that Jesus of Nazareth gave to his disciples, as recorded in the Gospel of Matthew, to "Go ye into all the world, and preach the gospel to every creature."[10] God directed the English to conquer and colonize a land already inhabited. But in so doing they did not wrong anyone because in carrying out the Great Commission they were carrying out God's will, which could not, Smith reasoned, be wrong or evil. God's will was that the English spread the Gospel to people hitherto ignorant of Christ, thereby bringing Good News of peace, happiness, love, and life to a people, it was presumed, who did not have them, and bringing as well a new culture, a civilization that far surpassed the sylvan culture of the American Indian. Smith's assumption, like those of his contemporaries in Jacobean England, was that civilizing a people went hand in hand with Christianizing a people.

For John Smith, adventure rather than thoughtful metaphysics was the best way to conform to God's will. Action more than passivity contributed to God's kingdom on earth. Smith, like many thinkers of the English Renaissance, believed that to glorify man was to glorify God. It was the human duty to discover and make fruitful what God had created. Human destiny was wrapped up in God's will and Creation. Smith's will, the human will, should conform to God's will. The characteristics that Smith described as the most important to be a conqueror, colonizer, and commissioner were "art, iudgement, courage, honestie, constancy, diligence and industry."[11] What humans were doing interacting with the Creation was great and wonderful. Humanity and human civilization were elevated by interacting with God's will and Creation.

Smith saw in Algonquian culture the interest in, worship of, and ability to survive in God's creation. They lacked only the Gospel, he thought. In Virginia, Smith and his men attempted to convince the American Indians of the truth of the Christian God. "Our order was daily to have Prayer," he wrote, "with a Psalme, at which solemnitie the poore Salvages much wondered." "To divert them from . . . [their] blind Idolatry," Smith and his companions "did our best endevours, chiefly with the Werowance of Quiyoughcohanock, whose devotion, apprehension, and good disposition, much exceeded any in those Countries, with whom although we could not as yet prevaile, to God as much exceeded theirs, as our Gunnes did their Bowes & Arrowes, and many times did send to me to James Towne, intreating me to pray to my God for raine, for their Gods would not send them any. And in this lamentable ignorance doe these poore soules sacrifice themselves to the Devill, not knowing their Creator; and we had not language sufficient, so plainly to expresse it as make them understand it; which God grant they may." Smith (like other writers of the time) referred to the indigenous people as "salvages," a word meaning not so much the pejorative *savages* but, based on the Latin *silva*, referring to those who live in the forest. Forest dwellers would be less sophisticated than city dwellers, lacking accoutrements of civilization such as literacy and metallurgy. Forest dwellers were not necessarily savage, though Smith was not afraid to use that word; but he preferred the less judgmental *salvages*.[12]

Although parts of Smith's threefold identity of conqueror, colonizer, and commissioner, might appear at odds today, they were consistent in his time. Adventurers and explorers of the sixteenth and seventeenth centuries, feeling that their activities served a larger, divine purpose, sought justification for their activities with contemporaries, themselves, and God. Edward Haies (Hayes), for example, who wrote the account of the 1583 voyage of Sir Humfrey Gilbert, argued that planting "the seed of Christian religion . . . must be the chiefe intent of such as shall make any attempt that way"—"whatsoever is builded upon other foundation shall never obtaine happy successe nor continuance." He admonished adventurers who prosecuted such voyages to beware such journeys for material rather than spiritual gain. Hayes associated the fulfillment of the Great Commission to all corners of the world with the Second Coming of Christ; hence he believed that God had chosen the Elizabethan age as the time to begin to prosecute the Commission in earnest. Moreover, a contemporary of Smith, James Rosier, who voyaged with and wrote accounts of the journeys of Bartholomew Gosnold and George Waymouth, wrote of the ultimate goal of the Waymouth voyage: "a publique good, and true zeale of promulgating Gods holy Church, by planting Christianity, to be the sole intent of the Honourable setters foorth of this discovery." Likewise Smith, in all his works, was self-righteous in his dealings with his friends and enemies, including the Native Americans. "But we chanced in a Land even as God made it, where we found onely an idle, improvident, scattered people, ignorant of the knowledge of gold or silver, or any commodities, and carelesse of any thing but from hand to mouth, except bables of no worth; nothing to incourage us, but what accidentally we found Nature afforded. Which ere we could bring to recompence our paines, defray our charges, and satisfie our Adventurers; we were to discover the Countrey, subdue the people, bring them to be tractable, civill, and industrious, and teach them trades, that the fruits of their labours might make us some recompence, or plant such Colonies of our owne, that must first make provision how to live of themselves, ere they can bring to perfection the commodities of the Country."[13]

In addition to a passage from Smith's *General History*, the inscription on side three of the pillar erected in 1864 includes an inexact passage from Smith's *True Travels*, in which Smith provided an account of defeating three challengers in single-handed combat: on one occasion over a three-day span the Turkish warriors fell sequentially to Smith's bloody sword. The Christian prince for whom Smith fought, Zsigmond Báthory of Transylvania, rewarded the victor with his own coat of arms—three Turks' heads, a memorial to Smith's services to Christianity and his own pursuit of fame, wealth, and social standing. The inscription complemented three stone heads of Turks atop the pillar.[14]

Captain John Smith was a violent man living in a violent age. His was a time of conquerors and the conquered, when a person might make a fortune by dipping a sword in blood, when horsemen dressed in armor riding into the fray contended for vast expanses of land, when foot soldiers carried the cumbersome arquebus into battle, when fighters waged hand-to-hand combat and fought contests for little more than honor and glory. His was a time when torture, massacre, and war settled religious disputes, when Christians battled Muslims and Catholics battled Protestants, when political and religious controversy were one and the same. This was a time when life was usually short and death often bitter, when famine, epidemics, plague, and war destroyed lives and dreams. This was an age of the arrogant and vain backing their boasts with the back of a hand, of princes and nobles squandering fortunes in gold and blood for a minor slight to personal dignity or a slight religious indignity. Countries were torn apart over the Bible and the Mass, the whims of petty rulers, the disagreements among aristocratic families and neighbors. Violence pervaded all aspects of life, in church, family, government, community, school, marriage, child rearing, and lovemaking. The English called such people lusty: they were acquisitive about everything and they used any means possible to acquire what they wanted.

The True Travels, published in 1630, was a wonderful adventure story of such a lusty farm boy turned soldier and adventurer. As a soldier Smith believed that whoever was in the way of his interest, that is, England's interest, was to be persuaded to change or be prepared to stand and defend. He lived his life according to the motto *Vivere est Vincere*—"to live is to conquer." Smith accepted without question that England was the Elect Nation, working for God and its own power and wealth toward a common goal. Smith showed his resolve on the battlefield time and again. Even before he sailed to America, bound for Virginia in 1606,

Smith had seen much of Europe, and had fought against Catholics in the Netherlands and Muslims in the Balkans. Smith knew that warriors are made great by adversity, which compelled him to journey to the Mediterranean, where he joined forces with Christians fighting the Turks for control of the Balkans. Smith quickly earned a reputation, among Christians as well as Turks, for resourcefulness, leadership, courage, and skill with the sword. The reputation of Smith's exploits made him an especially worthy prize to kill or to capture. The latter was Smith's fate. Sold as a slave in Istanbul, he briefly served Charatza Tragabigzanda, a young noblewoman. English slave and Turkish mistress became friends, which caused her brother to take Smith away with him to the steppes of southern Russia. Smith could make slaves of others but was not one to accommodate it for himself. He was treated like a beast and had an iron ring about his neck. "But God beyond mans expectation or imagination helpeth his servants, when they least thinke of helpe, as it hapned to him." Smith strangled his tyrannical master and made his escape across western Russia to Europe where, aided by benevolent Christians, he wandered through the continent. Smith ended up in North Africa, where he joined a French ship that turned out, whether to Smith's surprise or not, for piracy. Smith augmented his fortunes and returned to England in 1604. He planned to join an expedition to Guiana, where there was a colony on the Courantyne River, but never went. The leader of the colony, John Ley, died, and Smith's interests were redirected. He was never reluctant to share his adventures with willing listeners, and pride in his accomplishments went a long way toward furthering his ambitions. He loved to elaborate wistfully and gloriously upon his great deeds, which drew some in admiration to attach themselves and their projects to such a man but repelled others who thought that Smith was trying to rise above his humble origins. Both types sailed with John Smith in 1606 to America.[15]

The winds and weather of Star Island had by 1874, ten years after the erection of the Smith monument, taken a toll on the pillar and its heads. A writer for *Harper's New Magazine* who visited the Isles of Shoals reported that "one of the Turks' heads upon the monument is still in good condition; a second much the worse for wear; the third has been destroyed by stress of weather, or been carried off by vandal hordes." Within a genera-

The remains of the monument placed on Star Island in 1864 by George Beebe and Daniel Austin. American Memory, Library of Congress.

tion the sea destroyed almost the entire monument. A writer in 1910 who visited the Isles of Shoals reported that "there stood until last year a slim stone shaft—three-cornered, and resting on a three-cornered base—a monument to Captain John Smith, to whom is given the credit of having discovered the Isles. A long inscription recited the chief facts—or what pass for facts—in the explorer's career. Although modern, the monument, from being in shape and material quite unsuited to so exposed a place, is rapidly wasting away before frost and gales. Three Turks' heads that adorned its top, in memory of the doughty captain's prowess in fighting the infidels in the wars in Hungary, disappeared years ago, and last year the shaft, having fallen, was carried off." Only the damaged "base of the monument" remained.[16]

The memory of John Smith would not, however, go away. Four years later, on July 29, 1914, the three hundredth anniversary of Smith's voyage of discovery, 238 antiquarians, historians, and dignitaries gathered on Star Island to commemorate a restoration of the base of the 1864 monument and a new tablet that proclaims:

Captain John Smith
1579–1631
After Proving His Valor in
Europe and America Became
Governor of Virginia
and
Admiral of New England
While Exploring the Coast in the
Spring of 1614 Made the First Recorded
Visit to these Islands, Named by Him
Smith's Isles
This Tablet is Placed
Three Hundred Years Later by the
Society of Colonial Wars
In the State of New Hampshire
1614[17]

"It was a beautiful day, and a fresh breeze blew all the clouds inland." The crowd surrounded the remains of the old pillar, standing on "a near-by eminence, directly overlooking the sea, where a bronze tablet was unveiled to the memory of Captain John Smith." Professor Justin Harvey Smith, a noted historian and "Governor of the New Hampshire Society of Colonial Wars," gave an extensive address in which, during the course of a brief biographical portrait, he painted Smith as a modest, adventurous, truthful man who had been unjustly attacked both in the past and recently by critics as a liar. Professor Smith did not name the critics, but there had been during the previous century a host of them. John Palfrey, for example, in his *History of New England* (1858), Henry Adams in an 1867 article in the *North American Review*, and Charles Deane in the *Magazine of American History* (1885), among others, argued that John Smith fabricated the story that Pocahontas, the young Indian princess, saved Smith from execution at the hands of her father Powhatan. Nor were these mid- to late-nineteenth-century critics the first to question Smith and his works. The earliest biographical portrait of Smith, in *The History of the Worthies of England* by Thomas Fuller, noted that there are "two witnesses to attest" to Smith's deeds, "the prose and the pictures, both in his own book"—"it soundeth much to the diminution of his deeds," Fuller went on, "that he alone is the herald to publish and proclaim them." The problem was and is, as Fuller pointed out, that there is little information about Smith apart from his own published accounts of himself. Such works are always suspect as a guide to feelings and personal motives, of course, and historians are rightly suspicious of the words of a man so concerned with his personal reputation as was Smith. Many of his contemporaries doubted his adventurous tales, as Smith well knew. Skepticism about his narratives continued long after Smith's death. John Oldmixon, for example, in *The British Empire in America* (1708), cautioned against accepting the Smith-Pocahontas tale at face value. On the other hand, one of the first biographers of John Smith, the American writer, historian, scientist, and clergyman Jeremy Belknap, believed Smith's accounts in his writings were largely true. Belknap, who wrote a lengthy biographical portrait of Smith in *American Biography*, published in 1794, was one of eighteenth-century America's best historians and an able critic of sources who saw a match between Smith's account of his heroic actions and his character. Belknap thought that the enterprising courage that emerges from Smith's writings provided strong circumstantial evidence of its veracity. Belknap's view was corroborated ninety years later by English historian and editor Edward Arber, who published a two-volume critical edition of Smith's works in 1884. Arber provided extensive scholarly commentary in which he argued for the veracity of Smith's writings. Arber also ably discerned Smith's worldview and motives, which makes his edition of Smith's works continuingly valuable. People of Jacobean England often wore their hearts on their sleeves, and Smith in particular was a passionate man who could scarcely hide his feelings of anger, despair, hope, and faith. Arber and Belknap knew that, as his published works are all that we have with which to reconstruct his life and work, it is best to scrutinize his words and to get under his skin, as it were, to discover who was the real John Smith and what were his motives. Historians who empathize with the past, in order to engage in a dialogue with past humans, can reach a level of understanding that echoes, fairly accurately, what really happened.[18]

The technique of building an intuitive dialogue between the present and the past was pioneered by ancient biographers, such as Plutarch, author of the *Lives*, and adapted later by Renaissance writers such as Francesco Petrarca (Petrarch) and Michel de Montaigne. Plutarch, for example, wrote in his *Life of Timoleon*, "the virtues of these great men [serve] me as a sort of looking-glass, in which I may see how to adjust and adorn my own life. Indeed, it can be compared to nothing but daily living and associating together; we receive, as it were, in our inquiry, and entertain each successive guest, . . . and select from their actions all that is noblest and worthiest to know." Petrarch used this same technique in his letters to past humans, such as the ancient Roman orator Cicero. In one such letter to Cicero, Petrarch wrote: "I searched long and avidly for your letters, and having found them where I least thought to, avidly read them. I heard you, Marcus Tullius, saying much, complaining of much, in various moods. I already knew what a teacher you were for others; now at last I learned that you did not know how to guide yourself." Michel de Montaigne took Plutarch and Petrarch's ideas one step further, arguing that such dialogue with a past human is the means to engage in a dialogue with oneself. Montaigne wrote in the essay *Of Experience*: "I study myself more than any other subject. That is my metaphysics, that is my physics. . . . I would rather be an authority on myself than on Cicero. In the experience I have of myself I find enough to make me wise, if I were a good scholar. . . . The life of Caesar has no more to show us than our own; an emperor's or an ordinary man's it is still a life subject to all human accidents. Let us only listen: we tell ourselves all we most need." Montaigne believed that the best way to uncover the past, especially one's own, was through building a dialogue with people who are dead, indeed, but people nevertheless, with the same feelings, emotions, thoughts as oneself: such humanness cuts across time and makes the cultural, social, institutional, political, and material particularities of a set time less important—time becomes bridged, as it were, and one can say, as Montaigne said of Plutarch, "I think I know him even into his soul."[19]

Building a dialogue with a past person such as John Smith helps to guard against unintentional anachronism. It is all too easy to judge people in the past by means of what happened after their deaths, and what their actions led to in time. This is particularly true of the relationships between Europeans and the American Indians. The horrible things that happened to American Indians cannot be forgotten: the spread of disease among them, brought by the invaders; the aggression in words and actions of the invaders toward the Indians; the destruction of a way of life over the course of centuries. Humans do not, however, always know what their actions will result in. Does anyone know what their words and behavior will lead to in ten years, twenty years, or further in time? No, and neither did Smith and his contemporaries. Smith could not peer ahead in time to see a future United States of America, a future of Indian despair, a future of what has come to be called genocide perpetrated by whites against the Indians. He can hardly be held to blame. His worldview was circumscribed by his experiences and the experiences of the English up to that time. He was a young child when the Spanish Armada set sail in 1588 and grew up knowing how precarious was England's position in the world. He was born at a time when Elizabeth I was attempting to solidify the foundation of the Church of England against a strong Roman Catholic presence and growing Puritan presence in England. In his world, Christians were struggling to compete against each other as well as other religious systems, the believers of which were aggressive and just as convinced that they knew the truth. Christ's Great Commission was still very much a commandment yet to be realized. Smith lived before biblical exegesis of the nineteenth and twentieth centuries brought people to doubt the infallibility of the Bible as well as the constancy of Divine Providence in human affairs. To Smith, God was watching his actions even as He compelled time forward, and Christ was the Savior welcoming a valiant man home after the work of his life was complete. Civilization as Smith knew it was Christian—there were few if any alternatives. Jesus commanded the spread of His Word, and who was Smith or anyone else to challenge Him? Although the society and culture of the Indians had value, such that they "live as long, and much more healthfull and hardy" than the English, nevertheless the Indians were not civilized, that is, not Christian, did not make proper use of the land, and it was inconceivable to Smith that they would want to be left alone.[20]

In short, John Smith had little reason to hide his true motives or deceive his readers in the *General History* and his other works, for he wrote in the shadow of God's grace and could scarcely evade the searcher of hearts. He lived his life aware of Providence and aware that at some point he would have to account for his deeds. England was an Elect Nation that was clearly appointed by God according to His pleasure: at this time in human history the English were to settle America, make it productive, Christianize the native people, and bring them into the orbit of English civilization. What would happen in the future, what we know about the suffering of the American Indians, and what many now consider about the validity of the Bible, matters very little when trying to rescue the lives of people in the past, to consider them according to their own times—to peer into the past to get a glimpse, however fleeting, of what life was truly like at a particular historical moment, unencumbered by the future.

Professor Justin Harvey Smith used the technique of joining his experience with Smith's experience the day that he looked out across time and space from Smith's broken monument. "It was no grace or luxuriance that induced [Smith] to honor these islands with his name. Indeed, with but a little imagination, aided by the surroundings, we can see him step ashore here from his open boat, and climb to the summit of the isle; see him scan, with the wary but unflinching eye of a Ulysses, the shore of that New England which he named and loved, as it seemed now to come forward in a blaze of sunshine, and now to recede under the shadow of a passing cloud; see him bare his ample forehead and gaze upon the greatness of sea and sky with a spirit equally vast and equally free; and then see him retire calmly into a realm where every man of kingly blood has a throne, and where the voice of detraction and slander cannot penetrate, the realm of thought. . . . Though a doer of deeds he was, like all true men of action, essentially a man of contemplation; and where could he find a nobler opportunity to think than on a spot like this?"[21]

At this writing, another century has passed since the bronze plaque was dedicated. Today it is old, scarcely decipherable because of weathering. Visitors to Star Island can still see it, and ponder this man and his work. The monument still stands, looking out upon the sea to the south, north, east, and west. It is a monument of time, exploration, adventure. It is a sea mark.

TWO

London

Amid the many spires west of Newgate rose one of stone like a medieval fortress. The parish bell rang calling worshippers to St. Sepulchre, an old Roman Catholic, now Anglican church founded centuries ago and refurbished by the Popham family a hundred years before. It was Sexagesima Sunday, the second Sunday before Lent, February 27, 1614. When John Smith was in London, he worshipped at St. Sepulchre; there, in seventeen years, he would be buried. St. Sepulchre was in central London, north of and not far from the Thames, up the road from Newgate and St. Paul's, just east of Fleet River flowing south. Nearby was Smithfield, where martyrs once burned. John Smith was born and died in the Church of England, and never considered himself anything but an Anglican communicant. The *Book of Common Prayer* was his breviary. Its liturgy, prayers, and psalms formed a part of his thoughts and language that, in times of crisis, burst forth to still the fear. Smith and his fellow worshippers used the 1604 edition of the *Book of Common Prayer*, which provided for Anglicans throughout London and England a common worship experience, reading the same Gospel message, the same Epistle, praying the same Collect. This day, Smith enjoyed Eucharist for the last time for months—soon he was to put to sea again. The dangers of the deep always weighed on the minds of sailors and adventurers, so it was good to find solace in the Eucharist, the Word of the Lord, and prayer. The Collect this day seemed particularly appropriate for a man facing danger: "Lord God, which seest that wee put not our trust in any thing that we doe: mercifully graunt that by thy power wee may bee defended against all aduersitie, through Jesus Christ our Lord." Wind and waves, storms and swells, reefs and shoals awaited Smith and his crew. The

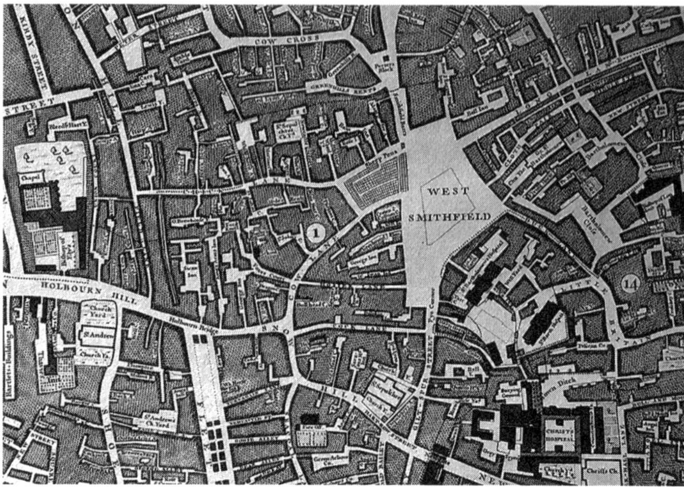

St. Sepulchre's Church, where Smith worshipped and where he was buried, is noted on this map just west of Gilt-Spur Street. John Rocque, *A plan of the cities of London and Westminster*. . . . Printed in London, 1746. Courtesy Cheatham's Library.

Epistle, from Paul's Second Letter to the Corinthians (11:19–31), described the Apostle's sufferings for the sake of Christ, the stoning, the beatings, the shipwreck: "In iourneying often, in perils of robbers, in ieopardies of mine owne nation, in ieopardies among the heathen, in perils in the Citie, in perils in wildernes, in perils in the sea, in perils among false brethren, in labour and travel, in watchings often, in hunger & thirst, in fastings often, in colde and nakednesse." The bread and wine, the body and blood, were a fit complement to the Gospel, from Matthew, that told the story of the householder who hired workers to labor in the vineyard; during the course of the day he hired successive workers, so that some worked more than others; then he paid all workers the same wages regardless of hours worked. Smith, a man who often felt that he did the work from which others shied away, that he was constantly trying to prove himself in an aristocratic, rigid world of rank and wealth, found solace in the concluding words of the Gospel: "The last shall be first, and the first shall be last. For many be called, but few be chosen."[1]

John Smith was a religious man living in a religious age. He was born two to three generations after Luther posted his theses on the Wittenberg

Church door and almost fifty years after Henry VIII broke ties with the Catholic Church. A generation before his birth, Bloody Mary burned Protestants at the stake, and only twenty years before George and Alice Smith brought forth John into the world, Queen Elizabeth I confirmed her role as supreme governor of the Church of England. John Smith grew up in the atmosphere of religious sacrifice, of John Foxe's *Book of Martyrs*, which told heroic tales of Protestants standing up to the wrath of Mary Tudor; of religious strife, when nonconformists were increasingly challenging the queen and the archbishop, preaching an unrelenting message of purification, urging return to the ancient Church of the Apostles; of religious growth, when under the stability of Elizabeth's long reign the Church of England, notwithstanding its opponents, grew powerful, orderly, and firmly established; and religious creativity, when the theologian and historian Richard Hooker published *On the Laws of the Ecclesiastical Polity*, seven massive, profound, and erudite volumes that argued the historical and theological justification of the Church of England. Hooker convinced his readers of the importance of an individual's subordination to the authority of the Crown, Church, and God, which was precisely what John Smith believed.

Four days after Sexagesima Sunday, Smith's little fleet of two ships lay at the Downs, awaiting fair winds, then getting under way. During the preceding several days, Smith and his men, along with captains Marmaduke Roydon and George Langam, had departed east from London Bridge, perhaps beginning at Deptford, a shipyard associated with Trinity House, of which Smith, perhaps, was a member. Trinity House was a corporation with a long history of supporting seafaring, protecting London, and controlling the Thames. If not Deptford, then perhaps Blackwall, where the three ships of the Virginia Company had set forth for Jamestown in 1606. Smith's ships followed the broad Thames downriver, letting the tide pull them gently along the winding route toward the sea. They might have anchored for the night, as many mariners would, awaiting fair winds and the tide, before pursuing the journey toward Thames Estuary, where fresh and seawater join in a briny mix. From the mouth of the Thames they journeyed south along Kent to the "Downes," a place along the coast where massive chalk cliffs provided cover from storms and contrary winds.

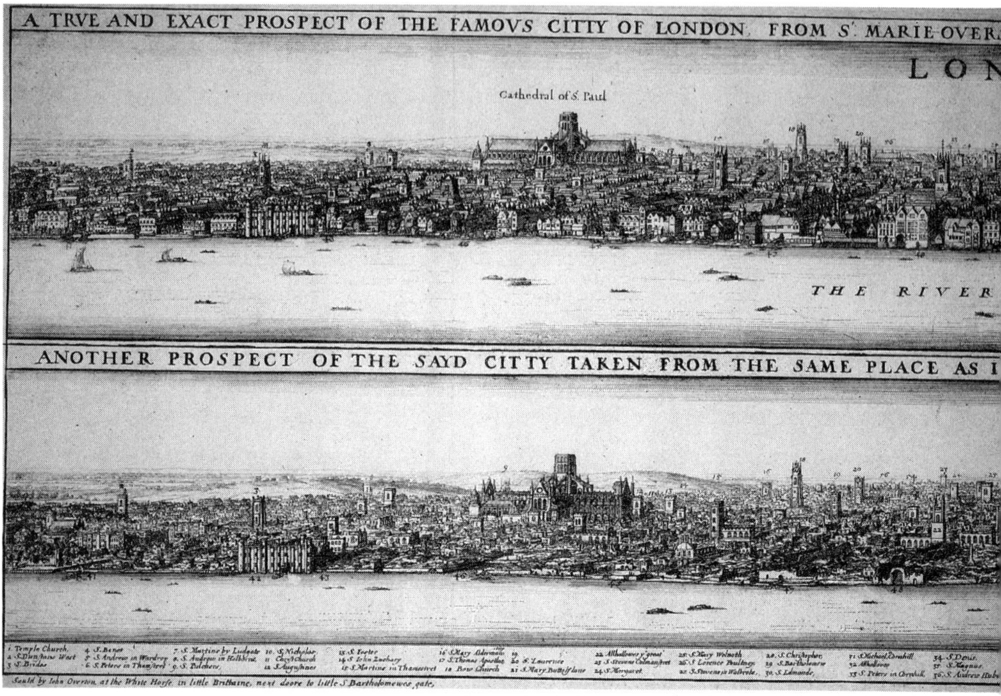

This view of London looking south of the city from across the Thames River shows the variety of river craft used during Smith's time. *Plan of London before the Fire*. Wenceslaus Hollar Digital Collection, University of Toronto.

They departed here southward on March 3. It was the time of the waning moon, so initially, along the coast, they sailed by day and moored their ships at night. The two ships, which Smith neither named nor described, were probably small barks of less than one hundred tuns each. He wrote in the *Description of New England* that he returned to Plymouth six months later at the end of August "in the Bark." The ships were large enough to quarter close to four dozen men and boys, along with food and other supplies including the parts to make seven fishing shallops.[2]

The English, since the end of Elizabeth's and beginning of James's reigns, had been seeking to establish a working colony in Northern Virginia between 41 and 45 degrees north latitude (that is, what would subsequently be called New England). Smith, in London before and after his journey to Jamestown from 1606 to 1609, had been among those concocting speculative plans and activities involving that region. Merchants and adventurers in London as well as Plymouth had learned about Cape Cod and the waters south of Massachusetts from Bartholomew Gosnold, about the rivers of Maine from Martin Pring, about the Penobscot region from George Waymouth, about the Sagadahoc (Kennebec) region from the survivors of the abandoned Popham colony. Even after the Popham colony failed while the Jamestown colony, founded the same year farther south, succeeded, there were a few hopeful and optimistic men and women of wealth and dreams who sought an advantageous financial return from an expedition to New England. Plymouth and London merchants sent trading vessels along the New England coast almost every year after the Popham debacle. What drove these ongoing attempts was not only perseverance in the face of continual failure, but more: it was the reality of successful Indian villages. Returning explorers such as Gosnold, Pring, and Waymouth brought reports of Indian prosperity as well as some of the Indians themselves to provide testimony. Waymouth in 1605 and Edward Harlow in 1611 brought kidnapped Indians to England, where they learned English ways, including the language, and informed their captors of the supposed wealth that New England offered. There were medicinal plants such as sassafras that formed an expanding English-American *materia medica*; furs and pelts from North American mammals such as the beaver, lynx, and mink; mineral wealth, perhaps even gold, that miners might find in the bowels of the earth; plentiful fish to dry and salt and pack in barrels for sale in a growing number of world markets; and crops such as maize. Smith had met and conversed with some of these captives, such as Dohannida, Tisquantum, and Epenow, and intended to use their knowledge, connections, and leadership among Algonquian tribes to establish a colony.[3]

On this voyage to America, Smith brought along as guide and interpreter Tisquantum, also known as Tantum, later called Squanto by the Pilgrims of Plymouth. Smith apparently knew Tisquantum through his captor Captain Edward Harlow, a veteran of the Sagadahoc colony who had sailed to New England in 1611 under sponsorship of "Henry Earle of South-hampton and those of the Ile of Wight." Tisquantum was a Patuxet Indian from Plymouth who could help Smith with the intricacies of Algonquian language and culture, of which Smith had a working knowledge based on his experiences in Virginia. Indeed, Smith was the expert on Algonquian among the colonists while he was in Virginia—but he was finished with that colony: "for all this, as I liked Virginia well, though not their proceedings, so I desired also to see this country [New England], and spend some time in trying what I could finde." Smith wagered on his success in New England because of Tisquantum, whom Smith called "a proud Saluage"; Tisquantum would be the "meanes," "I did not doubt," "but quickly to haue got that credit amongst the rest of the Saluages and their alliance."[4]

Besides Tisquantum, Smith knew another Algonquian Indian, Dohannida, "one of their greatest Lords, who had liued long in England." Dohannida (also called Tahenedo) was a sachem of the Wawenock tribe. Smith had in England met and communicated with Dohannida, who after his capture by George Waymouth in 1605 had lived in England for about a year and learned English. Dohannida had returned to his people in 1606 as a passenger on a voyage sent by Sir John Popham, who hoped to establish a colony in Northern Virginia the following year. The commanders of the expedition were Martin Pring and Thomas Hanham; they apparently brought Dohannida as a guide, and agreed to leave him behind with his people somewhere along the Maine coast.[5]

Failure to establish a working colony in New England, and a long line of less than profitable fishing and trading voyages, had resulted in "ill rumors and disasters" among the merchants and adventurers of England. But then Smith had met four London merchants, Marmaduke Roydon, George Langam, William Skelton, and John Buley, whom he had convinced that the prospects for wealth in America justified a renewed, if modest, attempt. They would try to bring about a profit by mining for precious metals and hunting whales for oil and bones; as a last resort they could profit from fishing and trading for furs. Notwithstanding that Smith could hardly help finance the expedition, he took charge, by his own account.[6]

Smith had enough experience with pirates, having been a passenger with a French privateer more than a decade earlier, that he was wary of the safety of two barks at sea in the English Channel.[7] He therefore hugged the coast from the Downs southwest and west toward the Isle of Wight where, taking the northern route between the Isle and England, called the Solent, they rode at anchor at the Cowes, the northern extreme of the Isle of Wight opposite Gosport, Portsmouth, and Southampton. Proceeding west through the strait, they passed the Castle at Yarmouth, where perhaps they gave and received a salute.[8]

Pursuing the journey west, they sailed between the mainland and the Needles, salt formations protruding from the sea just off the western extreme of the Isle of Wight. They hugged the coast toward Portland and Weymouth, then turned southwest toward the West Country, and Dartmouth, Plymouth, and Falmouth. They negotiated the dangers of the Lizard, a peninsula jutting into the sea known for dangerous reefs and rocks. From here, if they had a good northerly, they began their voyage into the seemingly endless waves and winds of the Atlantic. "Set the land," Smith would command, "how it beares by the Compasse that we may the better know thereby to keep our account and direct our course." The master and mates were to "steare steady and keep your course, so, you go wel." Smith knew that "every man [would] say his private prayer for a boone [bon] voyage," for prayers were apropos at such a time: "If Religion had not taught us what by the providence of god is brought to passe, yet daily experience might informe us, of the dangers of wars, and perils at sea, by stormes tempests, shipwracks, encounters with Pirats, meeting with enemies, crosse winds, long voiages, unknown shores, barbarous Nations, and an hundred inconveniences, of which humane pollicies are not capable, nor mens conjectures apprehensive." One must rely on God and accept His will.[9]

As captain of the little fleet, Smith set the course, the "height" as he called it, or latitude, leaving it to the masters of the two ships to take care of the particulars of the voyage. The typical route, established by Gosnold, Pring, and Waymouth, was to sail southwest toward the Azores, where supplies, if needed, could be acquired. Usually, unless the mariners had been long at sea, these islands could be bypassed; sailing a west-northwest course, about five hundred leagues, would then get them to America. The voyage was generally quick, lasting eight weeks if the winds were not terribly contrary and the storms were endurable. The two ships' complements included carpenters to make quick repairs and to put together the shallops when needed; "boteswaines," who kept track of all the materials to rig and sail the ships; a "chirurgion" for dressing wounds and caring for the sick, with a chest full of *materia medica* (materials of medicine) "for Physicke, and Chyurgery"; the steward, who kept track of food supplies, the barrels of salt meat, biscuit, beer, and water; a "cowper" (cooper), who kept barrels in repair and constructed them on demand; the "swabber," who made sure the deck was clean; ship's boys, who did varied and sundry jobs aboard the vessel for "a quarter can [of beer], and a basket of bread"; a trumpeter to "hale a ship, when you charge, booard, or enter"; and a marshal, who disciplined the recalcitrant and disobedient with punishments such "as ducking at Yards arme, hawling vnder the Keele, bound to the Capsterne or maine Mast with a basket of shot about his necke, setting in the bilbowes, and to pay the Cobty or the Morryoune." This mystifying list of punishments included dunking malcontents into the sea over and over until they learned their lesson; dragging a sailor, tied to a rope, under the ship; tying men to a capstan or mast and hanging a heavy weight around their neck; locking men in irons to a long rod, or bilbo, to restrict movement; beating the soles of the malefactor's feet with a stick (cobkey) or pikestaff (morryoune).[10]

On a typical day at sea in March or April 1614, Captain Smith emerged from the "Captaines Cabben," which the men called the "great Cabben." The ship was divided into two watch companies, starboard and larboard, on alternating duty for four hours, or eight turns of the hourglass, at a time. To keep them going the steward allowed them "a quarter Can of beere and a basket of bread to stay their stomacks till the Kettle be boiled." The captain saw a ship's boy run past, and called out, "Boy!" In response to which the boy said, "Holla Maister. Holla." Smith asked, "Is the kettle boyled?" to which the boy responded, "Yea, yea." The captain called out to the "Boteswaine"—"call vp the men to Prayer and Breakfast." Smith carried his prayer book, and he would lead the crew in morning prayer. At the turn of each watch the men "sing a Psalme" and "say a Prayer." The men repeated the same pattern "except some flaw of winde come, some storme or gust, or some accident that requires the helpe of all hands, which commonly after such good cheere in most voyages doth happen." The Anglican prayer book focused on the sinner before God, the redemption of sin, the majesty of God, and the dependence of humans upon God. The realization of their two little barks as but specks on the broad sea, which at any moment could swallow them, was always in the minds of the sailors. To go to their death, possibly at any moment, with wickedness in their hearts, would be intolerable. And so the words from the prayer book counseled, "To thee, O Lord God, belongeth mercie and forgivenesse." The men, daily, knelt and confessed their sins. They daily heard the Lord's Prayer and recited the *Venite,* Psalm 95: "The sea is his, and he made it: and his hands prepared the drie land. O come, let us worship and fall downe: and kneele before the Lord our maker." Smith led the men through other psalms and readings, concluding with: "O God make cleane our hearts within us," to which the men responded: "And take not thy holy Spirit from us." Morning prayer concluded, Smith called to the boy, "fetch my celler of Bottles," and upon their being retrieved, he offered "A health to you all fore and afte."[11]

The sailor's dream was for a kind wind and clear skies, whereupon the captain would say, "Faire weather, set your fore sayle," and the following breeze would fill the square sails on the foremast, mainmast, and bowsprit and take the ship along. Smith's two barks were rigged with lateen (or triangular) mizzen sails at the stern, for tacking into the wind. When on their western voyage they encountered a crosswind, the captain called out, "the wind veares" from the north, "git your star-boord tacks aboord," tack into the wind to make progress toward the northwest. The helmsman used the whipstaff, attached to the rudder, to steer the ship to port and starboard. To adjust the tension of the sails per the wind by adjusting ropes and braces, the captain ordered: "hawle off your ley sheats, ouerhawle the ley bowlin, ease your mayne brases." Smith's barks were outfitted with a spritsail, which with a following wind would bring forth the command, "out with your spret-saile." Should clouds approach, "we shall haue winde . . . take in the spret sayle, in with your topsayles, lower your maine sayles, . . . in with your maine sayle, lower the fore sayle." On comes "a storme, . . . lash sure the helme a ley," steer slightly into the storm. "How capes the ship?"—does she keep her course? "Cun the ship spoune," make her run, "before the winde"; "she lusts," or lists;

"she lyes vnder the Sea," adrift "trie her with a crose jacke," rig a sail on the mizzenmast, or steer her directly into the wind with "a hullocke of a sayle" as a last resort. Beware that the ship "put out a goose-winge," which is to change directions or tack from one side to another, which strains the sails and can cause masts to break. If so, "she will founder in the Sea." Such, owing to the skills and prayers of Smith and his men, was not their fate.[12]

Smith had crossed the Atlantic before, in 1606–1607 aboard the *Susan Constant*; Captain Christopher Newport had taken a southerly route to pick up the trade winds. Smith's 1614 voyage was his first journey in the North Atlantic to America. The cold northerlies, the frigid water, the fogs and storms, the cloudy days when all that could be seen were the endless rollers lifting the ship to peaks and tilting it down into valleys could make a person wonder who else would have hazarded such a journey—what possible motive could impel a person to risk such a lonely, barren crossing in the merciless sea? Stories were told in Elizabethan and Jacobean England of brave voyagers who many years ago had made the crossing to America. Storytellers talked of King Arthur, Malgo (Maelgwn), Saint Brendan, and Madoc Prince of Wales, who long before the technological advances to shipping and navigation available in Smith's age had set forth into the unknown Atlantic. The only story that had any credit to it, in Smith's mind, was Madoc's voyage to somewhere in 1170; the typically incredulous Smith wrote that "where this place was no History can show." Smith knew his history when it came to the English voyages of record. He knew both Richard Hakluyt and, later, Samuel Purchas, and read with interest of the voyages of John and Sebastian Cabot, Martin Frobisher, and Humfrey Gilbert, the latter swallowed by the cold Atlantic on his return voyage in 1587.[13]

To succeed where others had failed in crossing the Atlantic required knowledge, experience, the best instruments, and a little luck, acceptance of divine providence, and intuition. Smith had all these, especially the uncanny ability to survive. His two ships were provided with up-to-date nautical technology, some of it new and relatively sophisticated, some of it centuries old. Of the latter was the measuring of fathoms (six feet per fathom) with the "Dipsie line, which is a small line some hundred and

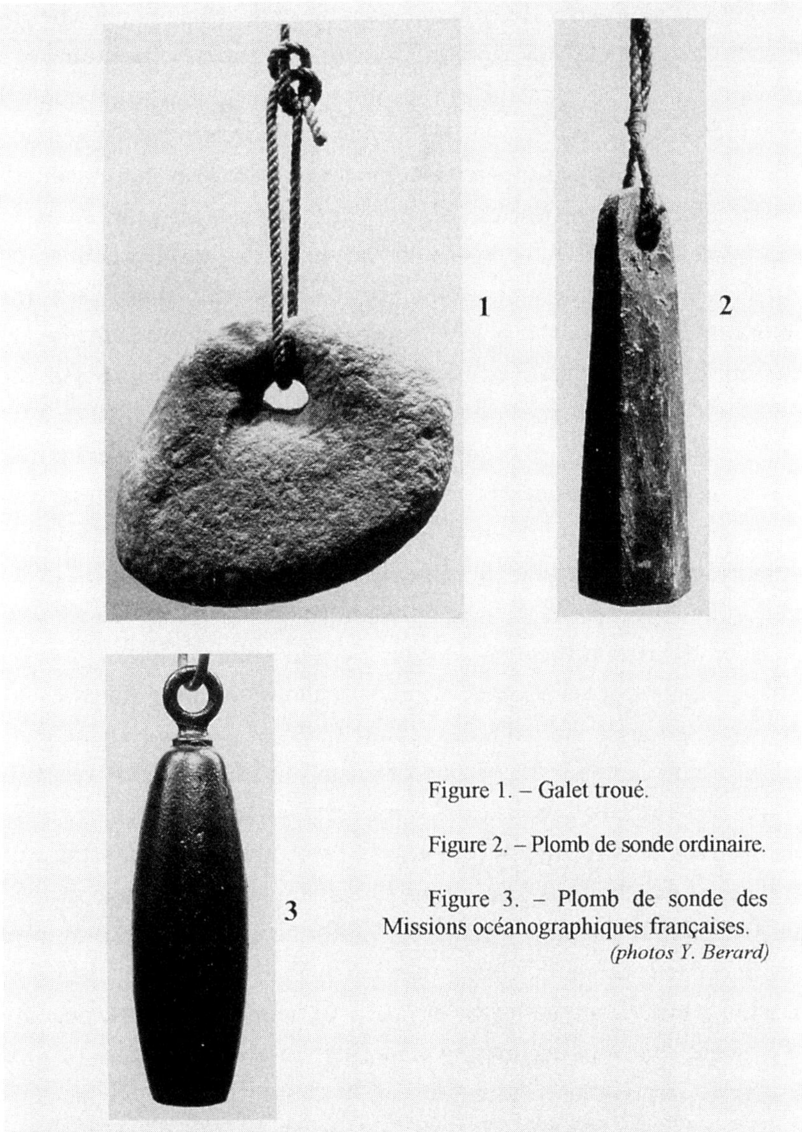

These three sounding leads were used in the past by sailors to gauge depth. Figure 2 has a hollow in which a sticky substance could bring up material from the ocean floor. NOAA's Historic Fisheries Collection.

fifty fadome long, with a long plummet at the end, made hollow, wherein is put tallow," a sticky substance to "bring up any gravell" or anything else indicative of the bottom. The line "is first marked at twenty fadome, and after increased by tens to the end"; small knots were fixed at intervals, "shewing it is so many times ten fadome deepe, where the plummet doth rest from drawing the line out of your hand; this is onely used in deepe water when we thinke we approach the shore, for in the maine sea at 300. fadomes we finde no bottome." In coastal waters, Smith used "the Sounding line," which "is bigger than the Dipsie line, and is marked at two fadome next the lead with a peece of blacke leather, at three fadome the like . . . ; at 5. fadome with a peece of white cloth, at 7. fadome with a peece of red in a peece of white leather, at 15. with a white cloth." As the sailor swung the line, fitted at the end with a "six or seven pound" lead that was "neere a foot long," he called out the depth per the black, white, and red indicators. To gauge distance, Smith and his men could rely on dead reckoning, that is, guessing speed and time by means of an accurate log and the eyes and sense of old sailors. A piece of wood tied to a long rope with knots at intervals allowed to play out from the stern gave a rough approximation of the speed of the ship. As the years passed Smith doubted the efficacy of the log and came to believe it was "not worth the labour to trie it." On clear days and nights, dead reckoning could be corrected by instrumental aids to navigation. "To learne to obserue the Altitude," or height, of the sun on the horizon at noon "or in the night the North Star," and "Latitude," the ship's comparative position north or south, Smith used a mariner's "astrolobe," a bronze disc hung by a ring used by the navigator at noon to gauge the position of the sun; a table of declination according to days of the year provided an estimate of latitude. Smith also used "a Crosse staffe," a long wooden staff with a scale and a wooden vane that moved perpendicularly to the staff; the observer positioned the staff between the sun or star and the horizon, then moved the vane until each end was placed exactly between object and horizon. Smith used "An Nocturnall" to track the position of stars so as to gauge the time at night. Smith also employed "two paire of Compasecs," one of which, perhaps, was the same compass that he had used to survive when he was captured by Opechancanough in Virginia

John Smith sailed to America with many nautical instruments, including two good compasses. This compass rose is from his *Map of New England.* American Memory, Library of Congress.

in 1607. It was "a round Ivory double compass dyall" that provided Smith not only with directions but, as it had a sundial, the time. Smith also had "Good Sea Cards," which he would "pricke," or mark, "to shift the Sunne and Moone" so "to know the tydes." Smith relied on half a dozen books, including the great Elizabethan explorer John Davis's *Seamans Secrets*, but he believed that "experiences must be the best Tutor."[14]

Much of the challenge of sailing a small boat across the Atlantic was to endure the extremes of weather and waves. "Foule weather" on the open sea, "the labour, hazard, wet and cold[,] is so incredible I cannot expresse it," Smith wrote. "Men of all other professions in lightning, thunder, stormes, and tempests with raine and snow may shelter themselves in dry houses by good fires, but those are the chiefe times Sea-men must stand to their tackling, and attend with all diligence their greatest labour upon the deckes." The only way to survive it was by recruiting a company of experienced sailors. "For if there be more learners then Saylers, . . . all the worke to saue ship, goods, and liues, must lye vpon them," the experienced men. If it is up to them to do all the labor, they will become exhausted and sick, and then everyone is doomed. Smith believed that a worthy captain must not skimp on supplies but provide what was best for the crew in terms of "victuals." His men ate well from March to May: "fine wheat flower, close and well packed, Rise [rice], Currands, Sugar, Prunes, Cinamon, Ginger, Pepper, Cloues, Greene-ginger, Oyle, Butter, Olde Cheese, or Holland, Wine, vinegar, Canary Sacke, Aqua vita, the best Wines, the best Waters, the iuyce of Lemons for the Scurvey, white Bisket, Oate meale, Gammons of Bacone, dried neates tongues, Rosted Beefe packed vp in vineger. Legges of Mutton minced and stewed, and close packed vp with butter in earthen pots." "Some it may bee will say," Smith continued, "I would haue men rather to feast then fight. But I say the want of those necessaries, occasions the losse of more men, then in any English fleet hath bin slaine in any fight since [15]88." Sick men need certain kinds of food and drink to help them recover. "After a storme, when poore men are all wet, and some not so much a cloth to shift him, shaking with cold, few of those but will tell you, a little Sacke," Spanish wines, "or Aqu[a]vitæ," brandy, "is much better to keepe them in health, then a little small beere or cold water." The sea offers "neither Alehouse, Tauerne, nor Inne . . . ; neither Grocer, Poulterie, Apothocary, nor Butchers shop": the captain must provide.[15]

Smith's ships, if indeed they were both barks, would normally have been lightly armed, but as the North Atlantic had a profusion of pirates—English, French, Spanish, and Dutch—he would have been a foolish captain if not amply supplied with military ordnance. Both boats undoubtedly had plenty of "Musquets, . . . Carbines, . . . long Pistols, . . . Charges, Cartrages, Match, Spunges, Ladles," and "Rammers" so that the entire crew could respond to an attack with small-arms fire, and small artillery such as falcons, falconets, and/or minions as well as the means to fire them upon an enemy including "a gunners quadrant, . . . a priming iron, . . . round shot, crosse-barre-shot," and "chayne-shot."[16]

"Within eight weekes sayling" the ships' crews knew they were approaching coastal America. When they dropped the lead, it hit bottom. They saw more birds in flight. Measurements of latitude indicated they were at about 44 to 43 degrees north. By the time they spotted land, they were in less than a 100 fathom of water. Fish were plentiful, and they feasted well. They spied ahead "*Monahigan,* an Ile in *America* in 43. degrees 39. minutes of Northerly latitude." The masters of the barks ordered the sailors to "trim the boate," to which they replied, "*vea, vea, vea, vea, vea,* who saies Amen, one and all, for a dram of the bottle."[17]

Having just traversed an unknown expanse of danger and mystery, Smith and his men prepared to embark upon another unknown, a terra incognita. "Of this 2000. miles more then halfe is yet unknowne to any purpose: no, not so much as the borders of the Sea are yet certainly discouered. But onely here and there wee touched or haue seene a little the edges of those large dominions, which doe stretch themselues into the Maine [mainland], God doth know how many thousand miles."[18]

How does a person prepare to enter the unknown? How to confront, challenge, and survive, let alone conquer, the vastness of the sea or the wildness of the land? Smith knew of many who had tried, friends such as Bartholomew Gosnold and Henry Hudson. Gosnold had been defeated by Virginia. Hudson had journeyed to the "frozen partes" of North America, inspired by Smith who, according to the seventeenth-century historian of the Netherlands Emanuel Méteren, had sent "Hudson . . . some letters and maps . . . from Virginia; and by which he informed him that there was a sea leading to the Western Ocean by the north of the southern English colony." Smith declared that Hudson had made "the greatest discouerie of any Christian I know of, where he vnfortunately died."[19]

Smith and his friends Gosnold and Hudson were joined by many others of their time in the exploring spirit. Elizabethan and Jacobean England comprised an era of experimentation, of trial and error, not just among the wealthy and educated but among commoners as well, of which Smith, he might reluctantly admit, was one. But he nonetheless soaked up the atmosphere of trying out ideas, of confronting the unknown, of facing fears that were a product of the imagination with the burgeoning empirical mind-set of sixteenth- and seventeenth-century England, of trying manifold solutions to the many problems of humankind, of seeing the potential in things, of risking failure, of investigating and discovering. It was an Anglican mind-set, because of the focus on experience and reason, a willingness to investigate God's creation, knowing that nature and the God's Word coexist, that an *Elder Scripture*, the scripture of nature, can reveal the mind of God.[20]

The English mind-set of Smith and his friends and fellow explorers was one of acceptance of the future and God's will, and not fear. Such willingness to embrace the future shows confidence, piety, and faith—accepting God's will as being realized through a person's own will. This is what Richard Hooker taught in the *Laws of the Ecclesiastical Polity*, and what Anglicans such as Smith embraced. Without risking the future one would stagnate, become savage. To plant seeds, cultivate, risk, grow, change, move, act, are what humans do. It was what John Smith did now, in the summer of 1614.

THREE

Monhegan Isle

At the end of April, when notwithstanding spring on the calendar the wind is sharp along the northeastern coast of America and the spray is icy from North Atlantic waves, John Smith and the other forty-five men voyaging in the two barks spied land in the distance. Mariners crossing the North Atlantic at 44 or 43 degrees latitude often sought Cape Sable (the southeastern extreme of Nova Scotia), the hills of Mount Desert Island or Isle au Haut, or if riding farther south, Matinicus Island or, just to the southwest, Monhegan. It depended upon the wind and weather, and whether or not fog lay about or the sky was clear enough for the captain to take the angle of the sun to the horizon to determine the latitude. Smith's account does not provide such details, except to say that they landed at Monhegan Island, whether by design or chance is not clear; but this island, lying about a dozen miles off the coast of Maine, became the base of their operations.

Captain John Smith was not the first European to sail coastal America wondering what lay within its forested interior. The obvious bounty of the land—its waters teeming with fish, its inland forests and furs awaiting exploitation—contrasted with the dangerous shoal waters of the coast, bitterly cold winters, and untenable pathways into the interior. The exploration and colonization of America required men and women who exhibited varying characteristics of audacity, patience, perseverance, and hunger for something more. This was true both for the immigrants from Europe as well as the indigenous tribes of New England, who continually waged war against privation and climatic extremes.

The first European explorers to sail the waters of the Northeast found the land and its peoples forbidding. The bays of coastal America centuries

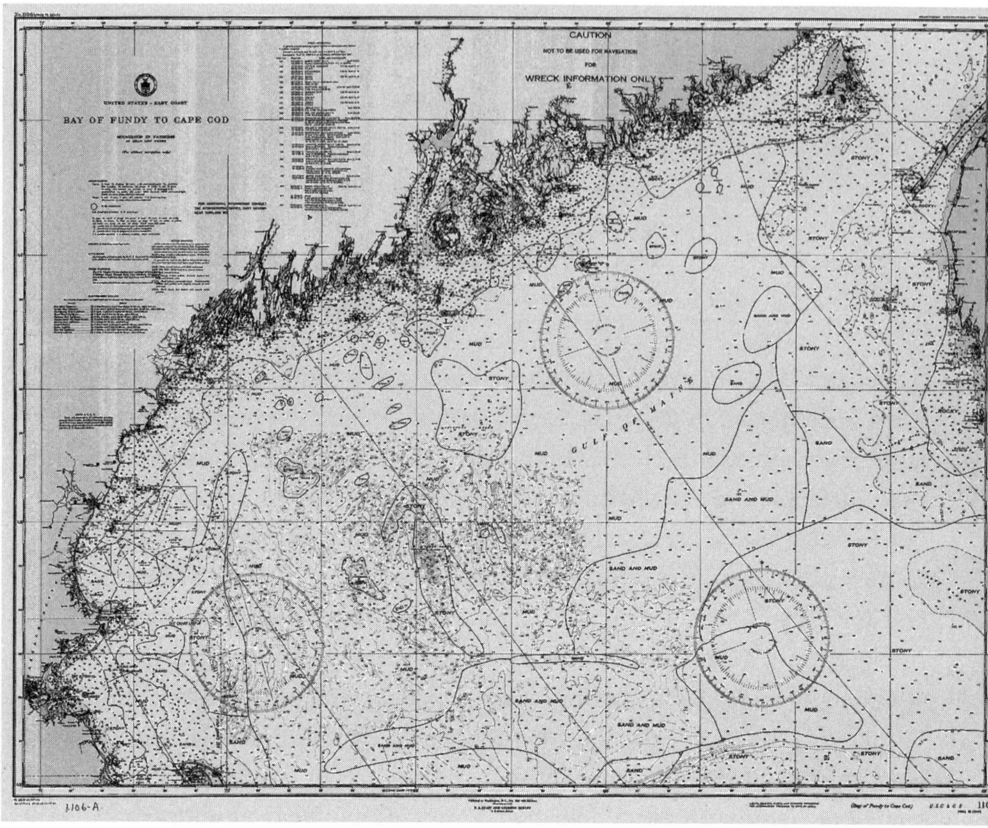

John Smith sailed into the Gulf of Maine in April 1614. NOAA Chart 1106-04-1947.

before had hosted single-masted warships from Scandinavia, Iceland, or Greenland. It is not known how far south along the coast the Vikings sailed; if they reached coastal Maine, south of Passamaquoddy Bay, they found rocky inlets similar to their homeland of Norway. The warlike Norse would have discovered native inhabitants of their ilk. The Viking ship used a single sail and oars to propel it before the wind; its shallow draft made it an excellent ship to explore narrow rivers, fjords, and intricate bays.

The first known Europeans to explore coastal New England were English, Portuguese, Italian, and French explorers of the late fifteenth and sixteenth centuries who were in search of a passage (the Northwest Passage) through the American continent that would take them from the Atlantic to the Pacific oceans and the lucrative trade of the East

Indies.[1] The Italian explorer Giovanni Caboto (John Cabot), sailing for the English in 1497 and 1498, explored Newfoundland and perhaps coastal waters farther south. Smith, who familiarized himself with his predecessors, believed that Caboto had "ranged a great part of this vn-knowne world," that he predated Columbus in the exploration of the North American continent, and that his son, Sebastian, had sailed the entire extent of North and South America.[2]

The Spanish and French came soon after. A Portuguese mariner, sailing for Spain in 1524, Estêvão Gomes, had gained notoriety sailing with Magellan a few years before. Gomes, who commanded one of the ships in Magellan's fleet, had deserted his captain in the uncertain waters of the Strait of Magellan in South America and sailed back to Spain. After a few years in a dungeon thinking over his cowardice, he hoped to redeem himself. On this voyage Gomes traversed the entire coast from Florida to Maine. Little is known of his journey, though he apparently ascended the Penobscot River to the fall line at present Bangor. The Spanish map of Diego Ribero, issued in 1529, referred to the region of northern New England as the Land of Estêvão Gomes.[3]

Notwithstanding Gomes's voyage, Spain was too preoccupied building its empire in South and Central America to spend significant resources on settling the northeast coast of North America. At the same time the French began to focus on the region. They sent the Italian explorer Giovanni Verrazzano in 1524 to explore the American coast. Verrazzano was a skilled mariner who made extensive explorations of the Carolinas, the coast of New Jersey, the mouth of the Hudson River at New York, and Narragansett Bay at Rhode Island. He made contact and traded with local tribes. Some were friendly, some fierce. But none of the Native American tribes could equal in ferocity the Abenaki of the Northeast. Verrazzano's ship *La Dauphine* coasted dozens of the islands of Maine, halting briefly at several locations to explore and attempt trade with the local inhabitants. Verrazzano probably made initial landfall at one of the promontories of Casco Bay. Verrazzano dubbed the region the "land of bad people" because of the hearty lack of welcome the invaders received. Nevertheless Verrazzano led shore parties of men who were not frightened by the Indians, who ranged through their villages taking what they wanted, and who despised the natives as uncouth, dirty, and barbaric. The Abenaki clearly wanted no part of the Europeans in their strange dress arriving in astonishingly large ships carrying great weapons of incredible lethality. As *La Dauphine* sailed away, the Indians felt free to taunt the Europeans with great cries and rude gestures. Departing Casco Bay, Verrazzano headed northeast paralleling the coastline. He noted the great numbers of islands, the numerous inlets, the daunting forest, and inland mountains. He cruised by Monhegan Island, Penobscot Bay, and islands such as Isle au Haut and Mount Desert Island, continuing northeast out of coastal waters.[4]

Verrazzano's voyage led to new maps appearing in Europe that instilled interest among able seamen and explorers in this hitherto unknown coast. Verrazzano learned that the Abenaki called their land *Norumbega*: the name appeared on maps throughout the sixteenth and seventeenth centuries. Norumbega became the goal of many shipmasters who set forth from the ports of England and France in coming years. One John Rut, an explorer sailing for King Henry VIII of England, searched the American coast for the Northwest Passage in 1527. His ship *Mary of Guildford* followed in Cabot's wake, exploring the coasts of Labrador, Newfoundland, Nova Scotia, and New England. The extent of Rut's journeys is lost to time. Similarly lost are records of most voyages of discovery of those who came to America in the wake of John Rut.[5]

One English sailor reported his fantastic travels up the east coast of America at midcentury. David Ingram claimed that he and two other sailors, marooned on the shores of Florida, had journeyed along the coast for hundreds of miles, fording rivers and wading through swamps. Eventually they arrived at the mouth of the St. John's River after having traversed Maine. Ingram described coastal America as a land of many riches—good weather, plentiful food, gold for the taking. Such stories inspired others, such as John Walker, who in 1580 explored Penobscot Bay, finding the same imaginary riches. A few years before, in the 1570s, Martin Frobisher had sailed farther north "to search for," in Smith's words, "the Northwest Passage and *Meta incognita*," the coast of Labrador and Baffin Island. Upon the bases of such reports, intrepid explorer Humfrey Gilbert determined to establish a viable English colony along the northeastern American coast. Tragedy, however, haunted his 1583 expedition to America. One ship wrecked off the coast of Nova Scotia. Gilbert himself, Smith wrote, "perished in his returne" to England, lost at sea. Not for twenty years would another English settlement along the northeast coast be attempted. For much of the sixteenth century fishermen from England, France, Portugal, and Spain frequented these waters; they found fishing banks off the northeast coast offered plentiful catches of cod and other fish. The many islands along the coast served as way stations for fishermen to take on water, make repairs, dry and salt their catch, escape from storms, and hide from enemies.[6]

It was not until the beginning of the seventeenth century that explorers again coasted the rocky shores of the Northeast. By this time the English as well as the French had postponed their designs on finding the Northwest Passage to focus their energies instead on exploiting other forms of wealth, real and imagined, of New England. Hence Bartholomew Gosnold ranged the coast from Cape Neddick to Narragansett Bay in 1602, about which Smith read in the "relation printed by Captaine *Bartholomew Gosnould*, of *Elizabeths Isles*," Gosnold's short-lived island colony south of Massachusetts. Smith and Gosnold were friends and fellow explorers. Smith likewise knew of the voyage in 1603 of Martin Pring, representing the interests of adventurers and merchants, including Richard Hakluyt, of Bristol in the West Country of England. Pring led an expedition of two ships, the *Speedwell* and the *Discover*, to the same locales that Gosnold had visited. Pring, on the *Discover*, spied islands along a rocky coast the first week in June 1603. Sailing past Casco Bay (to which Pring would return in the company of Sir John Popham in 1607), Pring explored four of Maine's southernmost rivers: the Saco, Kennebunk, York, and Piscataqua. He was most intrigued by the last river: its broad mouth and strong current indicated a route inland navigable for large ships with harbors for safe anchorage.[7]

There were several accounts of French voyages along the coast, which Smith, knowing French, undoubtedly read: Champlain's *Voyages* and Marc Lescarbot's *Nova Francia*. Samuel de Champlain sailed along the New England coast on three separate occasions from 1604 to 1606 as part of a larger French attempt to colonize the region from Maine north to the

St. Lawrence River. Serving as an explorer, journalist, and cartographer with the De Monts expedition, Champlain reconnoitered the coast of New Brunswick as far south as Passamaquoddy Bay and the St. Croix River. There, on an island in the river, he established the French settlement. Thereupon Champlain explored Norumbega farther southwest, with two local Indians as guides. In September 1604, Champlain and his men gingerly made their way along the rocky shores and island-studded waters of the Maine coast until they came to a large island with about a dozen peaks, which Champlain named Mount Desert Island. Next, Champlain explored the Penobscot, called by the French the Norumbegue River. The French explorers ascended to the fall line, near present Bangor, before descending and continuing southwest. Champlain briefly visited Monhegan Island and sailed toward the mouth of the Kennebec before deciding, upon the arrival of the cold winds of late September, that he must return to the shelter of the St. Croix settlement. The winter, however, was extremely severe; the French settlers were trapped on the island because of the partially frozen river; cold, hunger, and disease plagued them. Undaunted, Champlain, with the arrival of spring, pursued the Maine coast again, arriving at the Kennebec (Quinebequy), up which he sailed. This time he was accompanied by De Monts and an Indian guide, Panounias, and his wife. Champlain extensively explored the Kennebec and its mouth, coasted across but not within Casco Bay, and explored the Saco (Chouacoit) River. The indigenous people (called by Champlain the Almouchiquois) were accomplished farmers. From the Saco, Champlain voyaged south past Cape Porpoise and the mouth of the Piscataqua River between the New Hampshire shoreline and the Isles of Shoals, which Champlain noted though at which he did not pause. After cruising along the southern coast of New England, the French determined to return to the fort at St. Croix before the arrival of autumn. They halted briefly at the mouths of the Saco and Kennebec, and heard from the Indians of recent English visitors. Unlike the French, the English came not in peace, rather with intentions of violence.[8]

Smith knew of Captain George Waymouth's voyage in Maine from "a relation printed . . . by Captaine *Waymouth*, of *Pemmaquid*," as well as by conversing with men who had made the voyage and with the Indian

Samuel de Champlain voyaged along the New England coast almost a decade before Smith. Library of Congress.

sachem, or chief, Dohannida.[9] Waymouth had departed England in early March in a single ship, the *Archangel*, under the sponsorship of Sir Thomas Arundel. Arriving in May off the coast of Cape Cod and intending to explore regions farther south, Waymouth was instead forced north by strong southerly gales. He was able to escape the winds in the lee of Monhegan Island. Intrigued by the Maine coast, and particularly the hazy mountains in the distance, he explored Muscongus Bay, sailed up the St. George River, and explored Penobscot Bay. For a time the English futilely tried to march inland to reach and explore the beckoning mountains of the bay, which appeared much closer than they were. Around the area of current Thomaston, Maine, Waymouth claimed the land for England, backing up his claim with the violent kidnapping of five Algonquian Indians. These Indians survived the return voyage to England, where Waymouth presented two to Sir John Popham, lord chief justice, and three to Sir Ferdinando Gorges, military commander at Plymouth. One of these was Dohannida, whom Smith would later meet. Waymouth's explorations along with what they learned from the captive Algonquians inspired Popham and Gorges to pursue the colonization of northern New England. Acting upon the charter granted to the London Company and the Plymouth Company by King James I in 1606, both men planned extensive attempts to explore and establish settlements along the Maine coast. Popham and Gorges sent George Hanham and Martin Pring in 1606 to find out more about the region explored by Waymouth. They brought with them Dohannida, whom they left behind upon their departure.[10]

Smith was in Virginia in 1607 when along "the Riuer *Sadagahock,* . . . was planted the Westerne Colony, by that Honourable Patrone of vertue, Sir *Iohn Poppham.*"[11] In May, two ships organized by John Popham departed Plymouth, England, to cross the Atlantic. George Popham, nephew of Sir John, commanded the *Gift of God*; he was to be president of the colony. Raleigh Gilbert, son of the great Elizabethan explorer Humfrey Gilbert, commanded the *Mary and John*, the admiral (or flagship) of the expedition. The two ships rendezvoused at Muscongus Bay and continued on to Pemaquid, in the general area from which Popham's Indian captive, Skidwarres, hailed. There the captive was released to his tribe, but the Indians were nevertheless wary of possible continued English deception. Feeling unwelcome, the English departed to the south for the mouth of the Kennebec River. There, at one of the many pincers of land jutting into the Atlantic, a place that the Indians called Sagadahoc, the English established their colony. Construction began in August; the fort was ready when the winter winds hit. Meanwhile shipwrights set to building a pinnace while other colonists explored the area and tried to establish trade with the Indians. This latter goal was not very successful, as the natives remained skeptical of English protestations of friendship. The fate of the colony was set when Sir John Popham died in England and shortly thereafter the president of the colony, his nephew George, died in Maine; Raleigh Gilbert came into an inheritance, which determined his decision to return. The colony was abandoned during the summer of 1608.[12]

Further English attempts to settle Maine were delayed for several years after the Popham colony debacle. Ferdinando Gorges was disheartened, writing that the colony's failure provided a "wonderfull discouragement to all the first vndertakers, in so much as there was no more speech of setling any other plantations in those parts for a long time after." The French, more sanguine, continued their attempts. In 1613 two Jesuit priests, Pierre Biard and Enemond Massé, on their way to the Kennebec, halted instead at Mount Desert Island, where they found the natives welcoming and the soil rich. A small fort and houses were built, and the ground was cultivated by the Frenchmen who accompanied the priests. The new colony had a terribly short existence, however, due to an attack by Captain Samuel Argall of the English Jamestown colony. Argall had sailed up the coast reconnoitering for possible French settlements; he had orders to destroy any he found, as they were trespassing upon *Virginia*, the vast territory stretching from Georgia to Maine chartered by James I in 1606. Argall bombarded the settlement with cannon, forcing its surrender. After allowing most of the colonists their freedom, he eventually destroyed the settlement.[13]

John Smith was by birth an inquisitive explorer and an ad hoc scientist. He had journeyed throughout much of the known European world, including the Netherlands, France, Spain, Germany, Italy, Greece, Hungary, Transylvania, Romania, Russia, Turkey, North Africa, and islands of the Mediterranean. He had been the most active discoverer among the adventurers who founded Jamestown. Smith had explored the Chesapeake and tributaries, and had provided a detailed and accurate map of Virginia. One of his first publications, in 1612, was *A Map of Virginia, With a Description of the Countrey*. He had read about the Roanoke voyages of the 1580s, and knew Thomas Hariot and read his work (*A Briefe and True Report of the New Found Land of Virginia*). He took after Hariot and other journalists of voyages, such as Brereton, Rosier, and Champlain, in providing minute descriptions of the flora, fauna, minerals, people, and geography of America. His *Map of Virginia* provides an extensive Algonquian vocabulary of words and phrases, which Smith had picked up during his time at Jamestown. Smith believed he was in a line of "diligent obseruers" by whose work "posterity may be bettered." Yet notwithstanding the voyages of so many others, the region had no set name,

Monhegan Isle was the point of arrival and departure for Smith and his men in 1614. Library of Congress.

and was called variously "Norumbega, Virginia, Nuskoncus, Penaquida, Cannada, and such other names as those that ranged the Coast pleased." Smith, in short, concluded in 1614 "that the Coast is yet still but euen as a Coast vnknowne and vndiscouered."[14]

Monhegan Isle was a sea mark known to fishers and explorers for many years before Smith and his men moored their two barks in the harbor. Not only was the island a high outpost jutting from the sea, unmistakable with its rocky ledges that warned sailors to beware, but on its western side was a small harbor that allowed small ships and fishing boats to lie with some safety. Smith noted that on the lee side of Monhegan was a small island called Monanis (Manana), which formed "a small harbor where we ride." The harbor entrance is to the south, with Monhegan to the east, Manana to the west and obstructing the northern entrance, thus forming the third side to the cozy harbor, a rocky outpost called Smutty Nose Island.[15]

The initial and primary purpose of the voyage was "to take Whales and to make tryalls of a mine to find Gold and Copper." Smith candidly admitted in his *Description of New England* that, regarding the latter goal, "it was rather the Masters deuice [device] to get a voyage that proiected it, then any knowledge hee had at all of any such matter." Smith made some cursory searches for precious metals on his voyage along the coast; otherwise it appears that the search for gold and copper was quickly dropped in favor of whaling, which also became a problem, and fishing. The English were comparatively new to whaling. The Muscovy Company of England had sent a whaling expedition to Spitzbergen the year before, in 1613, with some success. Basque fishermen had engaged in whaling using shallops along the New England coast, and the Algonquians also sometimes hunted whales. The wealth in whaling lay in the oil, liquefied blubber, and in the whalebone, also called the baleen, and which Smith called the "finnes." The baleen is the means by which certain whales, such as the right whale, feed; it is a flexible cartilage, rather like human nails, that was used in corsets. Upon arriving at Monhegan, the mariners set to constructing fishing shallops that had been brought in pieces. Once they had constructed seven shallops, they began whaling. Of a crew of six or so men, four would row while one navigated and one wielded the harpoon. When the whale was harpooned, it would take off swimming and diving in pain and fear; the shallop had an extremely long rope to allow the whale to tire itself in its agony, when another harpoon, and another, would be thrust into the beast, eventually killing it. This was the theory. Whether or not Smith and his men had ever engaged in whaling is unclear, because of the result: "We found this Whale-fishing a costly conclusion: we saw many and spent much time in chasing them; but could not kill any." Even if they had succeeded, they got a good enough look at the whales to know that they were not the correct species. They sought right whales, or sperm whales, but Smith reported that those they chased were "a kind of Iubartes," probably the humpback whale (*Megaptera novaeangliae*), which was "not the Whale that yeeldes Finnes and Oyle as wee expected." After wasting the month of May in fruitless whaling, they decided to turn to fishing.[16]

Whalers became fishers during the month of June. The shallops were just as useful for fishing as for whaling. The fishers used poles and hooks and nets to catch cod, herring, ling, mullet, haddock, and mackerel. Whereas their plan had been to bring captured whales to Monhegan, where they could slaughter them and boil down the blubber into oil to be stored in casks, they now brought the fish to shore, where they split and dried them on wooden stages, which resembled wharves, called flakes. The fishers had limited success because of the growing warmth of summer. "Fish and Furres was now our guard," Smith wrote, "and by our late arriual, and long lingring about the Whale, the prime of both those seasons were past ere wee perceiued it; we thinking that their seasons, serued at all times: but wee found it otherwise; for, by the midst of Iune, the fishing failed." Many years later, when Smith penned *Advertisements for the unexperienced Planters of New England*, he blamed the "unskilfulnesse of our Pylot" for the misinformation. Fortunately, the fishing picked up again in July before they departed for England. Meanwhile Smith decided to take one of the shallops, with eight other men, to explore and to meet and trade with the indigenous people for furs.[17]

Was it by chance or design that Smith thus began his journey along the New England coast? Had the whaling paid off, all the days might have been filled with chasing, harpooning, cutting blubber, and making oil, and perhaps Smith's explorations would have been very limited indeed, for profit more than discovery of necessity ruled the voyage. Had the fishing been as wonderful as they anticipated, so that none of the forty-five men could be spared, then again, Smith's journey might have never happened or been much curtailed. As it was, nine men could be spared, as well as a fishing shallop, because one of two ways to make the voyage break even, much less make a profit, was to garner whatever furs they could. So Smith set forth for furs, which to find required exploration of isles, bays, and rivers to discover the indigenous people; then he had to meet with the people, to befriend them in order to trade, to converse with them by whatever means he could—in Algonquian such as Smith had learned in Virginia, by means of his interpreter Tisquantum, who spoke an Algonquian dialect of southern New England, or by means of sign language, the lingua franca of American Indians and Euro-American explorers and traders. A generation later, the English physician and explorer John Josselyn discovered, as he wrote in *New Englands Rarities Discovered*, that the Algonquian "language is very significant, using but few words, every word having a diverse signification, which is expressed by their gesture; as when they hold their head of one side the word signifieth one thing, holding their hand up when they pronounce it signifieth another thing. Their Speeches in their Assemblies are very gravely delivered, commonly in perfect *Hexamiter* Verse, with great silence and attention, and answered again *ex tempore* after the same mannter [*sic*]." Smith had learned in Virginia that information from the natives could supplement what he discovered by his own observations. Then one must make a map, must pen descriptions, in order to trace the way again in after years, when the initial visit was long past, more permanent colonies were to be established, and alliances with the local Indian tribes would be a necessity for safety and success.[18]

Smith, often more cryptic than clear in his many accounts of the exploration of New England, wrote about sixteen years after the fact that he and his exploring companions ranged the coast "by an houre glasse of three moneths." When he actually departed on his exploring expedition is unclear. Perhaps after the carpenters prepared the shallops in early May he made short voyages along the coast east and west of Penobscot Bay, to test the waters, as it were, while others engaged in whaling. If so, Smith explored the New England coast, perhaps off and on at first, from early May to mid-July, almost three months. The hourglass (or half-hour glass, as Smith kept on board his boats) was the best timekeeper on mariners' voyages during the Tudor and Stuart years. No doubt Smith kept one close by him on the journey from the Downs to Monhegan. And doubtless it accompanied him, and tracked time, from Penobscot to Cape Cod and back. These were months of intermittent cool and warm days, when the weather cleared after the summer solstice and the waters of the Atlantic grew warmer. The hourglass kept track of the longer days of summer as well as the daily tides, so that voyagers could plan the best times to ascend or descend rivers with tidal waters rushing in or out. The hourglass, unaffected by waves, winds, and storms, tracked constancy in a changing environment of newcomers ranging a strange coast looking for something, anything, by which to stake a claim for the future.[19]

FOUR

The Penobscot

Smith, his men, and his guide Tisquantum set forth from Monhegan Island in a small fishing shallop heading north toward the coast. It was late spring, and though the water was cold, cooling the breezes that skimmed over the waves, the sun beat down fiercely upon the men in the open boat. There are frequent rains along the coast in summer months, and some days the fog is sufficiently cool to require a heavy garment—and if the fog is thick upon the water the mariner is wetted by a cool mist before the appearance of the drying sun later in the day. It was a clear day when the Englishmen set their course to the wind, then proceeded slowly and methodically to make the voyage along the coast less perilous. The shallop was not built for comfort but for agility in negotiating shoal waters, narrow bays, and rivers. It had a shallow draft to permit safe sailing in relatively shallow waters with sandy bottoms. The shallop was about thirty feet long and eight feet wide. It had a single mast with fore and aft rigging for maneuverability if not speed, and oars to proceed in any direction notwithstanding a headwind or doldrums. One man handled a tiller attached to a rudder to guide the boat. Rowing benches provided the only seating, and there was no shelter against any of the elements with which the Gulf of Maine could challenge mariners. The shallop's vulnerability to the elements was similar to that of the larger Norse longboats that skimmed northeastern American waters six hundred years before the English. Smith and his men had to possess the same qualities as those Viking explorers, of courage, endurance, strength, will, and determination, to which they added an unhesitating reliance upon the will of God.[1]

Smith came prepared for his voyage with unnamed maps and charts

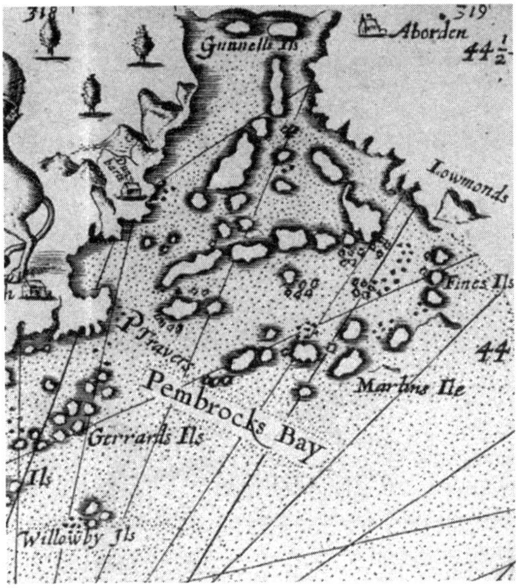

Smith provided an accurate representation of Penobscot Bay, which he denoted Pembrocks Bay, on the *Map of New England*. American Memory, Library of Congress.

drawn by his predecessors. He wrote in *Description of New England* that "I haue had six or seuen seuerall plots of those Northerne parts, so vnlike each to other, and most so differing from any true proportion or resemblance of the Countrey, as they did mee no more good then so much waste paper, though they cost me more. It may be it was not my chance to see the best." Extant maps that Smith might have examined included those by the French, such as maps of New France by Marc Lescarbot and Samuel de Champlain, both published in 1612; the Velasco Map, drawn (perhaps) by someone connected to the Virginia Company about 1611; a map of America by the Dutch cartographer Jodocus Hondius; and a map from the George Waymouth voyage of 1605, now lost. "Least others," Smith wrote, "may be deceiued as I was, or thro[u]gh dangerous ignorance hazard themselues as I did, I haue drawen a Map from Point to Point, Ile to Ile, and Harbour to Harbour, with the Soundings, Sands, Rocks, and Land-marks as I passed close aboard the Shore in a little Boat."[2]

Two years later, in 1616, back in England, Smith prepared his *Descrip-*

tion of New England for publication. It occurred to him to dedicate the book to the teenage Prince Charles: "I heere present your Highness the description in a Map; my humble su[i]te is, you would please to change their Barbarous names, for such English, as Posterity may say, Prince *Charles* was their Godfather." The dedication worked, and Prince Charles asked to see Smith and his map, during which meeting the prince acceded to Smith's request and, with Smith's suggestions, altered the indigenous names for English alternatives. Smith meanwhile had contracted the services of an engraver, Simon van de Passe, to draw the *Map of New England*, which was published with Prince Charles's appellations. The *Description of New England* having already gone to press, Smith requested that the printer strike off an extra page to be inserted in the published copies. The addendum reads: "Because the Booke was printed ere the Prince his Highnesse had altered the names, I intreate the Reader, peruse this schedule; which will plainely shew him the correspondence of the old names to the new." For readers of Smith's *Description* and *Map* ever since, perusing this addendum is necessary to make sense of the contrasting names in the book and on the map. Notwithstanding the confusion, the map is an essential tool in re-creating Smith's voyage. The accuracy of the map is remarkable considering the limitations of sailing an unknown coast in an open boat. As per his aim, the map fits snugly with his *Description of New England*. Much later in life, Smith discussed the theory and practice of sailing, noting the essential tools and methods of navigation, in *An Accidence or The Path-way to Experience*. What navigational instruments—the cross-staff, back staff, astrolabe, quadrant, and nocturnal—Smith and his men carried aboard the shallop is unclear, though Smith could hardly have been so successful paralleling the inhospitable coast of New England had he not had such instruments used for surveying and determining latitude.[3]

With these few instruments and assorted prayers Smith, his men, and native interpreter sailed along the coast using a trial-and-error approach, trying "those conclusions, not knowing the Coast, nor Saluages habitation." This region of the eastern extreme of New England was no doubt foreign territory for the Patuxet native Tisquantum; he and other southern New England Indians feared the Mi'kmaq tribe, the most daunting tribe of these northern parts. Tisquantum, like Smith, would have learned quickly through experience, which Smith preferred over theory anyway. He explained in *Description of New England* that he would have preferred the leisure of months, not weeks, for discovery, for he knew "there be many things to be obserued which the haste of other affaires did cause me [to] omit." His voyage was not supposed to be for exploration and discovery, to gain "knowledge by discoueries for any future good." Rather, having been "sent more to get present commodities . . . , I had not power to search as I would." "Yet," he maintained, "it will serue to direct any [that] should goe that waies, to safe Harbours and the Saluages habitations," which Smith and his men discovered by painstaking, patient navigation and inquisitive searching.[4]

Smith's *Map of New England* reveals that he and his men sailed to Metinic Island (which Smith called Metinicus and Prince Charles changed to Hoghton Ils) to the northeast of Monhegan, and Matinicus Island (which he called Matinnack and Charles called Willowby Ils), which is due east from Metinic. Smith's map fairly accurately placed these islands with respect to other islands and the coast, although he placed Monhegan Island (called Barty Ils on the map) too far west. Smith clearly wished to know the sea approaches to Penobscot Bay (which is called, on his map, Pembrocks Bay). The surrounding waters of all of these islands, especially Matinicus, require careful sailing to avoid rocks, ledges, and bars. The sailors knew when a ship entered into shallow, "fowle water," because the motion of the boat stirred the sandy, oozy bottom. Smith's map shows three islands and shoals that make up the group of Willowby, or Matinicus, Isles, which would indicate that he explored Ragged Island, south of Matinicus, as well as perhaps No Mans Land or Tenpound Isles. There are small harbors on Matinicus and Ragged in which Smith could have briefly anchored to explore these small, wooded islands. Metinic Island on Smith's map shows accurately that there are several islands next to Metinic, and plentiful shoal waters, which would have probably satisfied most mariners, including Smith, to sail peacefully by without attempting to find a mooring. Interestingly, Smith's map provides a very accurate representation of a series of about a dozen islands amid rocks, ledges, and other hazards that lie between Metinic Island and Owls Head (which Smith, and Prince Charles, dubbed on the map Point Travers). These islands have names today such as Crow, Pleasant, Graffam, Flagg, Hewett, Hurricane, Andrews, the Neck, Dix, Birch, Camp, High, Oak, and Otter. The rocks, ledges, and hazards among these islands are considerable, and it must have exercised much good navigating and a lot of hard rowing to avoid shipwreck. There are several harbors the men might have found amid the island maze for rest and exploration.[5]

Nothing in Smith's *Description of New England* counters the notion that the captain and his men sought first the easternmost of islands, bays, and capes. Logically, then, before entering Penobscot Bay to explore Penobscot River, Smith explored those many islands that bar the western and eastern approaches. Smith's map is not as clear here, showing a number of islands positioned horizontally across the entrance of the bay, which is not entirely accurate. He visited what Martin Pring had called Fox Islands, now a host of about a dozen islands dominated by North Haven and Vinalhaven. Smith likely sailed through the strait separating these two islands, since called Fox Islands Thoroughfare, and made it broader on his map than it is, at least, today. Smith (and Prince Charles) named one of these islands, on his map, Martins Ile, perhaps in honor of Pring's voyage. To sail amid the many isles surrounding Vinalhaven was no mean achievement, requiring dropping the lead and careful navigating to escape injury. Smith described this part of Penobscot Bay as "full of great Ilands, of one, two, six, eight, or ten miles in length; which diuides it into many faire and excellent good harbours."[6]

Smith sailed as far east as the Isle au Haut, which he called Sorico, claiming in the *Description of New England* that this was the "highest Ile" that he saw on his journey. The island, which rises to 553 feet, on its north side presents a bold cliff; there are several good harbors on its eastern coast that could have hosted Smith's shallop. Smith's name, Sorico, is perhaps based on his understanding of what the French called the native inhabitants of the place, the Souriquois. These people, the Mi'kmaq, lived in today's Nova Scotia, New Brunswick, and Bay of Fundy regions, and from the Passamaquoddy Bay west to the Penobscot. Smith, and other English explorers, referred to them as the Tarrentines, who lived with the French "as one nation or family." The French called the Algonquians

HOW PRINCE CHARLES CALLED THE MOST REMARKABLE PLACES IN NEW ENGLAND

The old names.	*The new names.*
Cape Cod.	Cape James.
The Harbor at Cape Cod.	Milforth Haven.
Chawum.	Barwick.
Accomack.	Plimoth.
Sagoquas.	Oxford.
Massachusets Mount.	Chevit hills.
Massachusits River.	Charles River.
Totan.	Famouth.
A great bay by Cape Anne.	Bristow.
Cape Tragabigsanda.	Cape Anne.
Naembeck.	Bastable.
Aggawom.	Southampton.
Smiths Iles.	Smiths Iles.
Passataquack.	Hull.
Accominticus.	Boston.
Sassanows Mount.	Snowdon hill.
Sowocatuck.	Ipswich.
Bahanna.	Dartmouth.
A good Harbor within that Bay.	Sandwich.
Ancociscos Mount.	Shuters hill.
Ancocisco.	The Base.

Smith's list of the old (Indian) names, and the new names supplied by Prince Charles, used on his *Map of New England.*

SOURCE: John Smith, *The generall historie of Virginia, New England & the Summer Isles: together with The true travels, adventures and observations, and A sea grammar.* New York : Macmillan, 1907. American Memory, Library of Congress

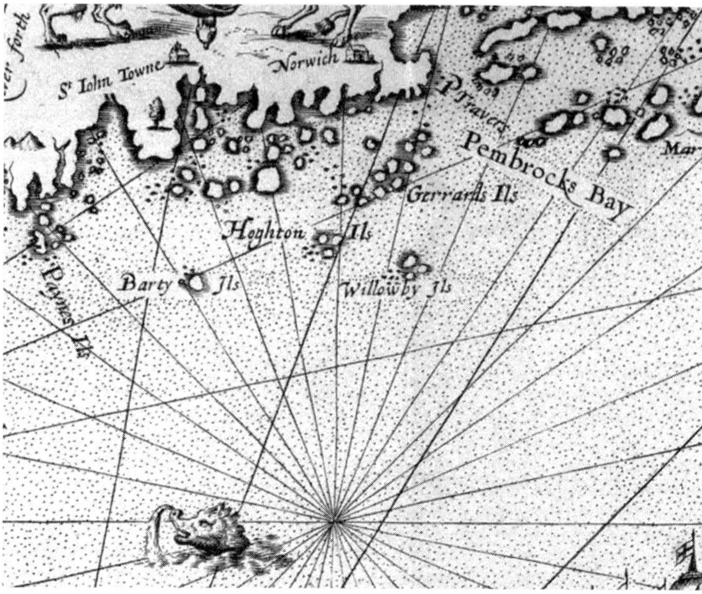

Smith referred to Monhegan Island as Barty Ils, and Matinicus Island as Willowby Ils, on his *Map of New England*. American Memory, Library of Congress.

from Penobscot Bay to Pemaquid the Etchimens, who sometimes allied themselves with other Algonquian tribes farther west, or the Souriquois to the east. Samuel de Champlain during his voyage the previous decade had met with the leader of the Western Etchimens and their allies, whose title was Bashabes (Champlain called him Bessabez). Smith heard about the Bashabes from the local inhabitants and the indigenous peoples to the south, such as his interpreter Tisquantum, who told him that "they hold the Bashabes of Pennobscot, the chiefe and greatest amongst them."[7]

The native inhabitants of the northeast coast of America were woodland peoples who had for centuries carved a plentiful existence from the northern forest. From Nova Scotia and New Brunswick south to Cape Cod, there were dozens of small tribes who spoke varied dialects of the Algonquian language. Although they sometimes differed in style of habitations, use of the land, means of transport, customs, and ceremonies, the New England Algonquians were united in relying on hunting deer, bear, and other mammals of the forest for food and clothing; catching and

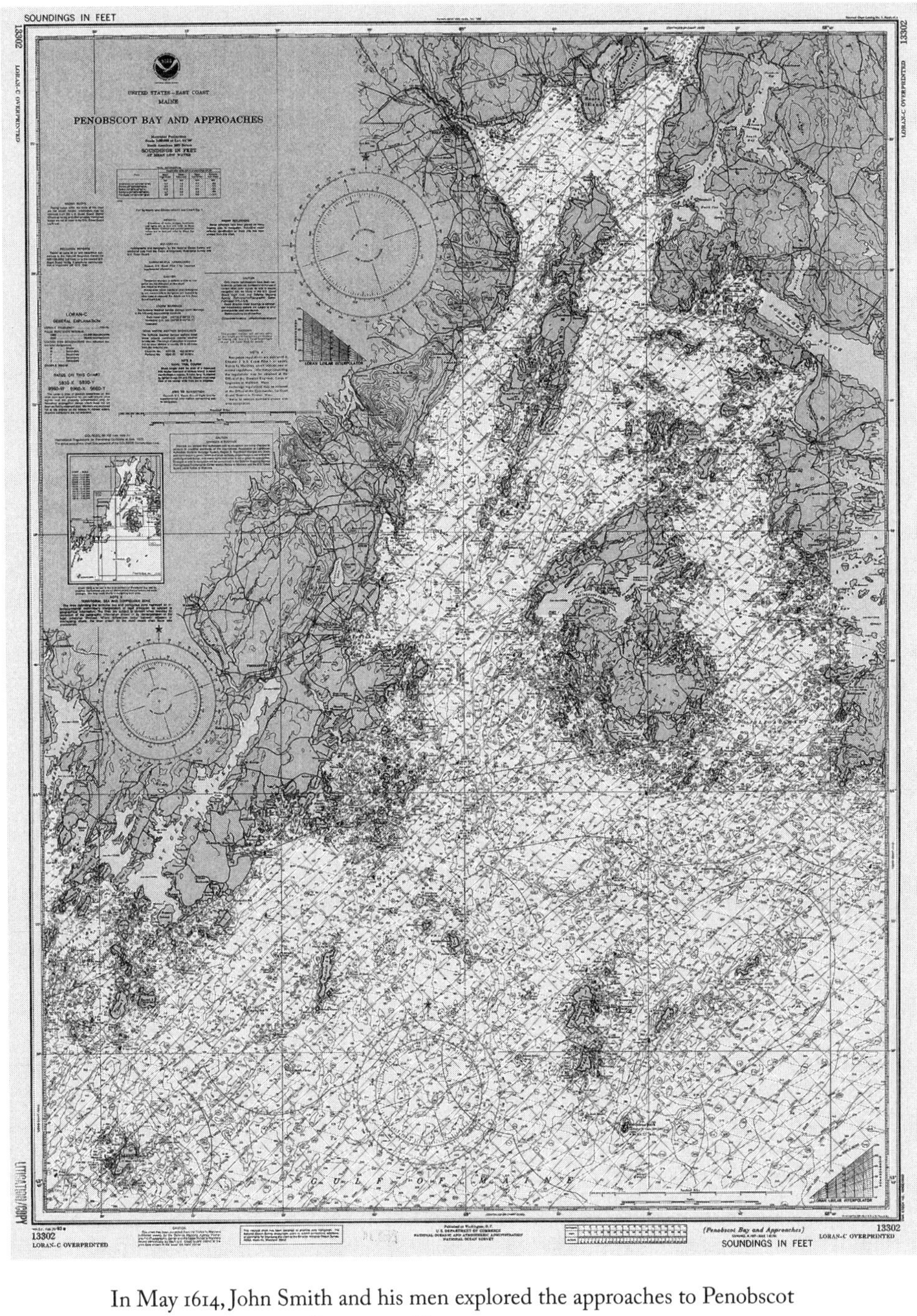

In May 1614, John Smith and his men explored the approaches to Penobscot Bay. NOAA Chart 13302-02-1983.

gathering fish and shellfish of the rivers and bays; foraging the meadows and forests for nuts, berries, and roots; and using the vegetation, bark, and wood of coniferous and deciduous trees for shelter, fuel, tools, and weapons.

Where precisely Smith met with the indigenous people of the Penobscot is unclear from his account. His map indicates several Indian villages, which Smith either heard about or visited. He explored throughout the bay, east and west, the dimensions of which are "more then ten leagues," though he did not ascend the river, as Champlain had, because of the constraints of time and because, although he learned that "the Riuer ranne farre vp into the Land, and was well inhabited with many people," "they were [away] from their habitations, either fishing among the Iles, or hunting the Lakes and Woods, for Deer and Beuers." He acquired this information from unidentified native inhabitants in the bay, "gathered from the niggardly relations in a broken language, to my vnderstanding, during the time I ranged those Countries." Changes in regional dialects along the coast made it difficult for Smith and Tisquantum to gather accurately everything that the Mi'kmaq said.[8]

Had Smith and his men ascended the Penobscot by rowing and sailing the shallop to the head of tide, they would have come to the Penobscot village at Old Town, where subsequent English explorers and colonists found about fifty native families living in birch-bark and spruce longhouses. The Algonquians up and down the coast used the birch bark not only for shelter but also for transport. Birch bark, stripped from the paper birch tree, was the chief material for making the preferred means of travel, the birch-bark canoe. Algonquians were adept at making these canoes quickly and efficiently. Birch bark is flexible and strong. The artisans stripped long pieces of the bark off felled trees. They fastened the bark to a wooden frame made of ash or similar hardwood, using pitch from pine trees as a glue; the roots of spruce trees sewed the seams together. The resulting canoe was light yet buoyant, able to carry more humans than its somewhat flimsy appearance would otherwise indicate.[9]

The Penobscot is the largest river originating and descending exclusively in Maine. The source of the Penobscot is the height of land that forms the watershed between Maine rivers and Canadian rivers flowing north to the St. Lawrence. The sources of the West Branch and East Branch of the Penobscot rise on either side of Mount Katahdin, the highest point in Maine, which cannot be seen from Penobscot Bay but can be seen from places just inland. Katahdin juts out of the forest, a solitary peak, a rocky crag, soaring skyward. The Maine Indians referred to it as the highest peak, Teddon, and feared to ascend it as being the home of evil spirits, such as the "night wind," or the "storm bird," Pamola, from which the climber would not return. The Indians of the Penobscot Valley relied heavily on fishing and trapping for their sustenance; they were successful agriculturalists, growing maize and securing it for lean times. "When the Corn is in the Milk," the Indian captive and English soldier John Gyles later wrote, "they gather a large Kettle full and boil it on the Ears until it is pretty hard, and then they take it up and shell it of the Cobb with Clam-Shells, and dry it on Bark in the Sun; and when it's thro'ly dryed, a Kernel is no bigger than a Pea, and keep Years—and boil'd again it swells as large, and tastes incomparably sweeter than other Corn." Perhaps Smith and his men enjoyed a friendly repast of such corn.[10]

Exploring the bay, the Isle au Haut was the farthest east Smith journeyed by shallop, from which, "as farre I could see Eastward of it," the coast was similar to the Penobscot region, "nothing but such high craggy Cliffy Rocks and stony Iles that I wondered such great trees could growe vpon so hard foundations." The white pine dominated coniferous trees and the paper birch deciduous trees along the coast and inland. The combination of massive trees along a granite coast amazed Smith, who declared it "a Countrie rather to affright, then delight one. And how to describe a more plaine spectacle of desolation, or more barren, I knowe not." "Yet," sailing and rowing the shallop from Monhegan to Metinic to Matinicus then among the islands at the entrance of Penobscot Bay, and seeing (and eating) the incredible numbers of fish among such otherwise desolation, "the Sea there is the strangest fishpond I euer saw; and those barren Iles so furnished with good woods, springs, fruits, fish, and foule, that it makes mee thinke, though the Coast be rockie, and thus affrightable; the Vallies, Plaines, and interior parts may well (notwithstanding) be very fertile." Can fertility exist next to barrenness? Of course, since "there is no kingdome so fertile [that] hath not some part barren: and

Isle au Haut, which Smith called Sorico, was the "highest Ile" he saw along the New England coast. Library of Congress.

New England is great enough to make many Kingdomes and Countries, were it all inhabited"—Smith discovered this at the Penobscot and all along the coast to Cape Cod. He revealed in his words his mixture of fear and awe as he beheld the land, which elicited in him a desire to know, and a sense of piety toward the Creator of such vast beauty.[11]

The Penobscot River enters the Atlantic in two channels, east and west. After exploring the waters about Isle au Haut, and its many hazards to avoid, Smith sailed north, exploring east Penobscot Bay. His *Map of New England* shows three small islands (Kimball, Merchant, Crotch) at the eastern extreme of the bay, which he and Prince Charles called Fines Ils; he saw and perhaps explored these along the island-studded route north from Isle au Haut to Deer Isle. The map designates a hill to the east, Lowmonds (named for Scotland's Lomond Hills north of Edinburgh)—perhaps Blue Hill—near which was an Indian village, Nusket. Smith's map next shows very clearly Deer Isle and Little Deer

Isle, and beyond them, to the west-northwest, Cape Rosier and, to the north, Castine. Smith's map is not as detailed here, and perhaps he did not explore this area, notwithstanding the many excellent harbors and coves. Whether or not the English, such as Pring or Waymouth, had preceded Smith to this region of Penobscot Bay is unclear from the historical record; the French undoubtedly had, and Smith complained that the French dominated trade from the Penobscot east along the coast.[12]

One suspects without clear evidence for or against that Smith's farthest inland penetration of Penobscot Bay was Cape Jellison and Sears Island—his map portrays several indistinct islands to the north (Gunnells Ils—named for his friend Robert Gunnell) that could represent these distinct landmarks where bay becomes river. He placed an Indian village east of the head of navigation on Penobscot Bay, which he either heard about or, doubtfully, visited, which he called Pennobscot in his *Description of New England* and Aborden (or Aberden) on his map. Smith's map is very suggestive that he sailed around, perhaps visited, the long thin island of Isleboro, west of Castine and Cape Rosier, as well as Seven Hundred Acre Island. Although it is not clear that Smith went as far north as Fort Point, or visited Belfast Bay and the mouth of the Passagassawakeag River, the many mountains portrayed along the western edge of Penobscot Bay on his map indicate that Smith saw, and perhaps observed firsthand, Mt. Megunticook, Camden, Rockport, Rockland, and Owls Head. Smith's map shows five hills extending north of Owls Head and Rockland Harbor; there are quite a few more, and some of significant height: Ragged Mountain, Spuce Mountain, Pleasant Mountain, Bald Mountain, Bald Rock Mountain, and Mount Megunticook. This latter peak, which Smith called Mecaddacut in the *Description of New England* and Dunbarton on his map, was the highest in this small range north of Camden. Smith's map shows indentations along the western shore consistent with Camden, Rockport, and Rockland. He doubtless explored these harbors and at least gazed upon, if he did not approach to explore, the peaks. Smith described "Mecaddacut" as an Indian village "at the foot of a high mountaine." He probably had some contact with the indigenous people of Mecaddacut, as they informed him that they used the mountain as a defensive fortification, "a kind of fortresse against the Tarrantines" the Mi'kmaqs. This mountain, subsequently called Megunticook, adjoined "the high mountaines of Pennobscot, against whose feet doth beat the Sea." Smith had been witnessing these great hills during his exploration of Penobscot Bay: "ouer all the Land, Iles, or other impediments, you may well see them, sixteene or eighteene leagues from their situation." On the other hand, from the perspective of a hill such as Megunticook, the distant bay, sprinkled with so many forested islands, appears calm and peaceful.[13]

Smith's voyage south allowed him to investigate three beautiful harbors on the western shores of Penobscot Bay. Camden Harbor was small, with a few hazards but with good anchorage; Rockport Harbor likewise was practically shoal-free, and provided excellent mooring for ships; Rockland Harbor had a few more shoals but offered excellent protection from storms. Sailing east, rounding Owls Head, the mariners had to avoid a few hazards but were able to make it quickly and without incident to Owls Head Harbor, across from Monroe Island. The Maine coast south of Owls Head was less certain, the hazards greater, at least close to shore. That Smith's map does not portray any isles off Owls Head (or Point Travers as he and Prince Charles called it) indicates that he explored neither Monroe Island nor Sheep Island—though he could see their wooded prospect in the distance. Continuing south-southwest, the men sailed past Ash Point with Ash Island to their port (or larboard) side. The passage here and farther, as the coast turned west-southwest, was shoal-ridden, extremely dangerous, and the sailor at the tiller had to take care not to hit a rock or ledge or run aground. Smith recorded no incidents; hence they probably had a safe passage. His map indicates several headlands, such places subsequently called Ash Point, Otter Point, Sprucehead, and Mosquito Head, their names suggestive of resident flora and fauna; and harbors, such as Seal Harbor, Whelier Bay, Clark Cove, Long Cove, and Tenants Harbor. One river along the way, Weskeag River (once called Wessaweskeag), did not promise an easy entrance for exploration, so was bypassed. Along the coast the lee of many large islands—Sprucehead, Rackliff, Clark, High, Northern, Mosquito—provided safe places to moor a boat—perhaps the English took advantage at night.[14]

The shallop approached Muscongus Bay through an island-studded waterway dubbed Gerrards Ils on Smith's map, since called Georges Is-

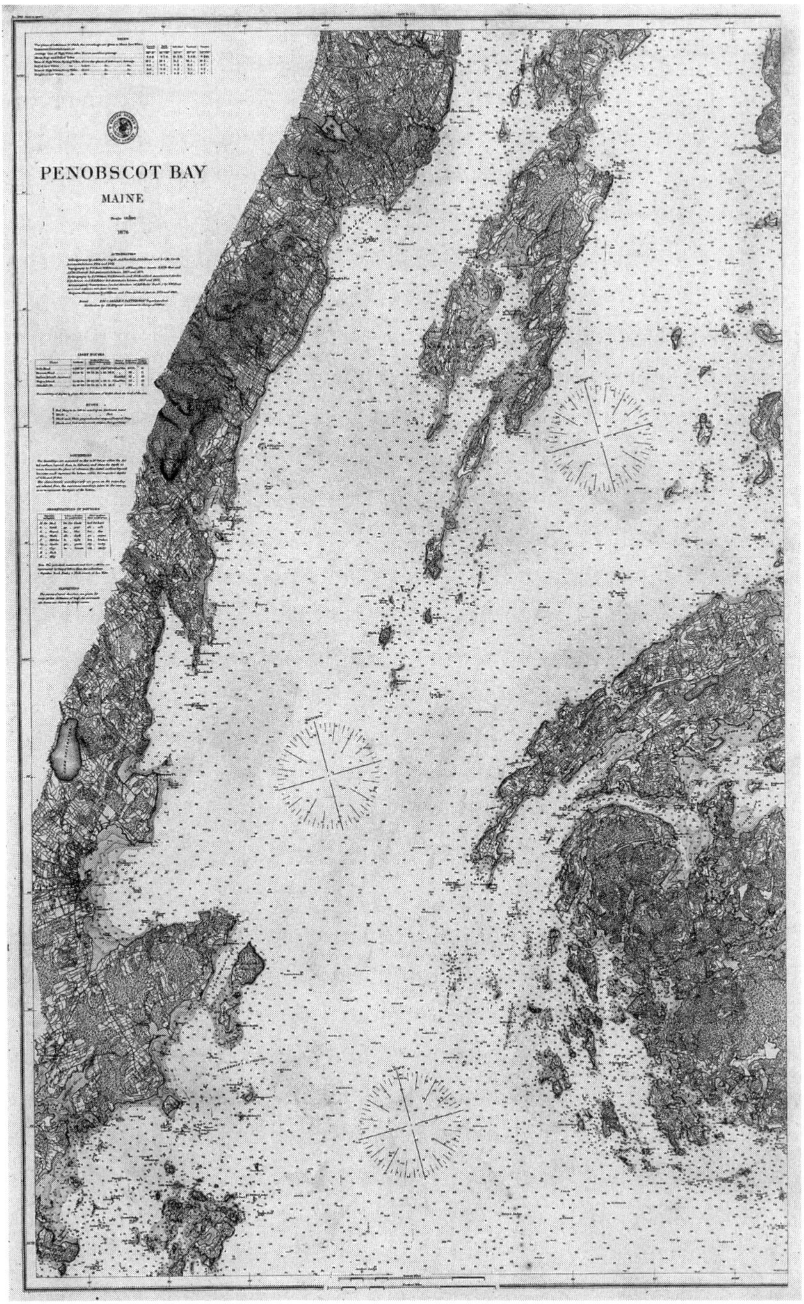

Penobscot Bay, based on the surveys and soundings of the nineteenth-century U.S. Coast Survey. NOAA Chart 293-08-1876.

lands. The coast was rocky and forested east and west, and up the many rivers flowing to the sea. This was particularly true of St. George River, shown on Smith's map north of Gerrards Ils. To approach the mouth, the men in the shallop had to wind their way through one of the most rock- and shoal-ridden places along the Maine coast. Once they had made their way safely past these hazards, they steered north following the fresh water of the river, sailing or rowing against the current, allowing the tide to carry them. They could have taken one of two passages, either east or west of Hupper Island, both of which had dangers enough. Once this passage was made, the river opened into a wide bay with few hazards.[15]

Smith knew something about the St. George River from George Waymouth's account of his voyage nine years earlier, and from Dohannida, the Wawenock sachem whom Smith knew from England. Smith hoped to find Dohannida, who could provide an opening for friendly trade and communication with the Wawenock and others tribes of the coast. Smith knew that Dohannida could most likely be found between the Penobscot and Pemaquid, particularly at the Indian villages of Segocket or Pemaquid. When the ships *Gift of God* and *Mary and John* sailed along the coast in 1607, Popham and Gilbert and their men met Dohannida at Pemaquid, where he was sachem.[16]

Whether or not Smith met up with Dohannida is not clear; Smith hinted in the *Description of New England* that he had met with Dohannida, and that the two agreed that the English assist the Wawenock in their conflicts with the Mi'kmaq. His search for Dohannida, as well as his intent to explore the coast and navigable rivers and to trade with the indigenous inhabitants, led him up the St. George River to the Wawenock village of Segocket, called Norwich on Smith's *Map of New England*. The St. George has a broad channel, like many of the chief rivers along the New England coast, with few hazards beyond the mouth save the wind and current. There are many secure coves along the way that could host small ships like Smith's shallop in case of trouble. The native Wawenocks, called Etchimens by the French, were part of the confederation led by the Bashabes of Penobscot. The year after Smith's voyage, in 1615, the Souriquois or Mi'kmaq (called by Smith Tarrantines) to the east attacked the Penobscot Indians, killing the Bashabes. In the

The dramatic cape of Owl's Head at the western extreme of Penobscot Bay. Library of Congress.

wake of this disaster an epidemic spread down the coast, destroying large numbers of the indigenous peoples. In 1614, however, these people of the St. George were still strong and confident, and wary of the bearded men who came from across the sea.[17]

The Maine coast south of the St. George River looks on a map like great crooked fingers penetrating into the Atlantic. Smith and his men experienced long, fjord-like inlets, bays, and rivers. Exploring the Maine coast required patience for the Englishmen, as they sailed and rowed in and out, around headlands and peninsulas, up rivers and bays, avoiding ledges and rocks, skirting shoal water, seeking harbors, astonished by the pine-tree coast, wondering what lay within the great interior forest. Smith and his men allowed the outgoing tide to waft their shallop down the St. George River into Muscongus Bay, a coastal water with plentiful islands, shoals, rocks, and ledges. Perhaps it was at this point in his journey that Smith met with "a Ship of Sir Frances Popphames," the son and heir of the late John Popham; Sir Frances had for "many years" sent trading vessels along the coast of Maine south of Penobscot River. Smith would naturally have plied the captain with questions of the best places to trade for furs and pelts. One well-known place for trade was the Indian village of Pemaquid. Smith's *Map of New England* is imprecise in its picture of the coast between St. George River and Pemaquid Neck. There are several important rivers south of the St. George, such as the Meduncook and the Medomak, which are not indicated on his map. It appears, rather, that Smith sailed among the islands of Muscongus Bay toward the great headland that he could spy to the south: Pemaquid. Smith's map shows almost two dozen islands in Muscongus Bay, which is fairly accurate, as is the portrayal of islands across Muscongus Sound from Pemaquid Neck. Assuming that the accuracy of the map indicates experiences and observations on the voyage, Smith perhaps anchored at New Harbor, on the eastern side of Pemaquid Neck, as other English mariners had before him. The harbor was dangerous to enter, but after sailing through Muscongus Bay, Smith's men undoubtedly found such a comparatively easy challenge most refreshing.[18]

If we agree with the Maine historian Henry Burrage that Smith met the Popham ship at New Harbor, perhaps Smith heard from traders, English or Indian, where the Pemaquid Indian village was located. Smith put the village, which he called St. Iohn Towne, not on the Pemaquid River, or in Pemaquid Harbor, rather northwest of Muscongus Sound, west of Broad Cove on the Medomak River, to near Pemaquid Pond. Either Smith decided to sail north of New Harbor through Muscongus Sound to the Medomak River, or he continued south along Pemaquid Neck, then around Pemaquid Point, where the lighthouse now stands, north up the neck in Johns Bay to Pemaquid Harbor. A decade later the English established a fishing and trading outpost at Pemaquid, mooring their sloops and shallops in Pemaquid Harbor at the mouth of the river. A half century later, the English constructed Fort Charles at Pemaquid

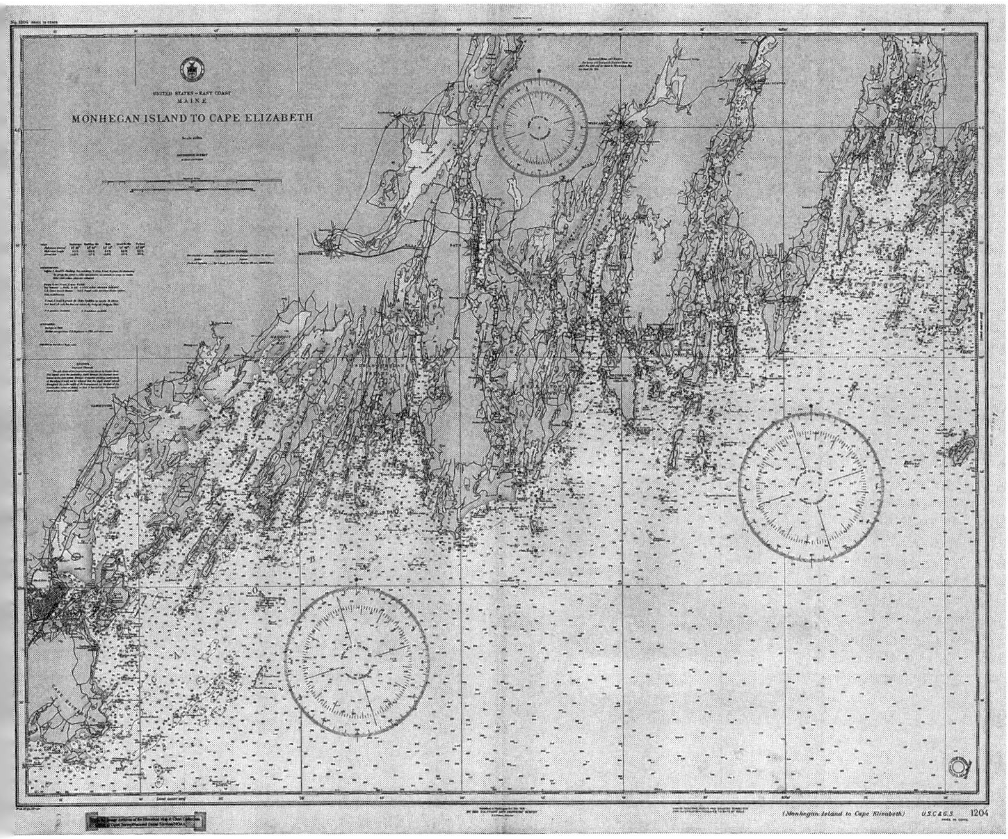

U.S. Coast & Geodetic Survey map from 1933 of the coast west of Penobscot Bay to Cape Elizabeth. NOAA Chart 1204-10-1933.

Harbor in 1677 because of the sporadic attacks and counterattacks of King Philip's War. Long before such conflicts, Smith and his men departed Pemaquid, continuing west to the Damariscotta River, which they ascended, allowing the tide to take the shallop upriver to a point parallel with Pemaquid Pond. Indian trade paths from Penobscot south went through the St. George River Valley to the upper Medomak Valley, south to New Harbor, west to Pemaquid Harbor, and north to the Damariscotta River Valley. The Indian village of Pemaquid located at Pemaquid Pond would be perfectly situated along this trade route.[19]

If we continue to poke into the mind of John Smith using his *Map of New England* to hypothesize his itinerary along the coast of Maine, we

The lighthouse at Pemaquid Point, Bristol, Maine. Library of Congress.

see that he pictured three great headlands between Pemaquid and the Kennebec River. He portrayed rivers between two of these headlands, and to the south, multiple islands, which Smith and Prince Charles designated Paynes Ils. Several mountains lay inland. Smith acquired by experience the representations on the map, but not without error, as he formed an inaccurate approximation of the size of Johns Bay, making it much broader than it is. He mapped Damariscotta River, and the islands at its mouth and to the south. One of these islands, called Damerils Ils on Smith's map, is now known as Damariscove Island. Perhaps he knew that fishermen sometimes bivouacked here; likewise Smith moored the shallop at a small harbor on the southern end. From Damariscove Island, Smith continued west through a maze of peninsulas and islands, and hazards of every conceivable sort. His map implies that he did not explore Booth Bay Harbor, rather went south of Southport Island, evading two barren islands, the Cuckolds, from Booth Bay to Sheepscot Bay, in which sailing north he entered Sheepscot River, a deep if narrow channel heading north. Small hills lay in the distance. There are many harbors and coves along the way to Wiscasset at which Smith and his men could have put in to rest and find supplies.[20]

From Sheepscot River, Smith and his men returned to Sheepscot Bay and sailed south around Georgetown Island to the entrance of the Kennebec (Sagadahoc) River. The river is difficult to perceive from the sea, but a significant sea mark at the mouth, Seguin Island, called by Smith Satquin, heralded the river. The Popham expedition in 1607 had sailed past the mouth without realizing where the river was, and used Seguin Island as a lee in a storm; perhaps Smith did not make the same mistake, having learned of Satquin Island from his precursors.[21] The island appears unnamed on his *Map of New England.* When Smith saw it the island was forested, rising steeply from the sea; today it hosts a lighthouse. If the wind blew westerly from the land, perhaps Smith and his men moored their shallop for the night in the island's lee. If the breeze was still and fog overwhelmed islands and coast, as it often does in these parts, the men would have bivouacked for a while waiting better sailing conditions.[22]

Smith reflected on his journey from the east toward Sagadahoc that the coast "from Pennobscot to Sagadahock . . . is all Mountainous and Iles of huge Rocks, but ouergrowen with all sorts of excellent good woodes for building houses, boats, barks, or shippes; with an incredible abundance of most sorts of fish, much fowle, and sundry sorts of good fruites for mans vse."[23] He and his men had explored, in an open shallop, a complex, confusing, and fearsome array of peninsulas, bays, islands, and hazards, and had come away, not with foreboding, rather with an appreciation of the richness of the land, open to so many possibilities.

FIVE

Sagadahoc

When Captain John Smith and his companions rowed and sailed and gave themselves up to the incoming tide, entering the River Sagadahoc one fine June day in 1614, Smith believed this was a place of promise, a place where the English might fulfill their destiny in planting a permanent colony in North Virginia. He was, of course, aware of the history of this place, that six years earlier the English, having planted a colony at the mouth of the Sagadahoc, had departed in failure after only "one yeere," branding "the Country . . . as a cold, barren, mountainous, rocky desart." But Smith had, during the previous fortnight, arrived at a different conclusion about the Maine coast. It was forbidding and daunting, to be sure, but knowledge vanquishes ignorance, the basis of foreboding, and the more he discovered about this coast, the more Smith realized that this was a place where the English could build thriving settlements mining the wealth of the land and sea.[1]

There were a few but not many obstructions when Smith and his men sailed north into the mouth of the Kennebec River. If they came from Seguin Island, they had to avoid the Seguin Ledges, as well as "foure or fiue Iles"—Pond, Wood, Stage, Salter—"in the mouth." Entering the river's mouth, where wind and tide often make for dangerous conditions, Smith and his men, if they experienced such difficulties, sufficiently weathered them. If the explorers needed to rest in a safe place, they moored the shallop west of Hunnewell Point, at the northern foot of Sabino Head, a place now known as Hossketch Point, where they could make use of the remains of the Popham colony, abandoned six years earlier. Smith called this place "the Westerne plantation"; it was, possibly, near the site of a village of the Wawenock Indians. On Smith's *Map of New England* it is

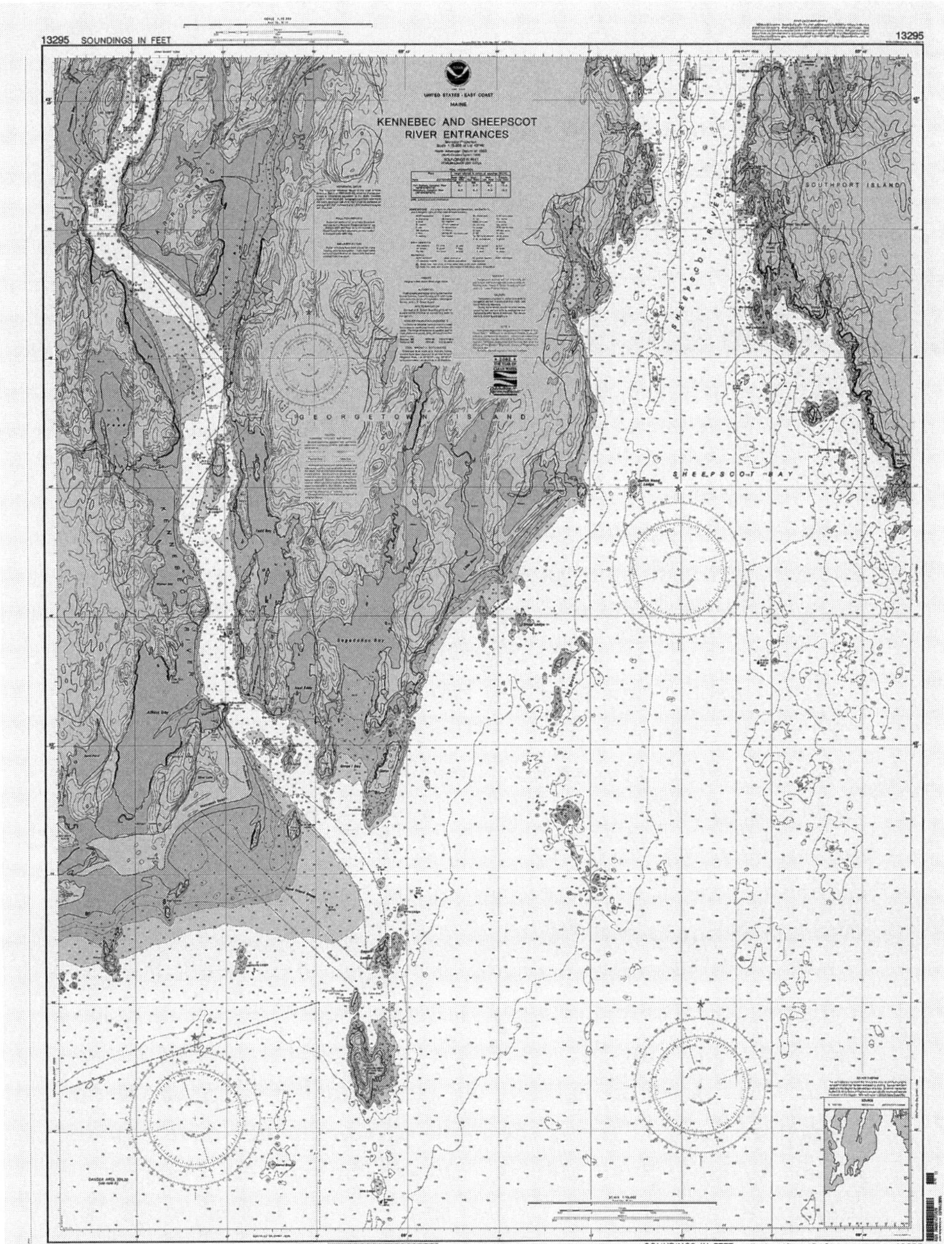

Smith's men traced the treacherous waters of the Maine coast from the Sheepscot to Kennebec rivers in late spring 1614. NOAA Chart 13295-10-2002.

The islands at the mouth of the Kennebec River, such as Smith's Satquin Island, seen from the perspective of Fort Popham. Photo by author.

called Leth. The point of land where Smith bivouacked and the Popham colony had been founded lies north of a hill, west of a peninsula, and south of a bay dotted with wooded headlands enclosing the broad Kennebec River. Today's explorer can mentally re-create Smith's experience by standing at the remains of Fort Popham, a Civil War relic due east of the Popham colony site that looks out upon the mouth of the river. The "great high cliffes of barren Rocks, ouergrowne with wood," of the river valley offered forests of oak, walnut, birch, and pine; fish-filled waters; "ground" that was "exceeding fat and fertill," in Smith's words, "where the Salvages dwelt" and planted their fields of maize; and woods teaming with fur-bearing animals.[2]

From the old Popham colony the men followed the broad, deep river upstream, Smith estimated about "40 or 50 miles." He appears to have decided to explore this river (unlike the Penobscot, Piscataqua, and Merrimack) because the account of it was familiar to him from the previous journey of Raleigh Gilbert of the Popham colony up the Kennebec to the fall line. Likewise, Smith and his crew in the little shallop rowed against the current and sailed with the tide and the wind blowing upriver. The men followed the channel past forested Long Island, across from which is Cox Head, also forested, a peninsula jutting into the river. Farther north, past Parker Head, they came to a river—Back River—flowing into the Kennebec from the northeast. The channel of the Kennebec

The Kennebec River looking upriver from Fort Popham.
Photo by author.

here jogs a bit to the northwest, along what is today the town of Phipsburg. Smith and his men, moving north, paralleled the massive Arrowsic Island, along with other islands separating the Kennebec from the Sheepscot River to the east. The channel of the river was deep, with few hazards, and almost due north until the men came to what became known as Fiddler's Reach, where they ascended the Kennebec due west between two headlands, before proceeding north into a broad channel between a rising landscape on both sides. Eventually they came to the site of modern Bath, where the Kennebec meets the Sasanoa River, a short, narrow, treacherous connector to Back River to the east. Above Bath, the river twists and turns and courses about islands on its southerly journey. The shallop could have made an easy voyage if the wind and tide were right. The tall forests on many headlands and the rich intervales fascinated Smith and his men as they continued the voyage upstream to the narrow way called the Chops. The Chops forms the southeastern extreme of what later inhabitants would call Merrymeeting Bay, where two rivers, the Kennebec and Androscoggin, join, the former descending from its source at Moosehead Lake, Maine's largest lake, fed by the Dead River, the latter descending from Umbagog Lake, fed by waters, such as Peabody River, descending from the White Mountains. At the Chops, the ascending tidal river meets descending freshwater, providing a lively habitat for fish such as salmon and sturgeon. Smith's map shows that he clearly sailed through and accurately observed Merrymeeting Bay. The town of Cambridg, on Smith's map, is situated near the mouth of the Androscoggin at Merrymeeting Bay, where the Pejepscot Indians lived at a place called Aumoughcawgen. If Smith chanced to row up the Androscoggin to the falls of Pejepscot, he would have arrived at the site of modern Brunswick.[3]

The men continued north past Abagadasset Point toward Swan Island, which divides the river into two smaller streams, both of which were navigable. Smith might have learned from the Indians, or guessed right, that the eastern channel was swifter, deeper, and followed it. Toward the northern half of Swan Island, the river narrows between Little Swan Island and Goodwin Point, which was about as treacherous a place as the men navigated. At the northern extreme of Swan Island, the river channel broadens and turns northeast and then, at Courthouse Point, north. The English were entering the land of what Smith called the "Kenebeck" or Cannabis Indians, who lived along the upper Kennebec River.[4]

Smith sailed as far as present Augusta, the site of which was probably inhabited by the same Algonquians that Gilbert dealt with eight years earlier. This place is called Edenborough on Smith's map. Perhaps Smith visited the Indian village of Kenebeck and heard from the locals that the people called themselves Wawrigweck.[5] The appeal for Smith, always on the lookout for a potential place to colonize, included the same features noted in Gilbert's report, of the wonderful fishing at the falls, the massive white pines that could help outfit a king's navy, and the fertile soil for growing diverse crops. In time, indeed, the Maine forest would give way to teams of axmen who felled the white pines and dragged them to the river, down which they floated to towns, such as Bath, where ship carpenters made war frigates and merchant schooners out of native oak masted with the white pine. Smith would neither see nor hear of this, dying in England seventeen years hence, but he imagined and anticipated it.[6]

The return voyage down the Kennebec to the bay was quicker, especially if Smith and his men descended with the outgoing tide. This would doubly make sense as the Kennebec is narrow, and much more shallow, at Augusta, which approaches the fall line. The river flowed along pleasantly between cultivated fields of maize, beans, gourds, and pumpkins. Once

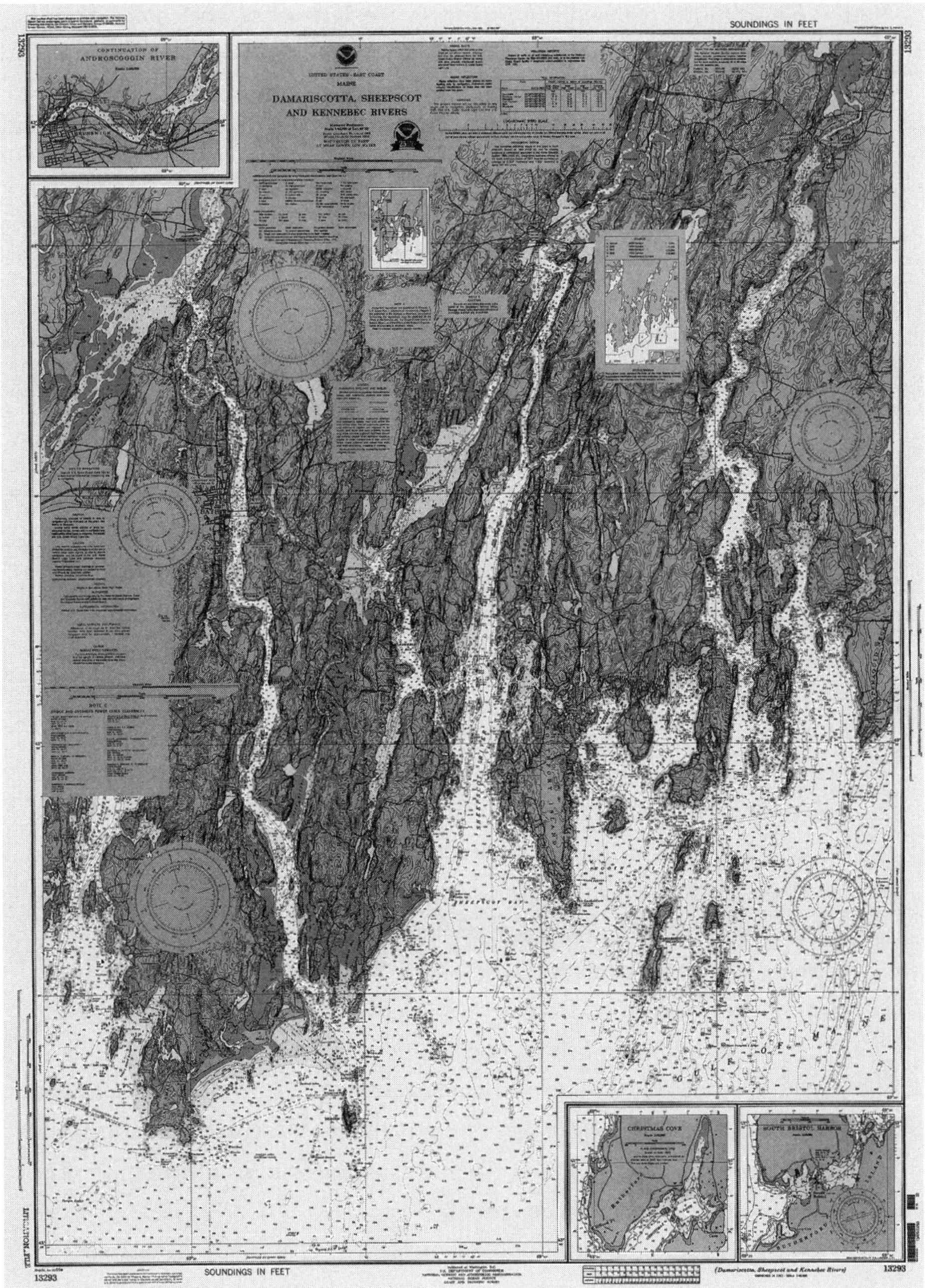

Smith and his men followed the incoming tide up the Kennebec River toward Bath. NOAA Chart 13293-04-1995.

the Englishmen reached the mouth of the Kennebec, they steered the shallop west around Wood Island, avoiding shoal water at Fox Islands and other such hazards off Cape Small (which on Smith's *Map of New England* is denoted Cape Elizabeth). Rounding the cape, Smith and his men entered Casco Bay. Smith wrote in the *Description of New England* that "westward of this Riuer," the Kennebec, "is the Countrey *Aucocisco,* in the bottome of a large deepe Bay, full of many great Iles, which diuides it into many good harbours." The only way Smith could have known of the many harbors of Casco Bay was to explore the coast, as he was wont to do, which at this point in his voyage meant a journey through a maze of islands, shoals, and other hazards too numerous to anticipate. Of the dozens of islands that crowd Casco Bay, Smith's map reveals just a few, which should not be surprising, as otherwise we should expect that the mapmaker was employing imagination rather than actual fact; for Smith and his men had neither the time nor the nautical ability to explore extensively the puzzle that is Casco Bay. Cape Small is at the southern point of a long finger of land that separates the Kennebec River from Casco Bay. Smith perhaps realized this and knew that as he sailed north he was, in a sense, paralleling the Kennebec. There were hazards aplenty but coves and harbors as well, should his men require rest and refreshment. Smith could have learned of the Pejepscot Falls on Androscoggin River, the site of an Indian settlement, the approximate place of "The Base" on his map. Was perhaps Smith, or Prince Charles, thinking of a foundational place to begin a settlement? On what must have been a haphazard journey west along the islands and coves of Casco Bay, Smith and his men saw one after another rocky, forested island, any one of which could maintain fishing operations for a time. Such a likely place was Harpswell Harbor on Merriconeag Sound, next to the long, narrow Harpswell Neck. If, farther west, Smith chanced to enter Maquoit Bay, he sailed into a tribal region of Abenaki Indians whose village lay on the traveling route west from Pejepscot.[7]

Smith encountered many of the Native American tribes that inhabited the Maine coast in the early seventeenth century, and he left behind a dazzling list of their otherwise unknown and obscure names. These included the Paghhuntanuck, Pocopassum, Taughtanahagnet, Warbigganus,

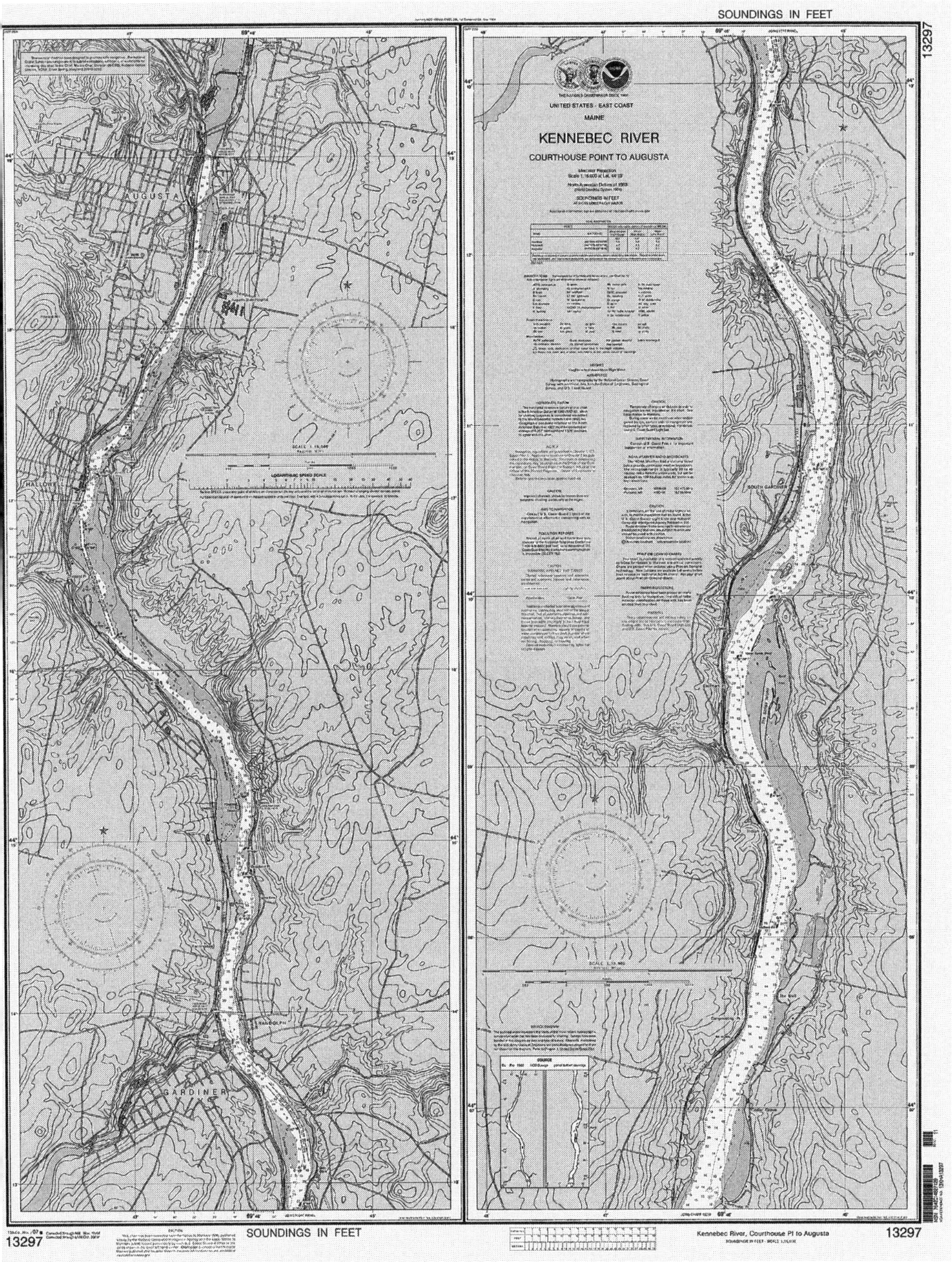

Smith journeyed up the Kennebec as far as Augusta.
NOAA Chart 13297-11-2007.

Nassaque, Masherosqueck, Moshoquen, Wakcogo, Passharanack—"&c," he added in the *Description of New England*, meaning many more![8]

Such tribes provided Smith with information to add to his own observations about the flora and fauna of the coast. "The hearbes and fruits are of many sorts and kindes," he wrote in *Description of New England.* Strawberries were an important food for the indigenous tribes, and Smith and his men availed themselves of these large, juicy fruits as well. Smith described a fruit that he called "curran[t]s, or a fruit like curran[t]s," which implied his uncertainty. There is an indigenous red currant in America (*Ribes triste* Pall.), which he might have picked and tasted; or, he might have confused the currant with the gooseberry, also found and used as food in New England. He saw and ate many ripe berries of the red mulberry tree growing along the coast; the fruit is not as tasty as other berries, though will still supplement a meager diet. The natives used the mulberry for a variety of medicinal purposes—perhaps they offered ailing sailors a bowl of root tea to invigorate them. Smith and his men gathered red grapes along the coast. Also prolific along the coast from Maine to Massachusetts is the beach plum, called by Smith the "plum tree," which went well with a piece of grilled cod around the campfire on a June or July evening.[9]

Of herbs, Smith recorded finding the "saxefrage" (saxifrage), any of a number of small wildflowers, some of which Indians considered a remedy for kidney complaints. Smith mistakenly saw a red berry that he believed was "alkermes," which was used in Europe as an additive to liquors, though it was not a vegetable, rather an insect; perhaps Smith's "alkermes" was the cranberry. Like many explorers before him, Smith thought he saw some of the spices of the East Indies, such as cinnamon and cloves, though what he actually mistook for such valuable spices, which he called "respices," is not clear.[10]

Smith could hardly but be impressed by the coniferous forests of New England, where "firre, pyne, . . . cypresse," and "ceder" grew. He was not the first Englishman to take note of the height and grandeur of the eastern white pine, as Captain Waymouth (or Weymouth), nine years earlier, had brought seedlings back to England, where they came to be called the Weymouth pine. The eastern hemlock, just as common, which Smith would have seen in Virginia, was used by the Algonquians up and down the coast for treating all sorts of illnesses, from arthritis to the common cold; perhaps Smith had enjoyed on his several excursions along the American coast a nice hemlock tea. Likewise, the eastern red cedar and northern white cedar are very common along the Atlantic seaboard, and were known by Indians and settlers alike as important materials of medicine. Of deciduous trees, Smith discovered that "Oke is the chiefe wood; of which there is great difference in regard of the soyle where it groweth." The most common used by Indians were the red and white oaks, the latter important for making dugout canoes and for medicinal purposes; the acorns of both trees were a food source. Algonquians also used the "elme" and "chesnut," Smith learned, for dugouts, food (chestnuts), and medicine (elm bark tea). Walnuts could in a pinch stave off hunger. Bark tea from the ash and hazelnut could stave off illness. The paper birch, besides it uses for canoes and wigwams, made a good medicinal tea.[11]

John Smith, in his *Description of New England*, did not describe his experiences with Native Americans in the same detail as other journalists of his time, but one can read between the lines and see that, as in Virginia, Smith sometimes enjoyed the hospitality of the tribes he met along the way. Meals would have included a repast of boiled "pumpions," as he referred to pumpkins, along with "beans, pease, and mayze," served in a hollowed-out gourd. Smith's dinner could have included flax seeds, which the natives cultivated, at least "a kinde or two." Besides eating the seeds, they spun the plant's fibers to "make nets, lines, and ropes both small and great, verie strong for their quantities."[12]

A dinner with indigenous hosts would include, at various seasons, fish, fowl, and meat. Of the former, Indians and English feasted on "Cod, Hake, Haddock, Cole [coal or pollock], Cusk or small Ling, . . . Mackerell, Herring, Mullett, Base [bass] . . . , Cunners, Pearch, Eels"—perhaps even "Turbut" and "Sturgion"—grilled or boiled on the beach or at a village campfire; men roasted shellfish such as "Crabs, Lobsters, Muskles, Wilkes [whelks], Oysters, and diuerse others, &c." Perhaps not eaten but seen along the coast from the perspective of the shallop were "Whales, Grampus [killer whale], Porkpisces [porpoises]," and sometimes in northern New England waters, sharks. The English observed as well on their voyage a variety of fowl, some of which were tasted, some observed from afar. Canadian geese and brants, roasted, along with their eggs, boiled, could ease hunger for a while. Likewise famished sailors ate "Ducks, Sheldrakes, Teale, Meawes [a gull-like bird], Guls, and Turkies," while they watched "Eag[l]es, Gripes [vulture], diuers sorts of Haukes, Cranes, Diue-doppers [dippers], and many other sorts, whose names I knowe not." America had a great variety of mammals, some of which Smith and his men knew from their experiences in Europe, England, and Virginia, such as the "deere, red and Fallow; Beuers, Wolues, Foxes both blacke and other; Otters, Martins, Wild-cats," "fitches [the polecat, or ferret]," and "Beares." Some of these animals, such as the "Beuers, Otters, Martins, [and] Blacke Foxes," could provide six to seven thousand pelts per year. Other mammals were quite new to the English—for example, the "Moos[e], a beast bigger then a Stagge"; "Aroughconds [the raccoon]," and "Musquassus [the muskrat]." Of the latter, the "Musk Rat may be well raised gaines well worth their labour, that will endeuor to make tryall of their goodnesse"—musk oil, soft pelts, and tasty flesh. "And," Smith added, there are "diuerse sorts of vermine, whose names I know not"—animals indigenous to North America include diverse species of rats, mice, voles, groundhogs, moles, chipmunks, opossums, squirrels, gophers, shrews, and so on.[13]

Smith learned from the Algonquians of New England about their tribal divisions, conflicts, and alliances; their healing ways and traditional customs; their villages where they built their wigwams and lodges and lived, at least part of the year; where they stored corn in storage pits; where they held religious ceremonies; and to where they returned after summer fishing or winter travels during times of want. Those villages about which Smith learned, he recorded on his map, christening each with a new, English, name.

For example, the region of what is today called Casco Bay, which Smith, along with Prince Charles, denoted Harrington Bay, was called by the indigenous people Aucocisco, a name that referred either to "muddy bay" or to the great blue heron, which Smith saw along with a variety of other shorebirds amid the sandy shores and scores of islands in this bay. Smith and his men sailed and rowed amid the shoals and islands of Aucocisco, and put in at several harbors, exploring the Royal River where the city of Yarmouth is now located, where in 1614 an Algonquian village existed, called Sandwich on Smith's map. The Royal and Cousins rivers combine to form a fairly broad mouth, inviting the mariner to enter for supplies and refreshment. Sailing farther south, Smith and his men could have put in at Broad Cove, west of Cousins Island, or, winding their way amid numerous shoals between the mainland and several large islands, they headed for the mouth of the Presumpscot River, or Back Cove, or perhaps the mouth of the Fore River, where Portland is today, then the site of an Indian village, called Dartmouth on Smith's map. Somewhere along the way, at the Indian villages or perhaps bivouacking on an island with a small eminence and freshwater springs, such as Great Chebeague Island, on a clear day, Smith looked inland and saw distant white mountains, almost like clouds on the horizon. The English explorer and Yorkshireman Christopher Levett, exploring Saco Bay and river ten years later in 1624, learned from the local Abenaki tribe that the river originated "100 miles in the country," flowing from the slopes of "a great mountain called the Christall Hill." Levett discovered further that this mountain, though so distant inland, "yet is it to be seen at the sea side, and there is no ship arrives in New England, either to the west so far as Cape Cod, or to the east so far as Monhiggen, but they see this mountain the first land, if the weather be clear." Smith called it "the twinkling mountaine of Aucocisco" after the Indian name for Saco Bay, when he spied the mountain, and though he did not depart from the coast to journey inland to find its supposed riches, he must have imagined such a journey of over three score miles into the highlands of what became New Hampshire, ascending the Great Mountain, the White Hill, in time called Mount Washington, from which great rivers of Maine, the Androscoggin and Saco, flowed.[14]

Smith's *Map of New England* portrays the jagged peak of Aucocisco, called Schooters Hill on the map, and just above it a lone wild animal, a mountain lion. This is the only place on Smith's map that portrays the wildlife of America. Smith, one supposes, conceived of the great wilderness from which such a grand peak emerged as teeming with great beasts and potential wealth for those with the courage to journey forth. Perhaps he was thinking of the "twinkling mountain" when he speculated on the mineral wealth of New England; he had heard, from whom it is not clear,

Chart of Casco Bay, from the U.S. Coast Survey. NOAA Chart 315-6-1892.

of possible "Mynes of Golde and Siluer, Copper, and probabilities of Lead, Christall and Allum"—though, Smith said wryly, "I could say much if relations were good assurances." The bane of all accounts of America at this time, Smith knew, was to promise more than could be realized, to exaggerate for the sake of acquiring more support, more money, more patronage. Smith kept to what he knew was "true indeed," that he had "made many trials" for ore (where or when he did not record) "according to those instructions I had." Someone in England, perhaps "that learned *Mathematician* Master Thomas Heriot," had informed Smith of what to look for. Notwithstanding the lack of evidence of precious metals, the English had convinced themselves they would be found in America, which more than anything else "doe perswade mee I need not despaire, but there are metalls in the Countrey." "But," Smith admitted, "I am no Alchymist, nor will promise more then I know."[15]

Cape Elizabeth, a peninsula that juts into the Atlantic and separates Casco Bay and Saco Bay, is called Point Kent on Smith's *Map of New England.* To approach Cape Elizabeth, Smith and his men sailed along the coast from Portland southeast around Portland Head, graced today by one of the most picturesque lighthouses along the Maine coast, to which giving a wide berth, the shallop proceeded south along a coast with few obstructions. A few small coves along the way offered protection from meteorological hazards; the land rose from the shore with an unending spectacle of coniferous and deciduous verdure. Cape Elizabeth itself had a few small peninsulas jutting into the water but was otherwise relatively shoal free. The winds tended from the south, and the air at midday was delightful in the sun, cool in foggy weather, which was a frequent occurrence in summer months. Rounding the southern extreme of Cape Elizabeth, the mariners found themselves in an extensive cove, since called Seal Cove, with a sandy beach to put in to for the night. Pursuing the journey west between Richmond Island, which Smith probably explored, and the mainland, they entered into a large bay. Smith wrote, in *Description of New England*, that "betwixt Sagadahock and Sawocatuck there is but two or three sandy Bayes," one of which was Saco Bay. Smith's map portrays, if not quite accurately, the characteristics of the bay. Sailing past Prout's Neck, he mistook it for an island, which, from the perspective of a

Smith's *Map of New England* refers to Casco Bay as Harrington Bay, the Kennebec River as the River Forth, and the inland peak Aucocisco as Schooters Hill. American Memory, Library of Congress.

shallop sailing east to west, is understandable. Smith probably also missed Scarborough and Spurwink rivers, both of which would be hidden from the sea. On the other hand, Smith's map provides an accurate picture of what is today Old Orchard Beach south to Fletcher Neck. The map surprisingly portrays the marshy Goosefare Brook, not a notable landmark, perhaps because there Smith and his men went fowling.[16]

Farther south, they came to the mouth of the Saco River. The Saco, a natural highway connecting the Atlantic and Indian trails north of the White Mountains to the Connecticut River, which forms the boundary between Vermont and New Hampshire, hosted a variety of Indian communities, such as the Pequawket and Sokokis. Smith and his men steered the shallop upriver, perhaps to the head of tide, only five miles inland. Here in later years the towns of Saco and Biddeford were built (the former originally called Pepperellborough after the great eighteenth-century hero William Pepperrell), from which the river would host the largest ships loaded with tons of oak and pine logs that had been conveyed from upriver for export. At the falls, where the rapids and their echoes formed pretty music, Indians caught plentiful salmon and lampreys. Fishing for the former was best done in the summer in rapid water, taking the fish either with weirs or, at night, spearing them with the aid of a pitch torch. The Saco has a reputation for massive spring floods because of the melting snow at its source at Crawford Notch in the White Mountains, from which it flows south and east gathering the waters of dozens of mountain streams and rivers. During this summer of 1614, however, the men did not experience such freshets. Somewhere along the river, Smith visited the Algonquian Indian village of the Sokokis, which Smith called "*Sowocotuck*" and Champlain, Chouacoet. Smith described the regional geography as "in the edge of a large sandy Bay; which hath many Rocks and Iles: but few good harbours but for Barks, I yet know." Smith's map portrays the village of Sowocotuck, renamed Ipswich, southwest of the river and just west of a large tidal marsh and shallow cove, known today as the Pool. The map is very accurate respecting the geography of Fletcher Neck (which on Smith's map is called Point Reeves), a long peninsula jutting into the sea. To disembark on this neck would have required careful sailing to Wood Island Harbor; if they eschewed a landing, there were many hazards to avoid in sailing between Wood Island and Fletcher Neck, then around the neck toward Little River and Goosefare Bay, south of which was Cape Porpoise. Smith and his men must have given the cape a wide berth, as besides the peninsular shape of the land, consisting of Cape Porpoise and Cape Arundel, Smith's map reveals little knowledge of either the Kennebunk River or the Mousam River. They followed the coast as the land curved due west, then south, passing by Wells, taking note of Bald Head Cliff near Ogunquit, and passing by Cape Neddick, which Smith and Prince Charles named Poynt Dauies.[17]

Smith had undoubtedly heard of Cape Neddick from his friend Bartholomew Gosnold who, when he sailed New England waters in the bark *Concord* in May 1602, visited this promontory jutting into the sea. It was a great mass of granite covered with seaweed and other hardy

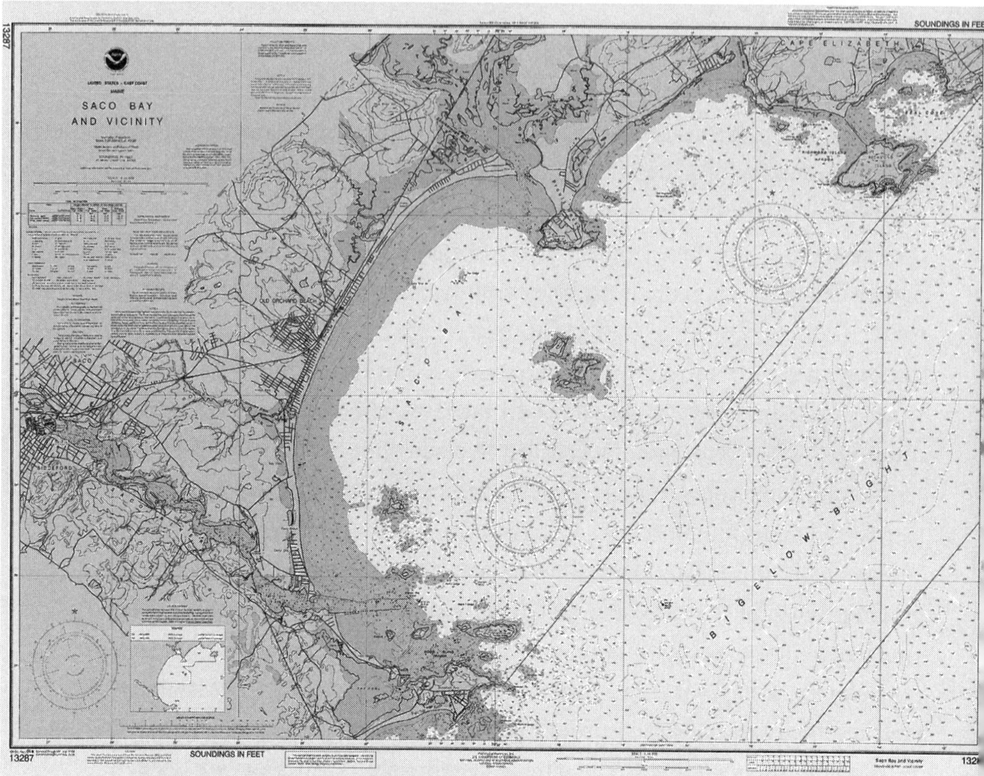

Smith and his men rounded Cape Elizabeth into beautiful Saco Bay, from which they departed south toward York. NOAA Chart 13287-2004.

vegetation. Gosnold and his men had arrived at Savage Rock on Cape Neddick, where today the Nubble Lighthouse shines a warning to incoming mariners. This region, encompassed today by the town of York, is one of rocky coast interspersed with white sand. The wonderful Long Sands Beach is just south of the cape. Beyond Long Sands lies York Harbor. At the northwestern part of the promontory is York Beach. The cape is today jammed with beach houses, restaurants, and gift shops. Four centuries ago the Algonquians greeted Captain Gosnold and his band of sailors. The Indians, surprisingly, approached the *Concord* in a "Baske-shallop," that is, a small fishing boat with a single sail. Basque fishermen frequented the coast of Maine—whether the Indians had acquired the shallop through Basque generosity or through more nefarious means is unknown, but it instantly put Gosnold and his men on guard.

This brief association of Algonquian and Englishmen was short-lived; Captain Gosnold ordered the sails unfurled, and the boat skidded south, leaving Maine waters for good.[18]

Twelve years later, Smith perhaps stood on "Savage Rock," though it is unknown whether or not he met with the local inhabitants. Smith's map accurately portrays Cape Neddick as well as the York River to the south. Here was the Algonquian village of Accominticus, called Boston on Smith's map. In the *Description of New England*, Smith denoted the harbor at the mouth of the river, now called York Harbor, one of "two conuenient harbors for small barks; and a good Countrie, within their craggie cliffs." Smith's map implies that he sailed up the York River, if but a short distance, and observed, perhaps explored, the small harbor. A significant sea mark along the coast, noted by Smith, was a mountain since named for the indigenous people: Mount Agamenticus. It is called Snadoun Hill on Smith's map. Mount Agamenticus is one of three hills visible from the sea. John Winthrop, on his voyage in the *Arbella* in 1630, passing along the Maine coast on the way to Massachusetts, noted three hills inland from York and Cape Neddick, calling them the "Three Turks' Heads." Long after Smith's voyage, when most of his names for landmarks had long been forgotten, seamen recalled the Three Turks' Heads lopped off by Smith, which became in part his claim to fame, though Smith commemorated his feat in three islands off Cape Ann. But as with much of what Smith experienced and described, those who came after him misconstrued, misnamed, and forgot.[19]

SIX

Smith's Isles

Although many mariners from long ago are thought to haunt places along the Maine coast, Captain John Smith is not one of them—after all, he died in England and from natural causes. Smith once envisioned himself ending his days in America, after having led a group of colonists to the islands off the northern coast to establish a thriving colony based on mining the wealth of the sea: fish. But the colony never came to be, as through misfortune and happenstance Smith never again returned to America.

In June 1614 John Smith, ignorant of what was to come, ever-observant, taking frequent compass readings, sketching headlands and bays, anticipating the dangers of the moment, looked for possibilities. Having sailed southwesterly from Accominticus harbor, keeping the mountain of the same name on the lee side, battling the easterlies driving the shallop toward the craggy shore, the mariners arrived at a likely place where to the west was an indentation between headlands and to the east, "against Agamenticus," distant dots rising from the sea. Eschewing the dangers of islands for the dangers of the coast, Smith cautiously sailed toward the indentation.[1]

Smith's map portrays a headland that separates Accominticus from Passataquack; he probably did not explore the region that came to be known as Kittery Point; otherwise he would have realized that two large islands—Cutts and Gerrish—in part make up this headland. If winds and surf or brushing against a hidden reef caused Smith and his crew to require a safe haven, they could have put in for a spell at Godfreys Cove, just south of York Harbor, and farther south along the coast, where a small inlet, Brave Boat Harbor, separates Raynes Neck from Cutts Island.[2]

Pursuing the way south along Gerrish Island, not knowing at first whether the indentation was a bay or river, the smell of fresh water soon informed Smith it was the latter. As they approached, the men guarded against the ledges, rocks, and sandbars that could be anywhere, just under the surface. Several men stood at the prow of the shallop with their eyes peeled; others reefed the sail to allow for careful navigation as they approached land; one man swung the lead and called out the fathoms; Smith called out orders and took everything in: wind, current, lay of the land, depth of the sea.

Subsequent mariners would discover by trial and error, often with deadly consequences, the hazards that hid from or appeared to Smith and his men. The coast from York Harbor to the Piscataqua River is sprinkled with submerged ledges and rocks that Smith and his men, sailing before modern aids to navigation, missed by unusual skill, chance, or the will of God. Smith always explained his success according to the latter, knowing the many times that he could have easily been sent to his death on land or at sea.

As the men in the small shallop approached land in about twenty fathoms, they sailed alongside the long, broad Gerrish Island, which appears like the mainland, though Chauncey Creek separates it from the main. The island is rocky, with some cliffs upon which the sea beats and crashes; forests of pine and oak stand above. Observing the shore while continuing south, they saw the dense forests beyond the rocky shore give way to a massive expanse of water, and a strong current coming from inland—this was the river of the land of Passataquack, or Piscataqua. Several islands lay within the broad mouth of the river, which emerged from between two headlands, which were actually islands—Gerrish and Newcastle, also called Great Island. The forested islands rose steeply from the sea. The wind blew stiffly from inland, following the river's course; the mariners could feel the tug and pull of outgoing river current and incoming tide. The sound of water currents and distant crashing waves mixed with the wind's roar and the incessant calls of gulls and other shorebirds. The channel beckoned inland even if the current and tides suggested due caution. The hazards off Gerrish Island were many, and Smith commanded a continuation of reefed sail and all eyes scanning the waters for shoals, shallows, and rocks; the shallop surged and swayed in the water. They passed a long bare rock emerging from the surf, hence called Whaleback, as well as other small islands and obstructions. The channel grew more narrow, and the men soon found themselves in a strong and deep river.[3]

Smith and his crew of eight were not the first English mariners to enter the Piscataqua River. Martin Pring, eleven years earlier in 1603, arrived to the Piscataqua from the English West Country in command of two ships, a bark and a shallop, seeking sassafras, a reputed panacea for all ills. Pring moored the bark and rowed the shallop up the Piscataqua, not trusting sails to the contrary currents and winds. He followed the main channel of the river through a maze of islands, bays, feeder streams, and good harbors to a confluence of waters, a place subsequently called Dover Point. Here the Piscataqua merges with two bodies of water, the Great Bay and Little Bay, formed from half a dozen small rivers that merge into a broad expanse of shifting fresh and tidal waters. Pring eschewed the bays to the west of Dover Point for the main river channel flowing from the north, which he followed past its confluence with other rivers that gather waters from the highlands of New Hampshire and Maine. Pring and his men explored riverbanks and forests in a fruitless search for sassafras. They saw signs of human habitation but never met with the local inhabitants, who either had fled at the approach of the English or had gone upriver to fish.[4]

Smith did not penetrate the Piscataqua Valley as far as Pring; he was, rather, content to explore inland just beyond the mouth to discover whether or not there were good harbors for ships. He likely put in at a small cove, such as Pepperrell's Cove on the Maine side, where he and his men perchance gathered supplies or looked about. Here, or perhaps elsewhere—for when and where Smith's story does not divulge—Smith and his companions learned from the local inhabitants that this land and its people were called Passataquack (denoted Hull on Smith's map), that in style of living and language they resembled those to the north, the people of Accominticus and beyond. Perhaps he learned that upriver were tribes such as the Squamscot and Newichawannock, living at the falls of the rivers that bear their names. These were agrarian peoples who grew maize, beans, and gourds, who fished for salmon, who hunted bear and moose, who thrived at the harvest though went through periodic starving times. They could have told Smith of the harsh winters, of the scarcity in January and February, of the hard-frozen forest ponds, and of the shifting waters of the Piscataqua, which never freezes.[5]

During the next decade colonists would arrive from England, sent by the proprietors of New Hampshire and Maine, John Mason and Ferdinando Gorges. Men such as David Thomson and Walter Neale established settlements along the Piscataqua, such as at Strawbery Banke, which in time became the city of Portsmouth, which boasts one of the best deepwater ports north of Boston. By the time of these first settlements in the Piscataqua Valley, during the 1620s, the Passataquack (or Piscataqua) and other local tribes were retreating inland to the highlands of New Hampshire and Maine, to the White Mountains and distant forests and lakes north toward Quebec. They were part of the general casualty of epidemic disease, tribal wars, and the onset of white settlement that swept the Algonquian peoples before them.[6]

Smith did not explore far enough up the Piscataqua to see Portsmouth Harbor. He was impressed, however, by the geography of the river's mouth, which would allow for excellent defense should the English ever settle this place. The entrance to the river is about a mile wide, between two highlands that could be (and in the future would be) fortified. South of Newcastle Island was a point of land, since called Odiorne's Point, a small, rocky peninsula that juts into the Atlantic, offering a particularly good place to fortify for defense, or in times of peace on hot summer days to stare languidly at the distant sea. From its vantage point, defenders and observers can look upon the broad mouth of the Piscataqua. Seven years after Smith's journey, the mariner and explorer David Thomson arrived at Odiorne's Point, then called Pannaway, to fortify the entrance to the Piscataqua and establish a colony for the proprietors of New Hampshire, Gorges and Mason. Thomson accomplished what Smith wished to do, but never could.[7]

In 1614, content to explore, map, observe, plan, and dream, Smith sailed the shallop about the broad mouth of the Piscataqua; Smith's *Map of New England* reveals several points and bays south of the Piscataqua, and it would hardly be surprising to discover that he explored the inlet Little Harbor, between Odiorne's, Frost Point, and Newcastle Island.

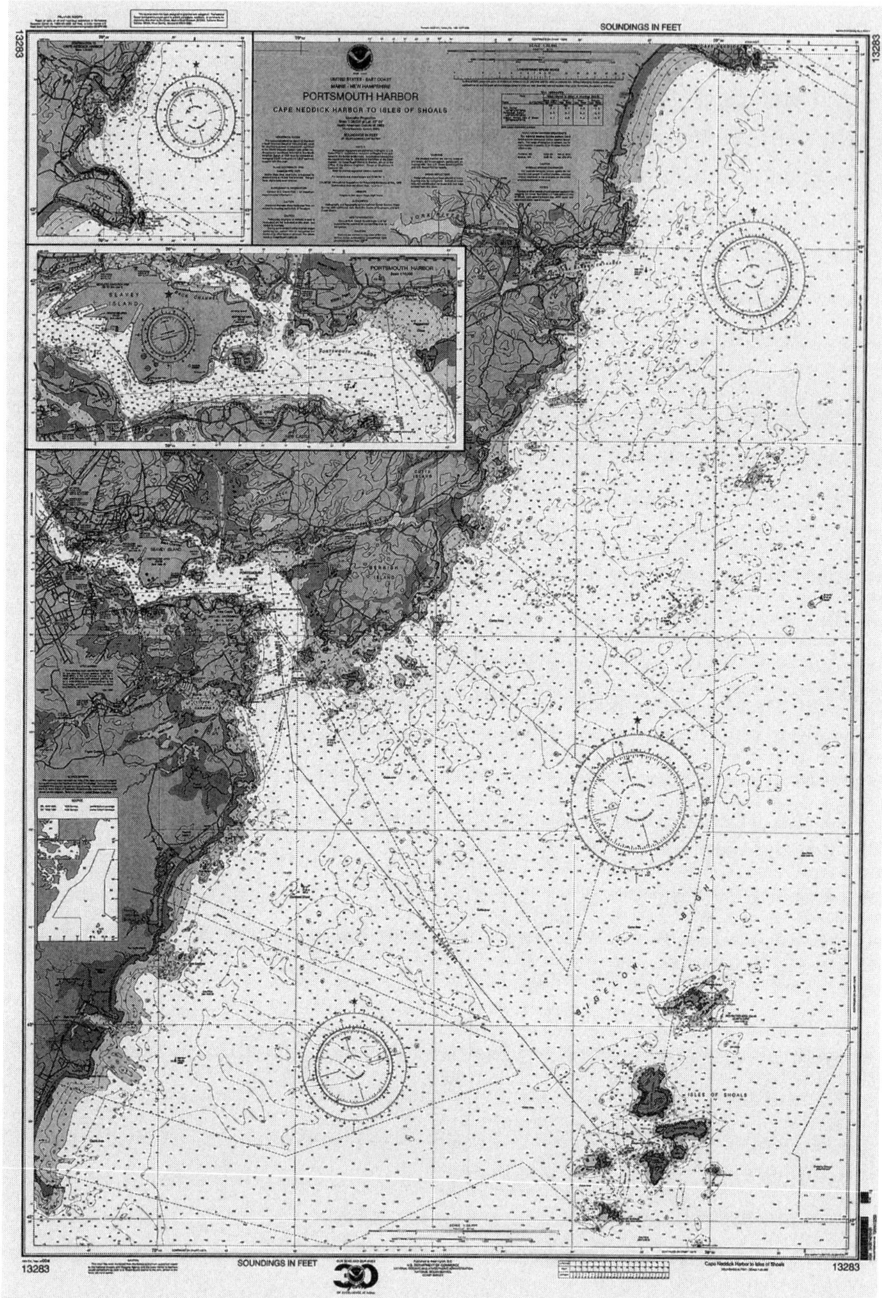

John Smith followed in the wake of Bartholomew Gosnold, visiting Cape Neddick, and Savage Rock, before proceeding south. NOAA Chart 13283-11-2000.

Smith examined all these places from the standpoint of defensive fortifications, and his imagination anticipated Fort William and Mary, later Fort Constitution, on Great Island, guarding the entrance to Portsmouth harbor, across from which at Kittery Point, just east of where the town of Kittery was soon to be founded, a rocky highland would in time be fortified as Fort McClary. But why did Smith not take the time to explore the Piscataqua farther upstream, as he had the Kennebec, to see whether the land was well cultivated, or to see what other harbors there might be? Clearly, his attention was turned elsewhere.

Departing the mouth of the Piscataqua, Smith set a course for the islands he had seen to the southeast. They appeared as "a heape together, non neere them."[8] Although thick fogs often lay upon the waters of the Piscataqua and the cold Atlantic, obscuring everything, bays, islands, and hazards, this June day must have been clear enough to allow Smith and his crew to approach the eight islands without incident. The Isles of Shoals betray in their name the hazards that await the mariner who attempts to approach them. Smith's experience sailing coastal waters and the cool seamanship of his crew enabled them to avoid the many traps that before and since caused shipwreck and heartache. Subsequent mariners were sufficiently wary of the Isles to give them a wide berth when passing. Smith and his men instead decided to investigate, discover what harbors existed, and disembark.

The first mention of the Isles of Shoals in the historical record is from Samuel de Champlain's *Voyages*. On his journey south from St. Croix in 1605 Champlain referred to "three or four rather high islands" as he sailed past the mouth of the Piscataqua toward Cape Ann.[9] The Isles had been a prominent sea mark for navigators for years. Basque, Portuguese, French, and English fishers had used the Isles as a base for drying their catch or finding a lee in storms. Smith knew some of the West Country fishermen of Plymouth and Bristol—perhaps they told him of the eight small islands six miles out from land, a solitary fishing base with fresh water and adequate harbors. John Smith was the first mariner to explore the Isles from the standpoint of a discoverer, who looks past the present moment to see what the future might bring.

His first task was to explore the seaways in and about the Isles to

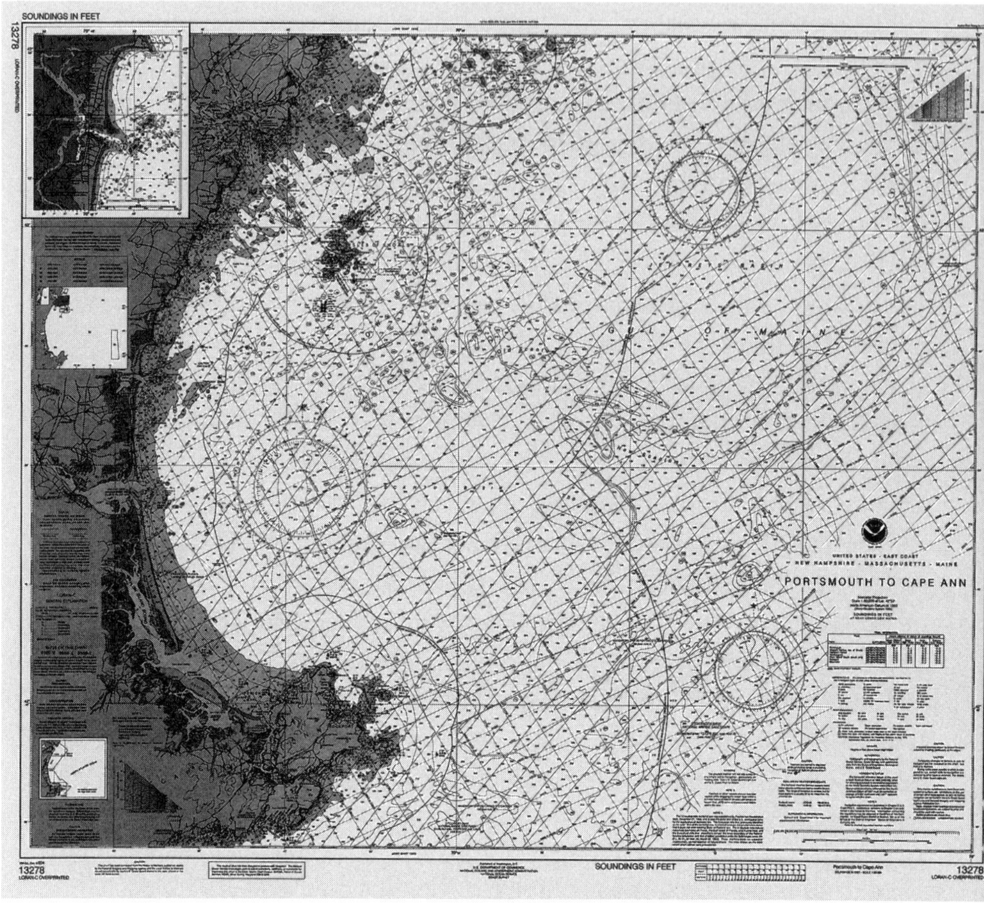

Smith sailed into the waters off the coast of New Hampshire at the beginning of summer 1614. NOAA Chart 13278-12-2000.

find the means to reach a safe shore. If the waves and winds had been high that day, "where waves doe seeme to sash the skies," Smith and his men would not have survived to tell of their experiences, of the massive swells that pitched small craft about in strange perpendicular angles to the sea, of the icy water that could kill in minutes, of the relentless wind driving ketch, pinnace, or shallop toward Halfway Rock, Cedar Ledge, or Anderson's Ledge, hazards that gave little warning besides the white spray of doom. The day was sufficiently calm to tack in and about the Isles to see what were possible harbors. There were very few, however.

The northernmost island, since called Duck, is surrounded with ledges and rocks. Smith and his men quickly determined that this was a place to avoid. Proceeding south-southwest of Duck Island, Smith steered the shallop toward what appeared to be the largest of the Isles, known within a few decades as Hog Island. This island has a long ridge that, to the mariners who often spent hours tacking back and forth waiting for the wind to relent so they could make port, appeared as a razorback. The water thereabouts is largely free from shoals and of sufficient depth to host a variety of fishing boats. On both the eastern and western sides of the island are adequate places to moor boats. Unlike some of the Isles, Hog Island has some soil and grass, as well as springs of water—the former Smith noted, the latter he might have guessed, when he set foot on this island. That Hog Island could support a fishing settlement was shown in subsequent decades; Smith perceived the potential and considered what such a settlement might be like.[10]

South of Hog Island is Smuttynose, a long, thin island with a few scrubby trees, grass, and sedge, and a few rocky inlets that could host an anchored shallop at high tide. Rocks tossed about by the ceaseless surf lie jumbled along the shore. Some days the wind unrelentingly scours the rocks and shrubs; other days a thick, moist fog hangs about, obscuring the surrounding isles in eerie muck. Seagulls, cormorants, ducks, and other fowl soar in the wind or dive under the waves searching for fish and crabs. Doubtless gulls squawked and taunted the men in their heavy boots, long shirts, and thick doublets who wandered about looking for food and potential on this June day.

Today, artificial breakwaters link Smuttynose to Cedar Island just to the southeast and Star Island to the south. In 1614, small expanses of water separated the three islands, and there were no artificial harbors. Star Island, bigger than Cedar, an island that hardly resembles the shape of a star except to the very imaginative, which is rocky with a number of granite lees for small boats, might have hosted Smith and his men. The description in *Advertisements for the unexperienced Planters of New England*, which Smith wrote years later, recalls what he saw at Cedar and Star: islands that have "many a barren rocks, the most overgrown with such shrubs and sharp whins you can hardly pass them; without either grass or wood but three or four shrubby old cedars." Smith's accurate and realistic appraisal of the islands was then tainted by disillusionment and age, yet true; these were inhospitable islands, and it took a great imagination to see them as something more. South and southwest of Star are two small islands that are continually beaten by the waves; White Island's eastern headland withstands the continual pounding—years later mariners selected it as a good spot to build a lighthouse, which still stands today. Navigation is tricky around White Island, and Smith likely examined it from the perspective of the shallop. Londoner's or Lunging Island is small, uninhabited then and now, and fit for birds; rocks and shoal water surround the island, which Smith likely avoided, as have mariners since.[11]

Perchance as John Smith wandered about Hog Island, Smuttynose Island, or Star Island, he saw the remains of Basque, French, or West Country fishing camps, of wooden stages used to dry cod and haddock taken from the sea, of shacks used for temporary shelters; old ropes and broken tackle, fish bones and charred wood, might have littered the shore. Signs of life, signs of fishing, indications of potential.[12]

Before this voyage, Smith had been keenly aware—which during the past several weeks sailing along the coast of America had grown to unbreakable conviction—that the key to English settlement in this land of "Northern Virginia" was fishing. The English had long known that off this coast lay shallow banks where fish spawned and schooled. The fish—haddock, cod, mackerel, herring, mullet—were fat and sweet. And there were markets throughout Europe, and in European colonies, for fish salted and dried and packed in barrels. Fishers chose rocky shores and barren islands as places to build their wooden stages, which resembled wharves, upon which they laid the fish, once split and sliced, to dry. Smith could see clearly that fishers using as a base these islands in the Gulf of Maine could exploit fishing that was essentially just outside their front door, much closer than the Grand Banks off the coast of Newfoundland. These Isles were much farther south than Monhegan Island, which was closer to the French sphere of influence. The isolated little islands would offer convenient access for fishers to come and go, daily, to catch and prepare fish. Smith thought that an island fishing colony had the advantages of being quickly accessible for fishers and at the same time separated from possible enemies on the mainland—the native tribes—who rarely attacked island encampments. Smith was at the same time wary of the French and Spanish, who would find such defenseless islands easy sport. But the islands were near the river of Passataquack, which Smith had noted during his reconnoiter of the river was a perfect place to fortify against sea invasion. Smith liked the situation of these islands so well that he named them for himself.[13]

Smith's (or Smyth's) Isles became the vanguard, as it were, of Smith's imagination, wherein a fishing colony headed by himself could capitalize on the hidden mine of the sea to bring wealth and power to England. Fishing represented a path to industry and virtue for the English—and personal fortune for John Smith. The English, suffering from poverty and apparent overpopulation, could relocate their idle paupers to America, where the opportunity for wealth through individual endeavor would elevate many an English man and woman from dependence to independence. The people of the Netherlands, Smith thought, were perfect examples of this. "Hollanders" were "hardy and industrious"—fishing had made them "mighty, strong and rich." Likewise, "so freely hath God and his Majesty bestowed those blessings on them that will attempt to obtaine them, as here every man may be master and owner of his own labour and land; or the greatest part in a small time. If hee have nothing but his hands, he may set up this trade; and by industrie quickly grow rich; spending but halfe that time wel, which in *England* we abuse in idleness, worse or as ill." Smith estimated that a three-hundred-man colony, where one-third worked to maintain the colony while the other two hundred fished, would thrive just on nine months of work out of the year. Already Smith had learned that the best season for cod, the spring, was ending, but sturgeon and mullet were plentiful in summer months; the season for cod would return again in late summer and fall. The New England fishing season was longer than the Newfoundland season. Although the people of Iceland thrived as fishers off Newfoundland, they had to leave shore for long periods at a time; here the English could have the advantage of using nearby island colonies. "But it is not a worke for every one, to manage such an affaire as makes discoveries and plants a Colony. It requires all the best parts of Art, Judgement, Courage, Honesty,

Constancy, Diligence, and Industrie, to do but neere well." Smith's ability to adapt and to survive, to stand alone against constant odds, to thrive in an atmosphere of want, made him confident that these islands, so like himself, could support a successful English colony.[14]

Years after Smith's voyage to New England, a thriving fishing colony did develop on the three main islands—Star, Hog, Smuttynose—and a fishing community emerged on Star Island at the town of Gosport. But by then the islands were known as the Isles of Shoals, befitting not their founder but their geography, and Smith had died long regretting that he had been overlooked in the fulfillment of his plan, which his fertile mind had generated during the summer of 1614, and which he put to paper in 1615 aboard the French corsair *Don de Dieu*.[15]

In time the fishing villages of the Isles of Shoals died away, replaced by tourists, artists, poets, and storytellers. Nathaniel Hawthorne enjoyed visiting the Isles, where he learned of specters that wander the islands on particularly dark nights when the surf is high and the wind howls a ghostly accompaniment. Ephemeral monuments to the Isles, such as the art of Childe Hassam and the verse of Celia Laighton Thaxter, are supplemented by granite monuments, the largest to the famous pastor John Tucke; a more modest, lonely one, at the southern tip of Star Island, in honor of Captain John Smith. The marker has stood for a century to recall Smith's brief visit to the islands four hundred years ago, when the only monuments on Star or any of the other islands were granite rocks protruding in all directions, hammered daily, yearly, for centuries, by the harsh elements of the cold sea.[16]

Smith and his men departed Smith's Isles to return to the coast and their task of surveying the waters, shores, headlands, and rivers. Departing Star or Smuttynose was tricky business, as there were hidden rocks and shoals toward the mainland that Smith and his men did not know about but had to anticipate. Halfway between Star and Londoner's Island was a rock below the surface that could have ended the voyage save for chance or destiny. Once free from the dangers of the Isles of Shoals, Smith directed the shallop westward toward the shore, where he could make out several small headlands.

When Smith and his men explored the short New Hampshire coastline

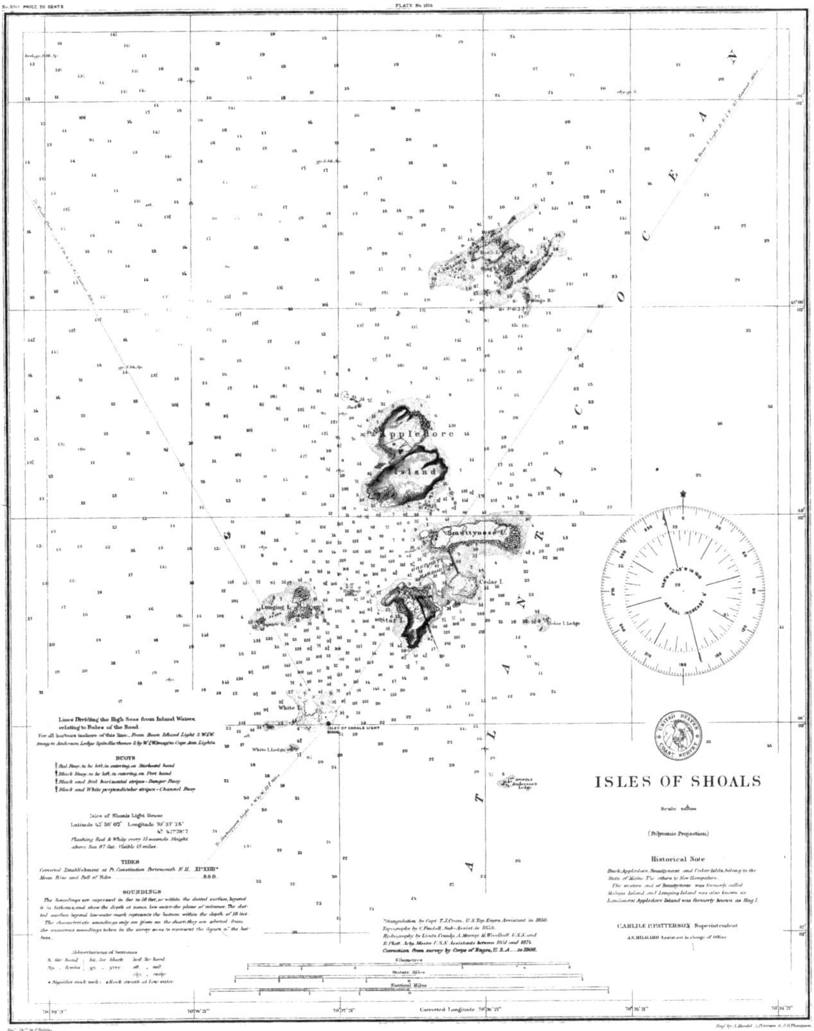

The Isles of Shoals, befitting their name, have dangerous waters challenging the hardiest sailors. NOAA Chart CP1016C.

they found a mixture of sand and rocks, long beaches interspersed with rocky outcrops and shoal water, and few hospitable shores at which to moor a ship. There were half a dozen places, however, that could host a shallop; one was the small cove of Rye Harbor, which Smith could have explored or at least noted in passing. The approach was shoal and dangerous, which Smith traced by sight and compass, recording unnamed

Since the 1800s, the lighthouse on White Island has guided mariners sailing north. Library of Congress.

indentations and headlands, and at least one river. There are a few small rivers along this coast: Little River, Blackwater River, and Taylor River, which becomes Hampton River, originally known as Winnecunnet. The mouth of the latter forms a small harbor, now Hampton Harbor, which Smith probably saw if he did not stop to explore. Shoal water marked the entrance to the harbor, which required careful sailing. If the breeze wafted in from the west, the smell of vast salt marshes along this flat coast simultaneously repelled and intrigued, for the pungent odor invited the husbandman who sought rich fodder for livestock as well as the adventurer on the lookout for fertile land that could support a colony.[17]

An Algonquian tribe, the Winnecunnets, resided in this place, living off the plentiful shellfish along the extensive sandy beaches and the ducks and geese and other fowl that frequented the marshes. If Smith saw, perhaps met, with any of the Winnecunnets he did not record the meeting, and it is more probable that he sailed south along the sands, marshes, and forests content to observe from afar. His map reveals two promontories that reached from the land into the sea: one, Little Boar's Head, smaller than the other, Great Boar's Head. If he chanced to halt on the sandy beach next to the latter to ascend its eminence and scan the horizon, he would have seen several harbors and rivers bearing to the south, and farther on a bold cape jutting dramatically from the land into the sea. If the day was clear, he would have seen the shimmering Smith's Isles to the northeast and, farther north, Mount Agamenticus. Many an adventurer and dreamer would in coming years likewise scan the horizon from Great Boar's Head. Within twenty years of Smith's voyage, the indigenous inhabitants vanished from the coast to physical places north and west or spiritual places beyond; in their wake came the English from Massachusetts traveling north, some hitherto living along the Merrimack or Charles rivers, who brought their nonconformist religion, their plows and scythes, their fishing shallops, and their mode of village living, calling the place Hampton.[18]

The landscape of sandy beaches giving way to marshland and a coast relatively free from shoal water continues south from Hampton Harbor to the mouth of the Merrimack River, where Smith halted to explore one day in June 1614. The approach to the river's mouth was uneventful, at least sailing from the north as Smith and his men did. The sandy beaches gave way to a small opening between headlands, where the current quickened and the smell of fresh water indicated a river. Here at low tide the water was very shallow and required an experienced mariner to navigate the way. Sunken rocks made the passage treacherous. Tidal conditions, winds, currents, shifting sands, and heavy seas have often made the entrance to the Merrimack deadly. Many a sailor has been fooled by the narrow verge between the river and sea. Upon entering the passage between sandy shores, the prospect opened to a massive bay of shifting currents. Here at its mouth, the Merrimack battles against not only the sea but several waterways flowing in and out: for example, Black Rock Creek and Shad Creek. Plum Island, "an Ile of two or three leagues in length," blocking in part the mouth of the Merrimack and extending southward, blocking as well the mouths of the Parker, Rowley, and Eagle Hill rivers, was an inviting place at which to anchor the shallop and explore. From the perspective of Plum Island Smith could see how river, harbor, and sea merged to make a satisfying place to live. Plum Island, which Smith left unnamed, was "the one halfe, plaine morish grasse fit for pasture," such as beach heather and beach grass, which thrives in the environment

Smith sailed along the sandy beaches of New Hampshire in early summer 1614. Photo by author.

of sand dunes; surrounding the island were acres of grassy marshland, where reeds and cattail were prolific. Smith also saw "many faire high groues of mulberie trees gardens" and probably black cherry trees as well. "There is also Okes, Pines," such as the black pine, "and other woods to make this place an excellent habitation."[19]

On his *Map of New England*, Smith and Prince Charles christened the place at the river's mouth South Hampton, notwithstanding that the Indians called it Angoam, or Agawam, meaning a place of good fishing. Indeed the mouth of the river teemed with sturgeon, a long and thin bottom-feeder that was difficult to catch. Indigenous people relied heavily on sturgeon for their diet; the colonists at Jamestown when Smith was there used sturgeon to stave off starvation. Although generally the English did not have a taste for sturgeon, Smith wrote enthusiastically in the *Description of New England* that the sturgeon fishing from May to August was good: sturgeon "roes doe make Cauiare and Puttargo," the latter a relish made from roe. Sturgeon tends to be a freshwater fish that spawns in tidal waters and estuaries, hence was prolific near the mouth of the Merrimack River.[20]

Just before its mouth, the Merrimack widens and forms a deep pool and secure harbor. This was one of the harbors that Smith guessed could

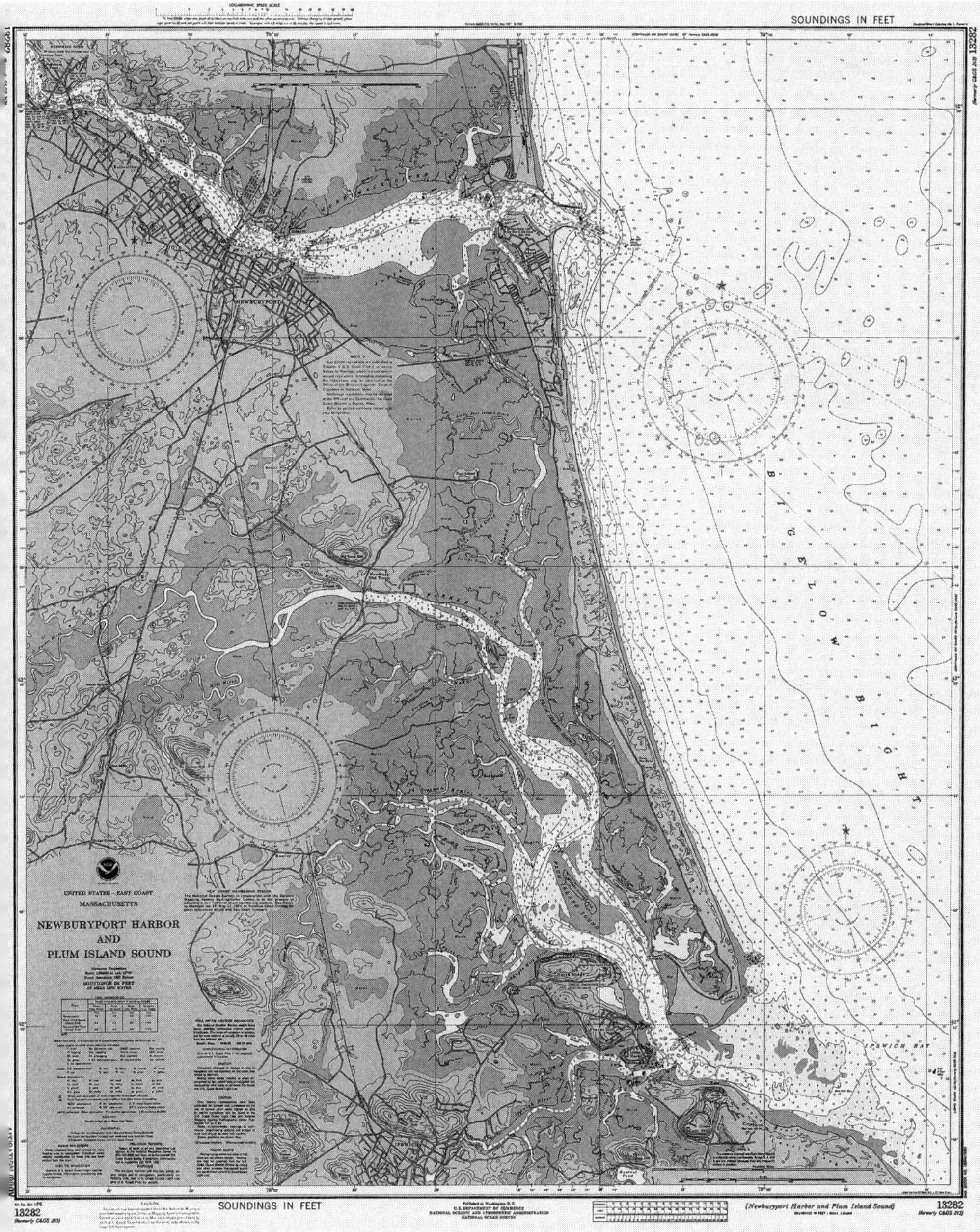

Smith sailed south into what are today the waters of Massachusetts, entering the mouth of the Merrimack River and exploring Plum Island. NOAA Chart 13282-04-1978.

The harbor of Newburyport as it appeared in the early nineteenth century. NOAA Historic Fisheries Collection.

host "500. sayle of ships of any burden." Not only was there sufficient fathom for mooring ships, but the anchorage was also secure from winds and surf thanks to the large sandy island at the mouth. Smith thought it a "good and safe harbour"; at the same time, however, always on the lookout for a superior fishing station, he countered that "there are many sands at the entrance of the harbour; and the worst is, it is inbayed too farre from the deepe Sea." Yet the beauty of the place impressed him: "This place might content a right curious iudgement."[21]

Exploring the harbor, Smith noted "many rising hilles; and on their tops and descents, many corne fields and delightful groues." The native inhabitants clearly knew how to yield fruits and grains from the land. These people of Agawam, like those to the north at Piscataqua and Agamenticus and those to the south at Cape Ann and Naumkeag, as far as Smith "could perceiue," differed "little in language, fashion, or gouernment: though most be Lords of themselues." The tribes of Agawam nevertheless, Smith reported, dreaded the power of the Tarrantines (Mi'kmaq) and indeed would be subject to raids in subsequent years. In their wake the English came to build towns, such as Newbury and Newburyport, which hosted, and still host, fishers who have daily sailed beyond the sandy mouth into the broad Atlantic.[22]

SEVEN

Cape Tragabigzanda

During previous days, sailing the coast south from the Piscataqua along sandy beaches, passing small harbors, exploring the mouth of the Merrimack and Plum Island, Smith and his men noted a "faire headland" lying to the southeast. On particularly clear days, along some places on the New Hampshire coast, Cape Ann appears unusually large, a massive land beckoning the explorer. The dramatic cape, explored extensively by Smith, engendered past recollections and feelings of grandeur revealed in the appellations he chose. The bays, harbors, and islands surrounding the cape made for dangerous sailing, but Smith, his men, and the shallop dodged hazards and escaped dangers all the while mapping and recording, meeting with the native inhabitants, and forming ideas and impressions of this *new* England.

Smith and his men sailed south along the eastern shore of Plum Island, avoiding the western shore, a haphazard mix of marshland, tidal pools, rivers, and creeks that makes up Plum Island Sound. The voyage along the length of the sandy shore was without hazard until they reached the southern extreme of the island, where they entered what was subsequently called Ipswich Bay. It is not clear from Smith's account whether or not he sailed west around the southern tip of Plum Island into Plum Island Sound and Ipswich Harbor. The maze of currents and shoals might have made him hesitant to dare fate. At the same time, discovery was an important aim of his journey. Hence unlike Champlain, who on his 1605 and 1606 voyages eschewed coastal exploration for a direct voyage from the Isles of Shoals to the northern tip of Cape Ann, Smith, we might expect, crawled along the southern extreme of Ipswich Bay, sailing through the mingling fresh water and brine at the mouth of the Ipswich

The sandy beach of Plum Island at the mouth of the Merrimack River. Photo by author.

John Smith explored Plum Island in early summer 1614. Photo by author.

River to the long peninsular Castle Neck, which had an extensive beach, subsequently known as Crane's Beach. Like Plum Island, Castle Neck featured trees such as the pitch pine, and Smith doubtless considered it a viable place for settlement.[1]

Continuing eastward, the shallop passed an opening where a small river (Essex River) entered the bay from the south, then after sailing along a sandy beach, another opening greeted the mariner from the south (Annisquam River). Both of these river mouths were treacherous, and one might imagine Smith would eschew exploring them; however, his drawing of Cape Ann on his *Map of New England* indicates two entrances on the northern side of the cape, which suggests that he did indeed enter the two rivers, if only to mark them. From Annisquam River, the cape juts dramatically to the northeast. There were few good harbors, and the crew was intent on tacking into the northwesterly breeze and dropping the lead repeatedly to avoid shipwreck. Cape Ann is beautiful, but deadly for the inexperienced mariner or newcomer. Smith and his men reached the northern tip of Cape Ann, since called Halibut Point (designated Point Wynthorp on Smith's map), where the entire expanse of the sea, north and south, opened before them. Champlain had come this way nine years earlier, in July 1605, and named the place the "Island Cape" in reference to the many islands and hazards that surrounded the cape.[2]

Smith realized that the winds, currents, surf, reefs, and shoals off Cape Ann could beat a small boat into splinters in an instant; but fear never conquered the urge to discover in John Smith. In his wake, the rocks and shoals of Cape Ann spawned many a tale of woe. For example, not long after Smith's voyage, in 1635, Anthony Thacher brought family and friends aboard a pinnace that set out from Ipswich for Marblehead, taking the same route as Smith. As they neared Halibut Point, a strong storm bore upon them, which drove the pinnace before a nor'easterly gale toward an uninhabited, rocky island off the coast of Cape Ann. The pinnace was set upon a rock emerging from the sea, where the waves beat it to shreds. All aboard, save two, died. The waves mercifully washed Anthony Thacher and his wife upon the island that would bear their name.[3]

There are numerous hazards as the mariner sails south along Cape Ann's eastern coast. Three islands mark the way: Straitsmouth, Thacher,

The distant hills of Cape Ann as seen from Plum Island Sound.
Photo by author.

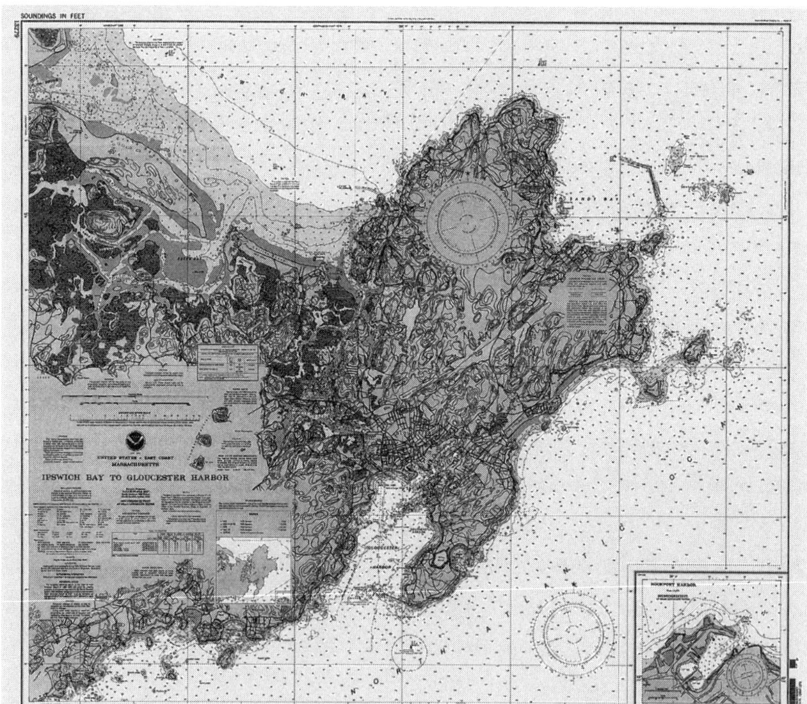

From Ipswich Bay, Smith sailed along the northern extent of Cape Ann, rounding the cape to Gloucester Harbor. NOAA Chart 13279-01-1998.

and Milk; all along are ledges, rocks, and reefs. John Smith and his men had to navigate these waters carefully. Smith, engaged in a battle with the sea off Cape Ann, recalled another conflict of a dozen years before when he had sold his sword to the Christian prince Zsigmond Báthory of Transylvania and had waged combat against three Turkish champions. On three successive days, rather like a medieval tournament complete with spectators, Smith engaged in single combat with a Turkish warrior. Day after day Smith emerged victorious, notwithstanding his many wounds. He decapitated each fallen Turk and presented the heads to his commanders, whereupon Prince Zsigmond awarded the English soldier money and a coat of arms with three Turks' heads. Smith commemorated this, his most noteworthy victory, in naming the three isles that barred the way to safe harbors "the three *Turks heads.*"[4]

It would have been natural for Smith and his men to have made port at the beautiful harbor eventually called Gloucester. The route from the three Turks Heads was southwesterly, through a maze of ledges and rocks that, miraculously, the mariners avoided. After coming about Eastern Point, one sees Gloucester outer harbor opening to the north. Champlain had come this way in 1606 and had found Indian villages and extensive crops, canoeists skimming the waters of the harbor and beyond. Smith's map of Cape Ann is not terribly suggestive of this harbor, and it is possible that he did not stop to explore. At some point, however, at Essex, Annisquam, or Gloucester, Smith and his men moored the shallop and disembarked to explore the rocky cape. During Smith's experience in the Balkans ten years before, after having defeated the three Turkish champions, he soon fell in battle. Wounded but alive, he was taken prisoner by the Turks and eventually transported to Istanbul, where he became slave to a young woman, Charatza Tragabigzanda, who subsequently treated the Englishman well. Smith, wanting to relive salient moments of his past by means of new experiences in new places, pondering how he had defeated the three Turks and then experienced the kindness of a superior woman, memorialized Tragabigzanda by giving her name to the cape.[5]

Exploring at least several places on Cape Tragabigzanda, Smith got a glimpse of the natural history of the place. The Turks Heads and Tragabigzanda, rocky, barren outcrops of granite interspersed with moss, ferns,

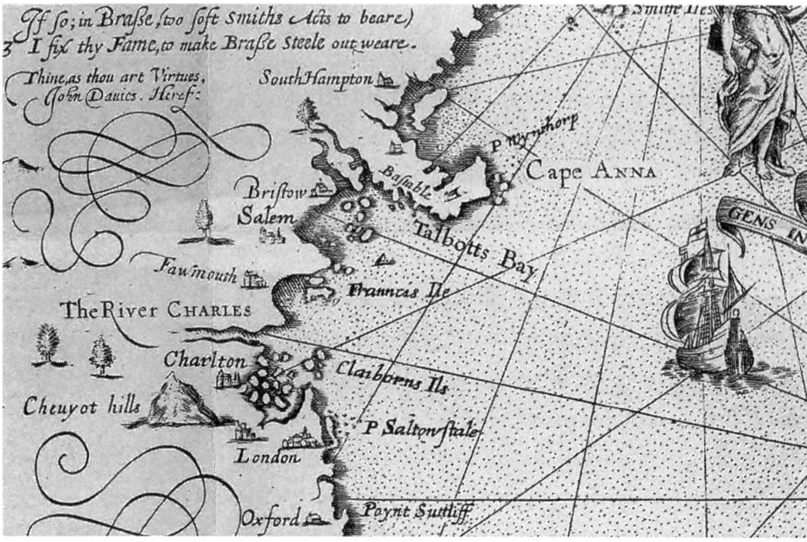

Prince Charles changed Smith's cumbersome name of Cape Tragabigzanda to Cape Ann. American Memory, Library of Congress.

and small trees, hosted thousands of screeching gulls, diving cormorants and grebes, crying loons, playful seals, a variety of migratory birds, and commensurate fish to feed upon. There was enough soil for gardens, which along with berry and nut trees and superior fishing comfortably supported an indigenous population.[6] Smith, like Champlain before him, communicated with the Indians, Champlain by means of a native interpreter he brought with him, Smith by means of his own "broken" Algonquian that he had picked up in the Chesapeake region as well as along the coast of Maine, subject to the amendments and editing of his native guide and interpreter, Tisquantum.[7]

Smith had noted on the way from Plum Island to Cape Tragabigzanda that there were Indian "habitations and corne fields." Asking for further information from the Indians, they told Smith and Tisquantum (as they had told Champlain and his interpreter eight years before) of "a great Riuer," the Merrimack, "and at least thirtie habitations, [which] doe possesse this Countrie." Smith either learned from his informants or deduced that "the *French* had got their Trade," so that he had "no leasure to discouer it." If Smith had had the leisure, he would have discovered that the waters of the Merrimack that flow into the Atlantic at Newburyport descend for several hundred miles largely through New Hampshire, gathering the waters of the foothills and hills of the White Mountains. The fresh, cool water of the Merrimack, good to the taste, confirmed for Smith what the natives told him, or what he suspected: the Merrimack was like many of the rivers of New England, "most pure, proceeding from the intrals of rockie mountaines."[8]

The "thirtie habitations" along the Merrimack were largely villages of the Penacook people, a large confederation of indigenous peoples throughout northern New England, centered in New Hampshire, who at the time Smith explored New England were led by Passaconaway, a wily and clever sachem who exercised great power in the lands between the Piscataqua and Connecticut rivers. There came to be many traditions about Passaconaway, whose reputed magical powers awed the indigenous peoples. Stories are told of his receiving the Puritan apostle John Eliot, refusing conversion to Christianity; that he met with the Pilgrims at Plymouth; that he was a great warrior leading his people against the Mohawks of Vermont and New York; that he lived in harmony with the English settlers; and that he convinced his son Wanalancet to peacefully move north away from expanding English settlements. Smith was sufficiently impressed by Indian sachems that he would have mentioned Passaconaway had he met him.[9]

Departing Cape Tragabigzanda, the men on the shallop sailed west toward Naumkeag. From the site of Gloucester, which would be settled within ten years by fishermen from England, Smith and his companions made their way southwest along the coast, which continued rocky, the waters treacherous. Perhaps they had a good wind from the north that pushed them along; perhaps they had excellent seamen aboard to avoid rocks such as Norman's Woe. They passed by a small harbor, subsequently called Magnolia, a ledge guarding its entrance and an island (Kettle) due south barely making space for the shallop to pass. Sailing westward, they passed a large cove, subsequently called Kettle, then sailed along a curving bay (Manchester Bay) from west to southwest. The coast alternated between sandy beaches and rocky outcrops and bold cliffs. The entire bay had islands, ledges, rocks, and channels that subsequent sailors denoted with such names as Misery Shoal, Misery Ledge, Misery Rock, Cutthroat Shoal, Hardy Shoal, Little Haste, Great Haste, Satan Rock, and Rams Horn Rock. The English boat had to tread gingerly with mostly furled sails, weaving in and about hazards to avoid shipwreck. This general area of the coast Smith called, based on how he understood the Indian designation, Naimkeck. It was generally known among mariners and colonists in subsequent decades as Naumkeag, and the Indians of the region were known as the Naumkeags. "*Naimkeck*," Smith wrote in *Description of New England*, "though it be more rockie ground (for *Angoam* is sandie) [is] not much inferior [to Angoam]; neither for the harbor, nor any thing [that] I could perceiue, but the multitude of people."[10] The Merrimack Valley would indeed guarantee more fertile ground, hence greater population density. Both Angoam and Naumkeag, like much of the New England coast, were extremely fertile. Moreover, "Cattell may here be bred and fed in the Iles, or *Peninsulaes*, securely for nothing." The English preferred islands for livestock, to secure them from raiders; many of the islands Smith had explored had sufficient verdure to support cows, sheep, goats, and hogs.[11] Notwithstanding the fertility of the land, within a few years, in the wake of epidemic diseases, the Indian population along the entire coast would be dramatically reduced. But not when Smith visited in 1614.

The shallop soon came upon a region of beautiful harbors amid a bay (Salem Sound) pockmarked with isles and shoals. Between the northern extremity of Cape Tragabigzanda to the opposing headland of Marblehead is an indented landscape of rivers and harbors. Two significant port towns would in subsequent decades be founded here: Beverley and Salem. Smith's *Map of New England* accurately reproduces this geography based on his observations and compass measurements. Clearly, Smith and his men carefully sailed these waters, investigating harbors and hazards, places to settle, prospective fishing communities, and the best means to sail from place to place. Smith estimated that numerous ships of many burdens could be moored in these harbors. In addition to Beverley Harbor, and the more extensive Salem Harbor, Naumkeag hosted many coves and river mouths to provide shelter for mariners. A dozen years after Smith came this way, Puritans led by Roger Conant, who tried to make a successful settlement on Cape Ann in 1625, relocated to Naumkeag in 1626, which was the foundation of Salem and, soon after, Beverley. Smith's map shows half a dozen islands in this sound, three of which were subsequently named Coney Island, Eagle Island, and Children's Island.[12]

Pursuing a passage south and east, Smith and his men came to an extensive promontory, which forms the eastern bounds of Salem Sound, since called Marblehead. The harbor at Marblehead is as extensive as Salem Harbor, bounded on the west by Marblehead and on the east by Marblehead Neck. The voyage from Salem Harbor around Marblehead to Marblehead Harbor involved some tricky sailing to avoid, again, ledges, rocks, and shoals. Rounding the northern extreme of Marblehead, from west to east, the mariner must avoid two ledges, Great and Little Aquavitae, named for the strong liquor that soldiers and mariners alike during Smith's time enjoyed imbibing. A series of other ledges and rocks greet the mariner who continues east to southeast rounding the tip of Marblehead, then proceeds south into the harbor. Two islands lay to the starboard as Smith and his men sailed south, exploring the vast and peaceful harbor. As Smith did not, in the *Description of New England*, describe meeting the sachem of the local Naumkeag tribe, Nanepashemet, it is doubtful that he disembarked and met with the local Indians. Nevertheless Smith would have seen the potential for this place to be a fishing station. The harbor is secure but of easy access to the fishing grounds of the Atlantic. Indeed, fifteen years after his voyage, fishers from England settled what became the town of Marblehead.[13]

The voyage leaving the harbor and around Marblehead Neck to the east was a continual trial, as all along the coast on the western and eastern shores of the neck were shoals and rocks. Rounding the southern tip of Marblehead Neck was particularly dangerous. It is possible that Smith and his men took a conservative, long way around this point, circumnavigating Tinkers Island to avoid the obvious shoals between the point and the isle. Sailing west with the peninsula that makes up Marblehead standing to starboard, they encountered a few obstructions on the way (Roaring Bull, Little Pig Rocks, Ram Rock) though the shore mostly presented a sandy beach with few shoals. However, as the coast turned more to the southwest and south-southwest, the shore grew more shoal,

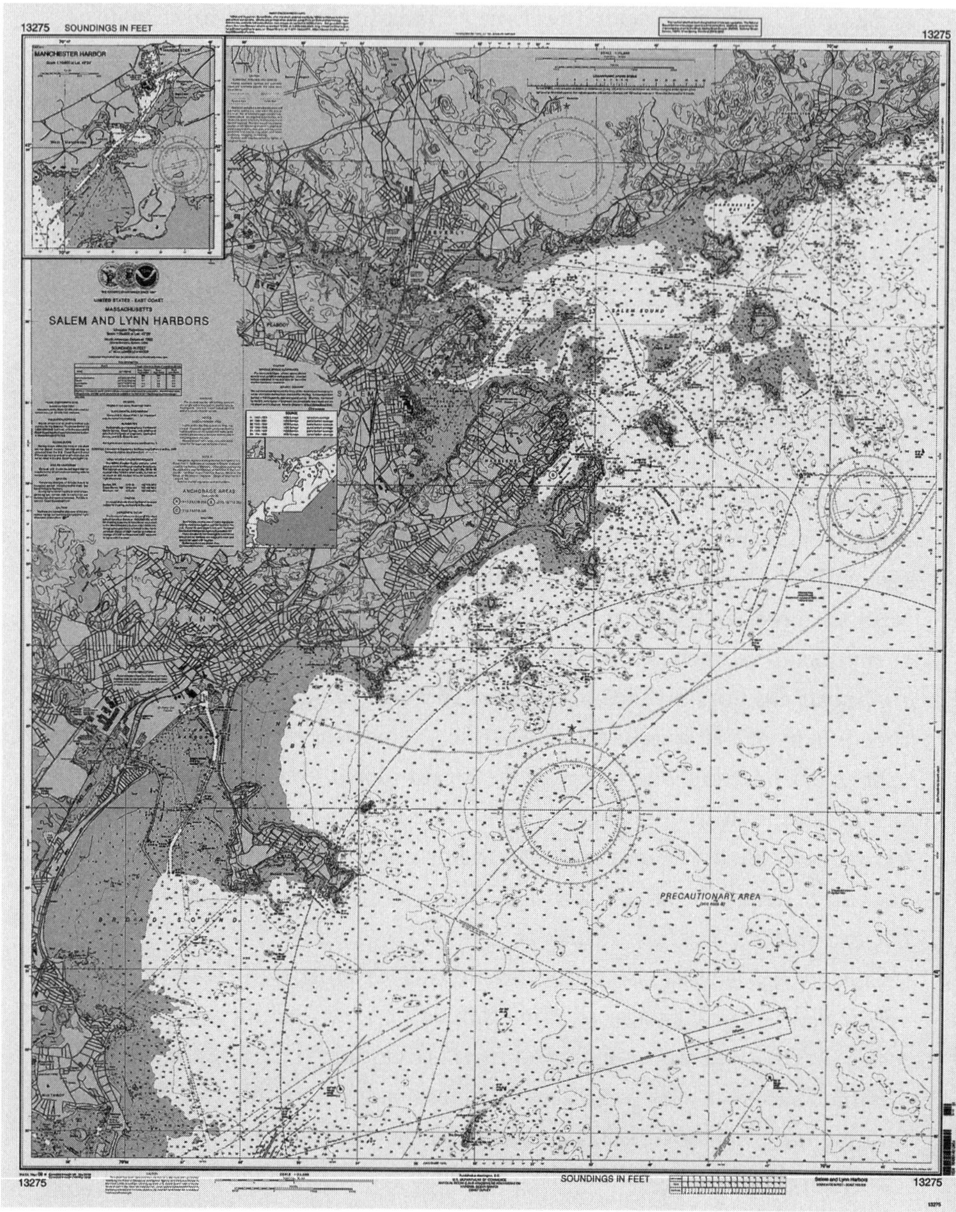

Smith sailed by and explored the beautiful Massachusetts harbors at Salem and Marblehead. NOAA Chart 13275-05-2008.

requiring greater caution. The shallop was entering the northern extreme of Nahant Bay, filled with ledges, rocks, and islands. Having reached a point jutting into the bay (Phillips Point), and making a wide turn west to avoid the shoals, they continued west along what is today Swampscott, Massachusetts. The shore curved southwest then south, and the shallop made its way along what is today Lynn. What struck Smith at the time was not Lynn Harbor, or the shore, so much as the islands in the bay. He recalled in his *General History*: "The Isles of Mattahunts [Nahants, called Fullerton Islands on Smith's *Map of New England*] are on the west side of this Bay, where there are many Iles, and some Rocks that appear a great height aboue the water like the Pyramides in Ægypt, and amongst them many good Harbours." In the *Description of New England*, Smith depicted Nahant as "two pleasant Iles of groues, gardens, and corne fields, a league in the Sea from the Mayne." There are two islands, the smaller called Little Nahant and the larger Nahant, an Algonquian word that implied that the islands were connected, and indeed they are; a narrow isthmus (or tombolo) connects Nahant to Little Nahant, and Little Nahant to the mainland. Although the larger island has a harbor, both islands are surrounded by shoal water, and it is likely that Smith formed his opinion based on observation from the shallop. He did not stop to investigate Lynn Harbor but noted that the shore had "questionlesse good harbors." The rocky shores of Nahant, and Massachusetts in general, convinced Smith that colonists would be able to find adequate building materials, perhaps even good mines. "Especial[l]y," he wrote, "the Coast of the Massachusets is so indifferently mixed with high clayie or sandy cliffes in one place, and then tracts of large long ledges of diuers sorts, and quarries of stones in other places so strangely diuided with tinctured veines of diuers colours: as, Free stone for building, Slate for tiling, smooth stone to make Fornaces and Forges for glasse or iron, and iron ore sufficient, conueniently to melt in them."[14] Perhaps Smith was thinking of the North Shore when he made this comment, in which case he anticipated by thirty years the development of the Saugus Iron Works near the mouth of the Saugus River at Lynn Harbor.[15]

Sailing south from Lynn Harbor, the shallop skimmed along a sandy beach (Revere Beach) with few shoals until arriving at a small point

The harbor at Marblehead as it appeared in the nineteenth century. NOAA Historic Fisheries Collection.

(present Beachmont) with dangerous shoals, avoiding which, Smith and his crew continued a south-southeast course along a marshy area filled with fowl. If the men anchored to investigate, perhaps looking for a hearty meal, they saw many of the ornithological specimens still found at Belle Isle Marsh.[16] During his voyage along the New England coast Smith killed many fowl that graced his rustic table, such as geese, including brants; turkeys; ducks, including sheldrakes and teals; as well as other water and shore fowl, such as gulls, including "meawes" (herring gulls); "gripes" (grepes or grebes); "diue-doppers"; cranes; cormorants; and hawks. Of the latter along the New England coast, a bird-watcher or falconer might see a red-tailed hawk, Cooper's hawk, and northern harrier. Smith was, like many people of his time, intrigued with hawking, or falconry, and enjoyed seeing the soaring, graceful birds hovering above fields and marshes. Falconry achieved the height of its popularity in Jacobean England, and many books were written, some of which Smith might have read. He knew the sport and might have practiced it, as most gentlemen were expected to do. It occurred to Smith that others might, like himself, enjoy the sport and wish to practice falconry in the wide-open wilderness of America. Still others might, like himself, enjoy watching wild hawks without the trouble of acquiring equipment (such as gloves, bells, leather ties, hoods). "For Gentlemen," he wrote, "what exercise should more delight them, then ranging dayly those vnknowne parts, vsing fowling and fishing, for hunting and hawking? And yet you shall see the wilde-haukes giue you some pleasure, in seeing them stoope (six or seauen after one another) an houre or two together, at the skuls [schools] of fish in the faire harbours, as those a-shore at a foule; and neuer trouble nor torment yourselues, with watching, mewing, feeding, and attending them: nor kill horse and man with running and crying, *See you not a hawk?*"[17]

A soldier, man of action and violence, who wrote with sometimes a hand not of grace but rudeness, Smith was at the same time a man of wit and humor, self-deprecating amid his bravado, knowing his fellow humans perhaps too well, mixing venom with his praise, and suggesting a way of life not altogether popular to the wealthy men and women of Jacobean England. His was a time when in words, deeds, clothing, and actions men and women portrayed life as more than they simply lived, constantly putting on airs of grandeur as a substitute for simply being, elevating art (that is, the artificial, the human creation) above nature (the plain, simple, natural, organic). America represented an opportunity to change, to live, to accept the natural, to simply be. Hawking had so many rules and regulations, so many pretensions of class and wealth, whereas watching wild hawks soar in the wind and dive for prey, perch in silent grandeur, represented the simplicity of America for Smith. Over and over he preached in his writings the solution to the arrogance, vanity, poverty, criminality, and violence of his contemporaries, which was to find a place to work, build, sweat, breathe, eat the product of one's labor, live in the results of one's work, glory in the unprepossessing enjoyment of a simple life. This was his vision of America, of the *new* England that he proposed.

EIGHT

"The Paradise of All Those Parts"

John Smith was a restless man in search of something. This restlessness, this search, explains his entire life, his pursuit of glory in European wars when a young man; his drive for adventure, knowledge, and wealth during his twenties in Virginia and the Chesapeake region from 1606 to 1609; his continual drive to return to America in subsequent years, even as he approached middle age; his dissatisfaction with English colonization schemes that were not his own; and his anger at the lethargy and apathy that he sensed in his contemporaries when considering what was in the best interest of England. Smith released his restlessness by means of action and thought: action as a soldier and explorer; thought as a planner, observer, cartographer, scientist, and writer. In his midthirties during his voyage to New England and subsequent attempts to return, Smith was at the pinnacle in his life of this restless searching for satisfaction, for the means to the end, for the superb accomplishment, the way forward, the object of his life's work. One senses, in his subsequent years of waiting and writing about what could be, what could have been, a man who sees this object fading. The restlessness does not depart even as the life's goal does. This is the time and place, then, New England in 1614, when John Smith has a singular opportunity to fulfill his restless searching.

Hitherto Smith had seen many places along the coast, from Monhegan Island southward, that could fulfill his dreams and ambition. The land is extremely fertile, he wrote in his *Description of New England*, "capable of producing any Grain, Fruits, or Seeds you will sow or plant." Land is so plentiful and fertile that "it seems strange to me, any such should there grow poore." Indeed, sufficient sustenance to live upon, and even more, the bases of wealth, could be much more easily acquired "heere" rather than in England, which was burdened by the tens of thousands with indigent paupers. In the *new* England there is "sweet content: for, our pleasure here is still gaines; in England charges and losse. Heer nature and liberty affords vs that freely, which in England we want, or it costeth vs dearely." So many people in England yearned for the simple "pleasure in planting one's own land, in fishing for one's own meal," which they could hardly do in the old country, where the enclosure movement of the sixteenth century replaced arable with grazing land, displacing farm laborers; this combined with population increase and rising prices led to such a large number of impoverished people in the Tudor-Stuart period as to threaten the social order. The number of criminals executed for stealing and other crimes of desperation were rising during Smith's time. Hunger, want, and suffering plagued the people of Jacobean England—but acquiring food was no chore in New England. "He is a very bad fisher [who] cannot kill in one day with his hooke and line, one, two, or three hundred Cods." It takes fishers only "an houre in a day, to take more then they eate in a weeke." "And what sport doth yeeld a more pleasing content, and lesse hurt or charge then angling with a hooke; and crossing the sweete ayre from Ile to Ile, ouer the silent streames of a calme Sea?" The fishing grounds lie "before your doors," and the fisher "may euery night sleep quietly a shore with good cheare and what fires you will: or when you please [fish], with your wiues and familie." Moreover, the fish are fatter, and the labor less—"halfe the labour in hooking, splitting, and turning is saued."[1]

Smith had seen the plenty of the New England coast, and had heard the Indians "compare their store in the Sea, to the haires of th[e]ir heads: and surely there are an incredible abundance vpon this Coast." There was nothing in his experience with which to compare it, save his time at Jamestown. "This is onely as God made it, when he created the worlde." Smith had seen what human labor and industry could do. He had been to Paris, Rome, Istanbul. "Mine owne eyes . . . haue seene a great part of those Cities and their Kingdomes." But they have no advantage over this *new* England "but this, They are beautified by the long labour and diligence of industrious people and Art." If humans were to use art to change this land blessed by God, if the land were planted and cultivated

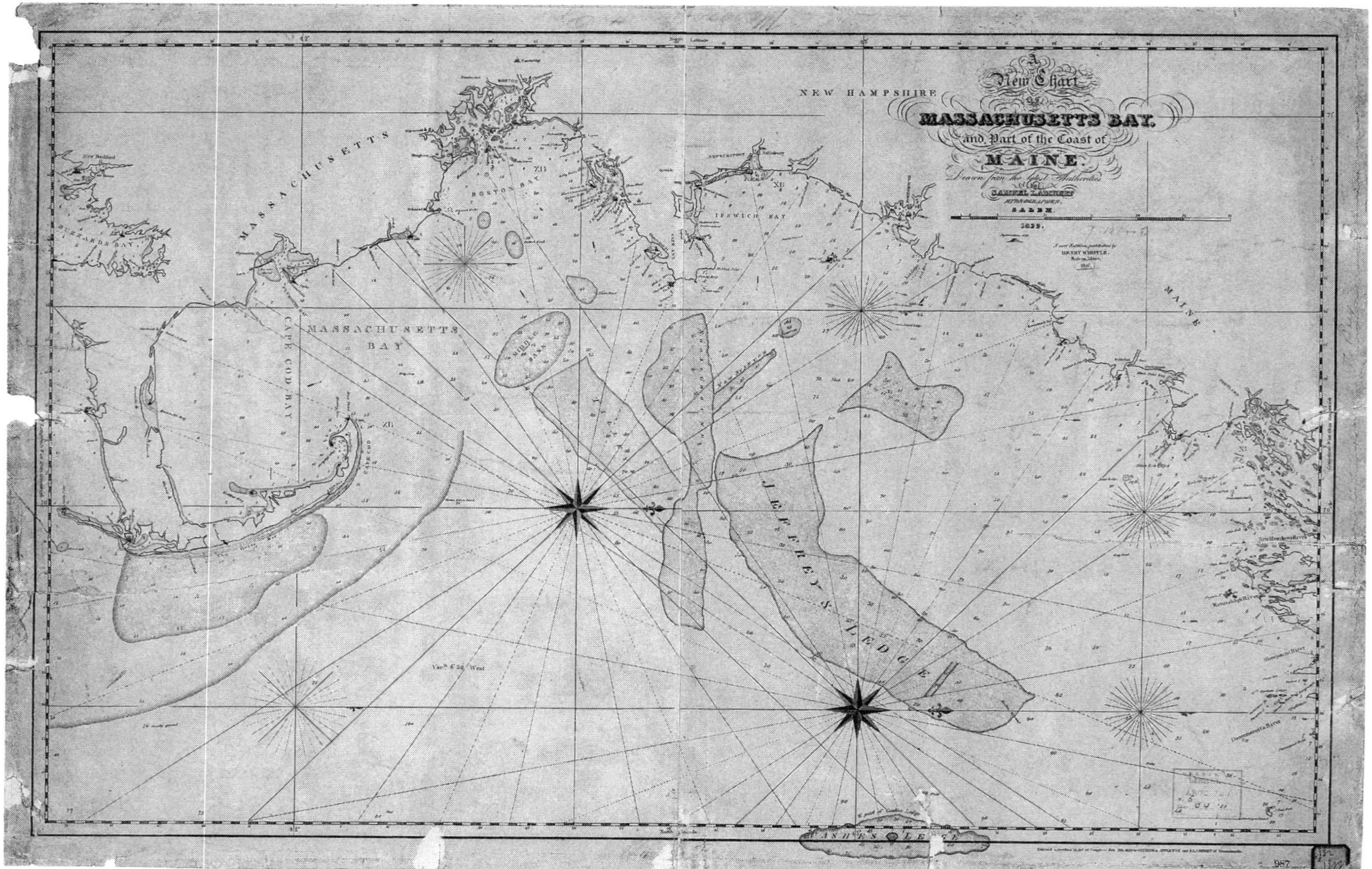

This chart of Massachusetts Bay, drawn in the early nineteenth century, portrays Boston Harbor before the massive landfilling and development of the midnineteenth to midtwentieth centuries. NOAA Chart 00-00-1847.

"by men of industrie, iudgement, and experience," would New England not therefore end up like the great civilizations of other places? For "her treasures" have "yet neuer beene opened, nor her originalls wasted, consumed, nor abused." God's blessing will afford the same wealth and society in New England as it has in those civilizations of anywhere else, Europe, Asia, or Africa.[2]

Smith's entrance into Massachusetts Bay was a completely different experience from that of a mariner today sailing a yacht to Boston Harbor. Boston has gone through several transformations during the past four centuries, so that the original island-dotted harbor leading to the peninsula of Shawmut is scarcely revealed on maps or by sea today. What used to be Dorchester Heights, which Washington occupied during the War for American Independence and from which he bombarded British-occupied Boston, is now vastly expanded and changed by means of landfill to South Boston. Logan International Airport in East Boston occupies land that was once part of three different islands in Boston harbor. The old peninsula of Shawmut, which was connected to the mainland by a narrow neck, is seen today only on ancient maps. The hills of Shawmut have been leveled and the dirt used to fill in the Back Bay. The islands, peninsulas, waterways, and mainland that Smith saw, which he denoted "the Countrie of the *Massachusets*, which is the Paradise of all those parts," would not be called Boston for another twenty years, would not see settlement for another decade, and were inhabited by Algonquian Indians who "planted with corne" the "many Iles" and maintained "groues, mulberries, [and] saluage gardens."[3]

Smith saw what attracted the Puritans to Massachusetts Bay in 1630. The island-dotted bay was fertile, defensible from attack by sea, and had "good harbours." The challenge was to make one's way through the maze of islands and shoals in a small boat without the benefit of charts or modern navigation to find those harbors. Smith and his men sailed south from Belle Isle Marsh along an extensive peninsula settled as Winthrop in 1630. Winthrop has changed since Smith saw it. Channels that surrounded it have been filled in, so ancient islands such as Hog Island and Deer Island no longer exist. Boston Harbor is so treacherous that there are numerous navigational aids to assist today's mariner. Smith and his men, however, relied on dropping the lead, keeping a close watch, and frequent use of the prayer book. Since Smith lived to map the harbor and tell of it, he obviously found a safe route. The approach from the north past Nahant Bay to Deer Island, around which south and west the mariner must sail to gain the harbor, is and was filled with rocks and ledges that careful seamanship avoided. The summer winds tend from the southwest, though sometimes a strong easterly would blow, so Smith and his men either had to tack gingerly westerly into the wind or furl their sails and let the wind drive them west. Their course undoubtedly followed that between Deer Island and Long Island to the south, voyaging west between Governor Island and Castle Island, the former now joined to the fill that made Logan Airport, the latter now part of South Boston. Proceeding west, the large Noodle Island (now part of East Boston) lay to the north, while Shawmut Peninsula lay to the south. Smith's *Map of New England* provides a vague outline of the many islands of Boston Harbor that he negotiated to reach Shawmut.[4]

The extent of Smith's explorations of the harbor is unclear. Perhaps he sailed north and west around Charlestown Peninsula to the mouth of the Mystic River, which the natives called the "MissiTuk or 'great tidal river.'" He doubtless sailed west and southwest between Shawmut and Charlestown following the fresh water that emerged from a great river that Smith subsequently named the Charles. He clearly disembarked somewhere, one imagines at Shawmut, where he conversed with the native Massachusett tribe, relying on the help of Tisquantum whenever his own growing vocabulary of Algonquian words was deficient. How much they understood each other is unclear, as Smith referred to the "Massachusets; of another language, humor, and condition" from other Indians he met along the way. Perhaps he learned the various possible meanings of Shawmut: "where there is a going by boat" or "fountains of living water" or "springs." Perhaps he met the sachem of the Massachusett, Nanapashemet. If so, he was among those "great troupes of well proportioned people." The natives, perhaps, shared their meal of maize and told Smith that there was "neer three thousand people vpon these Iles, and that the River doth pearce many daies iourneies the intralles of that Countrey." His *Map of New England* shows a disproportionately

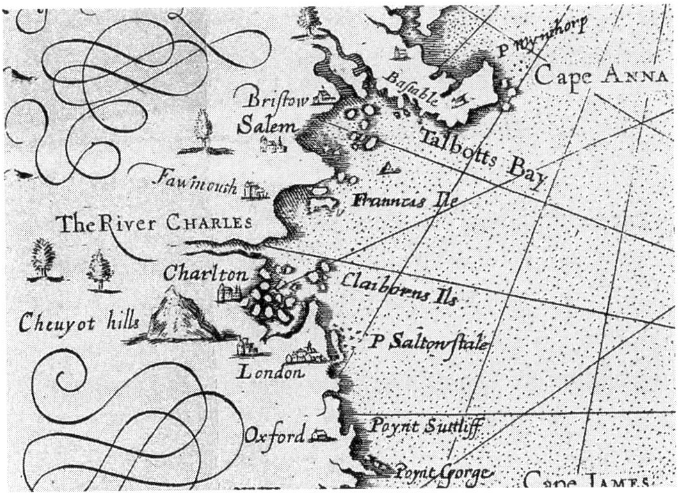

Smith's *Map of New England* accurately portrays the many islands of Boston Harbor and the majestic Great Blue Hill. American Memory, Library of Congress.

large Charles River, which reveals that it loomed large in the minds of the Indians as well as Smith, and tempts us into believing that he must have journeyed a little way upriver. At the same time, however, Smith complained that the French had been here before him, had left little in the way of furs to purchase from the natives, were perhaps still in the neighborhood, and Smith felt uncomfortable waiting around to see if the presence of the English might occasion a visit. The amount of words he spent on this place, that he called it a paradise, indicates some time spent observing, exploring, and communicating with the Massachusett. "For their trade and marchandize; to each of their habitations they haue diuerse Townes and people belonging; and by their relations and descriptions, more then 20 seuerall Habitations and Riuers that stretch themselues farre vp into the Countrey, euen to the borders of diuerse great Lakes, where they kill and take most of their Beuers and Otters."[5]

The indigenous peoples of New England told many of the explorers of this time about these great lakes far into the interior. Hearing about them fired the imagination of many people, such as Samuel de Champlain, who actually found them, and John Smith, who did not. It would take the English many years to reach the Great Lakes. A vast mountain barrier separated them from the interior lakes that many hoped might be the means to reach the great South Sea, the Pacific Ocean. The English for the time being had to be content with exploring the rivers that sourced at the foothills of the Appalachian Mountains. Smith explored some of these rivers in the Chesapeake region, such as the James and Potomac. In New England, he was content mostly to sail along the coast. Of the great rivers flowing from the interior—the Penobscot, Kennebec, Saco, Piscataqua, Merrimack, Charles—he scarcely explored any of them, save the Kennebec.

The Massachusetts Bay region hosted a series of hills that sailors used for landmarks. The Massachusett were "the people of the Great Blue Hill." Smith and his men had seen the Great Blue Hill (called Chevyot hills on Smith's *Map of New England*, named for Cheviot Hills in Northumberland) as they approached the harbor. Likewise Shawmut had a series of hills that sailors used as beacons to guide their approach: the tallest was Beacon Hill. It, along with two others (Mount Vernon, Pemberton), formed what Puritan settlers called the Trimount. In between the hills were valleys and lowlands; sweet freshwater springs made Shawmut a likely place for settlement. Shawmut had a variety of hard and soft woods—elm, oak, pine, birch, maple, hickory, and aspen—which England so desperately needed to break away from an expensive dependence on imports from Europe. The trees were here; only labor was wanting. Besides the forested hills were other useful flora that the natives used for food such as gooseberries, strawberries, blackberries, raspberries, blueberries, and whortleberries. As everywhere else along New England's coast, the fishing was good. Indians caught salmon, alewives, shad, and mullet with weirs up the Mystic, Charles, and Neponset rivers. Around much of Shawmut and elsewhere along the coast there were salt marshes that could provide feed for livestock.[6]

On departing Shawmut, Smith and his men wandered through the many islands and harbors to the south. Smith's *Map of New England* includes a group of islands just east of Shawmut, as well as nearby islands, denoted "Cary Ils" (perhaps named for the river of the same name in Somerset), which appear to the northeast of a large bay, which was Dorchester Bay and the mouth of the Neponset River. His route was probably west of Thompson Island, which in just a few years was to be used as a trading post by English colonist David Thomson, who traded with the Indians at Neponset. The men could smell the fresh water mingling with brine as the Neponset entered Dorchester Bay. They skirted Thompson Island to the south in the shallows north of Squantum Peninsula, then negotiated the waters east and south avoiding Moon and Long islands to the north. Proceeding south along Squantum Peninsula, they entered what is today called Quincy Bay, which after Houghs Neck (named for an early colonist) becomes Hingham Bay. On Smith's map, his route would be the narrows between the mainland and Cary Ils, which denote the dozen islands of outer Boston Harbor. The challenge that Smith and his men faced was to circumnavigate a long point, Nantasket Peninsula (where is today's Nantasket Beach), at the eastern extreme of Hingham Bay, avoiding the many islands and shoals along the way. Modern mariners use Nantasket Roads, which Smith might have used, though if he explored the estuarial Weymouth Fore River and Weymouth Back River, and Hingham Bay, he would have been forced to sail north through shoal water skirting five or six small islands. The voyage along the shores of Nantasket Beach, facing the Atlantic, was relatively free of shoals, until the shallop came to a quite different place, which Smith called Quonahassit, today's Cohasset Harbor.[7]

The granite rocks along the shore and coast forming ledges and dangers for mariners greeted Smith and his men as they left Nantasket Beach and now followed the rocky coast eastward. It takes brave and skilled mariners to sail these waters about Cohasset, but Smith and his men were up to it. The harbor itself is guarded by shoals and rocks, which require careful navigation and luck to avoid. Smith was the first recorded intrepid Anglo- or Euro-explorer to make his way to Cohasset. He wound his way into the harbor, passing Windhill Point and White Head, inching through the shoal water into the harbor past Bassing Beach reaching Cohasset Cove, where he set foot on land and met with the local Quonahassit people. English and indigenous had good trading, perhaps some lively conversation, and shared a meal. Smith recalled that "the people in those parts [were] verie kinde." Like other tribes of the coast, they grew maize, beans, and squash, gathered berries and nuts, netted fish, dug clams and caught lobsters for their feasts. They lived in birch-bark wigwams made snug and warm against the New England winter; they preferred dugouts made from white pine rather than birch bark for their canoes. Having had little contact with Europeans before Smith's arrival, they relied heavily on stone tools and weapons.[8]

The varied tribes along the coast alternately warred and made peace. The tribes of coastal Massachusetts "sometimes haue warres with" and feared "the Bashabes of Pennobskot." At times the Massachusett tribe, and perhaps the Quonahassit as well, were "not alwaies friends with them of Chawun," the Nauset Indians on Cape Cod "and their alliants." "But now," the Indians reported to Smith, "they are all friends, and haue each trade with other, so farre as they haue societie on each others frontiers." Tisquantum at this point could confirm or deny their profession of friendship, of which trade among tribes was a sign, a friendly alliance that allowed hunters to range and hunt on lands on the perceived verge of another tribe's hunting ground. A sign of friendly trade involved the exchange of wampum, decorative pieces of shells, used for a variety of purposes, even as currency, by American Indians at this time.[9]

Smith had firsthand experience with the Quonahassit war strategy and weapons. During his time with these people, one of the Quonahassit warriors became offended by some action or comment made by Smith, one of the sailors, or perhaps even Tisquantum. Smith, accustomed to the kind of "furie" that occurs when experiencing a perceived personal wrong, respected the "valiant" response of the Indian. For when the English took their leave from the Quonahassit and began to navigate their way out of Cohasset Cove, they had to pass the narrows between Bassing Beach and Hominy Point (Bryant Point). Here the offended Quonahassit warrior, "with three others," had taken a canoe to the point jutting into the harbor where they secretly lay in wait for the English. Such stratagems of subterfuge and surprise, guerrilla warfare, were typical of American Indian warriors. When the English passed by, the Indians stood on the rocky point and "there let flie their arrowes." The English returned musket "shot, till we were out of danger." Whether or not death or injury was the result to either English or indigenous, Smith did not say. Other accounts of English fighting New England Indian warriors reveal that they were excellent marksmen with the bow and arrow. The bow, made of a hardwood such as ash, had a cord made of animal sinew that was sufficiently taut to launch an arrow, also made of hardwood with a sharp chipped stone or bone on the end, over a hundred yards. Remarkably, this was the first, but not the last, occasion on this voyage along the New England coast where the competing aims of the Englishman John Smith and American Indians came to blows.[10]

Leaving Cohasset Cove and entering Cohasset Harbor, the Englishmen steered the shallop east through continuing treacherous waters toward Scituate Harbor. The eastern edge of Cohasset Harbor was framed by Scituate Neck, off which were ledges and rocks to challenge any seaman. Threading their way southeast, bearing toward land through shoals, they cleared, through chance or will, a particularly dangerous place known since as the Hazards, and another named Smith Rocks, until they reached a safer stretch of beach that they paralleled in a south-southeasterly direction. In time, as they got closer to Scituate Harbor, the water grew more shoal. If Smith and his men entered the harbor, they had to round Cedar Point and weave their way west through a narrow route into the harbor. More likely they explored North River, as Smith's *Map of New England* shows an extensive inlet south of Scituate that implies knowledge acquired either by observation or communication with the indigenous people. The North River, named by the English in the wake of the founding of Plymouth in 1620, is a tidal river that flows from inland about eighteen miles to the sea. Near the mouth it joins with the South River, flowing north near the sea, paralleling a long sandy beach. Both rivers flow through marshy land, in which the English, if they explored it, might have found some fat fowl for their supper. William Bradford, in *Of Plymouth Plantation*, noted that the coast had many wild turkeys, easy prey for the average marksman.[11]

South of North River is a point of land, which on Smith's map is designated Poynt Sutliff, off of which are rocks and shoals where the Green Harbor River enters the sea. Champlain had called this place Cap de St. Louis; it is known now as Brant Rock. Smith (or King Charles) named it after a friend and sponsor, Dr. Matthew Sutcliffe, Dean of Exeter, founder of Chelsea College, chaplain to the king, in time a member of the Council of New England. Smith made note of the point as an important landmark, a place of difficult sailing, and perhaps a place, at

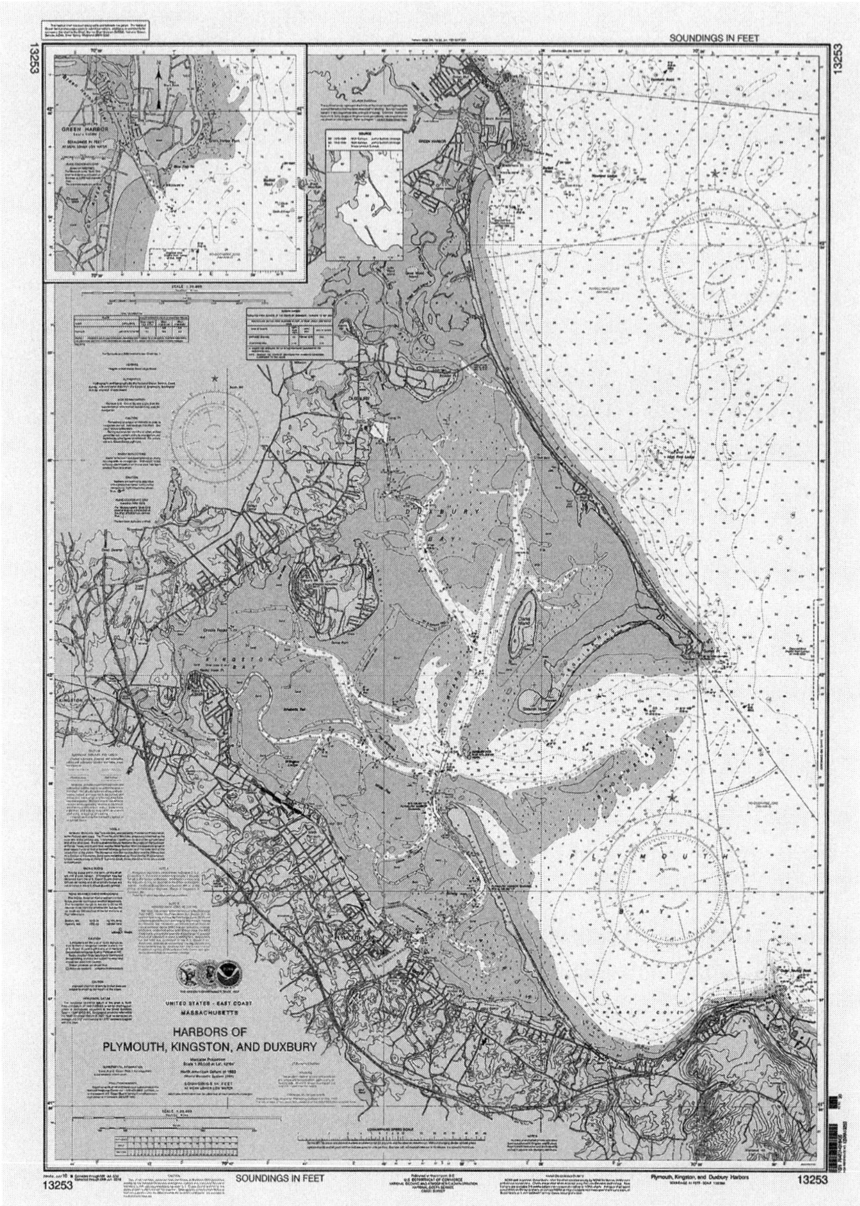

The Massachusetts coastline south of Boston, including Plymouth Harbor.
NOAA Chart 13253-07-2010.

the mouth of the Green Harbor River, to find a quick harbor. South of this point extends a long sandy spit, comparatively free of hazards, since known as Duxbury Beach, on the other side of which is an extensive marsh giving way to Duxbury Bay. Duxbury Beach comes to a point at Gurnet Point, which on Smith's map was named Poynt George. The way south was generally without hazard; when Smith and his men turned the point west, they followed another pincer of land, subsequently named Saquish Neck, leading to Saquish Head, which is the northern point of Plymouth Harbor, the southern point being the northern extreme of Plymouth Beach. This massive inlet consists of two bays named for two towns, Duxbury and Kingston, and, to the south, Plymouth Harbor.[12]

The English had now arrived at Accomack, the home of Tisquantum, where his tribe, the Patuxets, lived. The Patuxets were part of the Wampanoag Confederation of Indians of southern Massachusetts and Rhode Island. Several years after Smith's visit, an epidemic raged throughout the area, decimating the indigenous population, so that when the Pilgrims arrived in 1620 they found very few Indians and quite a few unburied skeletons. Martin Pring, who explored Accomack in 1603, had extensive interaction with the native inhabitants. He had sailed into Duxbury Bay, but not finding sassafras, the purpose for his voyage, he crossed over to the opposite side, Plymouth Harbor. He named Accomack, Whitson Bay. The native Patuxet tribe were friendly in response to Pring's men, who gave them trinkets as well as "Pease and Beans." One of the young men of Pring's company played melodies on his gittern for the Indians, of which "they tooke great delight," and gave the player many gifts in return for his song. Pring took note of their "Bowes of five or sixe foot long of Wi[t]ch-hasell, painted blacke and yellow, the strings of three twists of sinewes, bigger then our Bowstrings. Their Arrowes are of a yard and an handfull long not made of Reeds, but of a fine light wood very smooth and round with three long and deepe blacke feathers of some Eagle, Vulture, or Kite, as closely fastened with some binding matter, as any Fletcher of ours can glue them on. Their Quivers are full a yard long, and made of long dried Rushes wrought about two handfuls broad above, and one handfull beneath with prettie workes and compartiments." The Patuxet warriors were larger and stronger than the English, though they were terribly afraid of "two excellent Mastives [mastiffs]," such that, "when we

Plymouth Harbor as it appeared in the early nineteenth century.
NOAA Historic Fisheries Collection.

would be rid of the Savages company wee would let loose the Mastives, and suddenly with out-cryes they would flee away."[13]

In the intervening years since Pring's visit, the New England Indians experienced similar arrogant behavior from other English on other voyages. George Waymouth kidnapped five men in 1605 from Pemaquid, and Edward Harlow kidnapped Tisquantum and others in 1611. Such atrocities were long recalled in Indian villages. Smith, knowing of Tisquantum's history, was doubtless prepared for anger and revenge. Upon arriving at Accomack, Smith found "an excellent good harbor"; he and his men sailed the shallop into Plymouth Harbor, which was no easy task, probably done at high tide; the harbor could be sandy and dry at low tide. Smith's *Map of New England* shows an inlet or river just south of Gurnet Point, which could be several different rivers (Jones River, Bluefish River, Duck Hill River), any one of which Smith and his men might have explored. Smith likely did not explore the southern extreme of Plymouth Harbor, as he portrays on his map an island rather than the long thin peninsula of Plymouth Beach. The map of Champlain, who explored this area in 1604, shows an extensive river flowing into Plymouth Harbor. This was perhaps Town Brook. When William Bradford and the Pilgrims explored the land that would become the town of Plymouth, Bradford wrote that "they sounded the harbor, and founde it fitt for shipping; and marked into the land, & found diverse cornfeilds, & litle runing brooks."

Champlain, too, found the land well planted with extensive cornfields. Smith, likewise, wrote that Plymouth had "good land."[14]

Upon his arrival, Smith not surprisingly found a tribe of able warriors, jealous of their rights, suspicious of the whites sailing into their bay with their strange ship and arrogant ways. At first the two peoples got along, perhaps because of Tisquantum; Smith showed his knowledge of Algonquian, perhaps exchanged pleasantries, offered gifts. Something happened, however, to offend one or the other parties. Perhaps words were misunderstood. Perhaps two traders disagreed on the value of items to be traded. Perhaps seeing Tisquantum alive and well brought forth angry memories after the initial pleasure of reunion. Whatever the cause, "after much kindnesse; vpon a small occasion, wee fought also with fortie or fiftie of those." The odds were five or six to one, but though the English were outnumbered, they had more fearful weapons. The Patuxets had the worst of it—"some were hurt, and some slaine." "Yet," in the strange world of seventeenth-century war and peace, "within an hour after they became friendes" again, perhaps through the mediation of Tisquantum. Smith had agreed to bring him home, but strangely, Tisquantum did not stay at Accomack when the English departed; perhaps Smith requested or demanded that Tisquantum continue on to Cape Cod; perhaps Tisquantum was not welcome at his home.[15]

John Smith's impressions of Accomack, like Champlain's before him, were positive, and Smith noted that this would be a wonderful place for a colony. Six years later, the Pilgrims on the *Mayflower*, some of whom had read Smith's *Description of New England* and had his *Map of New England* as a guide, had a very different perspective of the new land. To them, Bradford wrote, this was "a hideous & desolate wildernes, full of wild beasts & willd men. . . . The whole countrie, full of woods & thickets, represented a wild & savage heiw [hue]." Smith, on the other hand, had this to say about the coastline that became the English colony of Massachusetts: "And of all the foure parts of the world that I haue yet seene not inhabited [Europe, Asia, Africa, America], could I haue but meanes to transport a Colonie, I would rather liue here then anywhere: and if it did not maintaine it selfe, where wee but once indifferently well fitted, let vs starue."[16] To be sure, one person's wilderness is another person's paradise.

NINE

Cape James

When John Smith returned to England in 1604 after several years of adventures in Europe—fighting against and being enslaved by the Turks, living in the household of Charatza Tragabigzanda, being forced to work for her brother in Russia, killing the brother and escaping through Europe, crossing over into Morocco, joining French privateers in piracy, and returning to England with some money in his pocket—he was looking for adventure, wealth, and glory when he met a kinsman of his patron Lord Willoughby.[1] This man, Bartholomew Gosnold, who was just as enterprising and bold as Smith, convinced the younger man that the place for the sword, energy, ambition, and faith of a Jacobean soldier was America, specifically Virginia, the coast named for Queen Elizabeth. Indeed, while Smith was fighting in Europe, Gosnold had been sailing the New England coast, attempting to establish a colony in Northern Virginia. In 1606, Smith joined Gosnold and other adventurers who formed the London Company in their ambitious attempt to establish a colony in Southern Virginia, at Jamestown. Although Gosnold would never return to England, succumbing to illness in Virginia, he and Smith shared many of the same personality traits and ideas, and no doubt Gosnold told Smith about his journey along the northern coast.

Bartholomew Gosnold had not visited Accomack, hence would have had limited knowledge of the great bay that separates Plymouth from Cape Cod; so perhaps Smith, in ignorance, when he and his men in 1614 departed the harbor and bay of Accomack in their shallop, followed in Champlain's wake, sailing south before discovering, in time, that the apparent islands to the east were in actuality a massive landmass, a cape, around which to circumnavigate he had to retreat back to the north. If he did take this uncertain route, he found, like Champlain before him, that the bay had very few obstructions or shoals, at least away from shore, and if, when he determined to change directions, the wind cooperated, it was quite a pleasant voyage. Or, perhaps, Tisquantum was sufficiently familiar with the bay to inform Smith that the correct path was due east to reach the northern tip of the cape. Whichever way Smith arrived at the farthest northern extent of the cape, he realized, if he already did not know it from friend Gosnold or from Tisquantum, that "this *Cape* is made by the maine Sea on the one side, and a great Bay on the other in forme of a sickle." King Charles, on Smith's *Map of New England*, designated the bay, Stuards Bay (after the Stuart royal family), now known as Cape Cod Bay. Gosnold (or at least John Brereton, the journalist of the voyage) had a middling view of the cape: "in some places plaine," in others "full of goodly woods." Unlike Champlain, who saw beauty in Cape Cod, Smith observed "a headland of high hils of sand ouergrowne with shrubbie pines, hurts," or whortleberries, "and such trash." Gosnold had not explored the shores of New Hampshire and Massachusetts, coming to the cape directly from Maine, so when he found the numbers of cod that his sailors caught, so that many had to be tossed back, he naturally named the place Cape Cod. Smith ignored Gosnold's appellation when he met with Prince Charles, honoring the king by suggesting it be called Cape James. William Bradford, writing some time later, noted that "it retains the former name," Cape Cod, "amongst seamen"—and so it has hence stood.[2]

If Smith was not impressed by the white sands of the cape, he nevertheless found "an excellent harbor for all weathers." There are several harbors along the eastern and southern shores of Cape Cod. Champlain had explored, on the eastern side, Nauset Harbor, which he named Mallebarre because of its dangerous shoals, and on the southern side, Stage Harbor. The Frenchman met with the native inhabitants at both of these places and had a conflict with those at Mallebarre. Nauset Harbor, Chatham Harbor, and Stage Harbor are all difficult to access because of shifting sands and shoals and tricky tides and currents, which challenge even today's mariner, much more those of four hundred years ago sailing in ignorance in these risky waters. Smith called the people of lower Cape

The bark *Mayflower* sailed into Plymouth Harbor in 1620. Library of Congress.

Cod, Pawmet, and southern Cape Cod, Chawum—both were Algonquian peoples of the Nauset tribe. These people thrived on the cape, were sometimes aggressive, grew crops and fished for their sustenance, and lived in sturdy wigwams. Champlain had a difficult time conversing with the Nauset, but Smith, because of his partial understanding of Algonquian (which had improved on this voyage), was able to communicate with them, to such an extent as to get their impressions of the route around the cape to the south and west. "The Saluages say there is no Channell," Smith wrote, perhaps referring to Tisquantum's information as well as that of the Nausets, "but that the shoales beginne from the maine at Pawmet, to the Ile of Nausit; and so extends beyond their knowledge into the Sea." By experience, Smith discovered that they were wrong, though it required sailing "towards the South and Southwest of this *Cape*" through "a long and dangerous shoale of sands and rocks." Rather than trying to negotiate the passage between the southern extent of Nauset Beach and Monomoy Island, which would have taken him to Stage Harbor, as Champlain did, Smith appears to have sailed south along Monomoy Island and west into Nantucket Sound, as did Gosnold. But unlike Gosnold, who continued to explore Nantucket Sound and eventually set up a temporary colony on Cuttyhunk Island, Smith went no farther. "So farre as I incircled it," he wrote, referring to Monomoy

Island, "I found thirtie fadom [of] water aboard the shore, and a strong current; which makes mee thinke there is a Channell about this shoale: where is the best and greatest fish to be had, Winter and Summer, in all that Countrie." If he was correct, and a strong westerly channel drew the sea and its fish along the southern coast of New England, and had Smith followed the "Channell," he would have perhaps found his way to Capawack, later called Martha's Vineyard, which he heard from the natives was one of many "abounding Countries of copper, corne, people, mineralls." But such would be another voyage, for another time.[3]

Somewhere along the coast of the cape, Smith allowed Tisquantum to depart, perhaps to stay with the Nauset tribe. Several weeks later, Tisquantum was one of a number of Patuxet and Nauset Indians who were kidnapped by Thomas Hunt, one of Smith's associates, who had stayed, ostensibly to trade and fish. Smith, in *Description of New England*, lamented that Hunt "abused the Saluages where hee came, and betrayed twenty seauen of these poore innocent soules, which he sould in Spaine for slaues." In *General History*, Smith argued that Hunt was jealous of Smith and aimed "to prevent that intent I had to make there a Plantation, thereby to keepe this abounding Countrey still in obscuritie, that onely he and some few Merchants more might enjoy wholly the benefit of the Trade, and profit of this Countrey." Tisquantum eventually, as William Bradford wrote in *Of Plymouth Plantation*, "got away for England, and was entertained by a marchante in London, & imployed to New-foundland & other parts, & lastly brought hither into these parts by one Mr. [Thomas] Dermer, a gentle-man employed by Sr. Ferdinando Gorges & others, for discovery." In 1620 he met and befriended the Pilgrims.[4]

Meanwhile Smith's voyage along the New England coast, which began earlier in the spring, and as a brief journey of discovery by which to establish more solid plans for a plantation, a self-sustaining fishing colony that would be a successful vanguard of the English in this northern Virginia, was nearing its end. Smith had traded with the indigenous peoples from the Penobscot to Cape Cod, and had a shallop filled with pelts and furs. It was time to return to the rendezvous point at Monhegan Island, to see what the fishers and sailors who were left behind had accomplished, to load the cargo and prepare for the return voyage to England before the end of

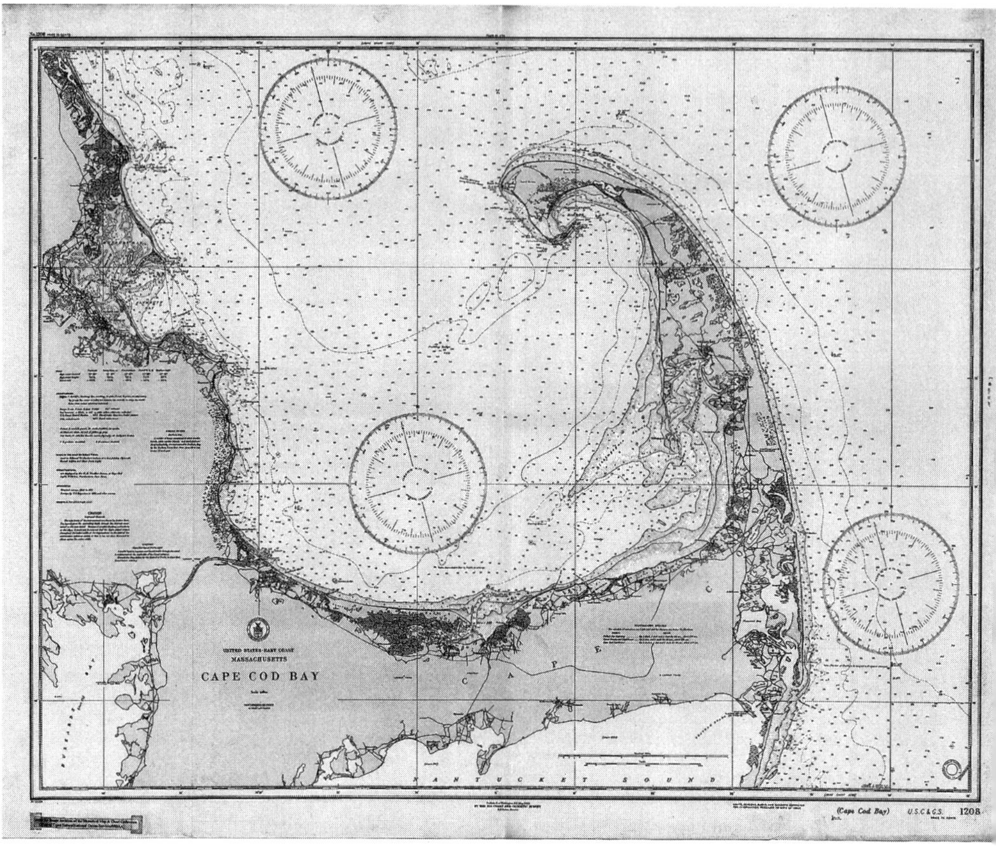

John Smith explored Cape Cod a dozen years after his friend Bartholomew Gosnold first visited. NOAA Chart 1208-08-1933.

summer. So Smith and his men put about, set their course northerly, and eschewed exploration of the coast for the quickest and safest way back, one with few hazards save the waves, currents, and winds. If the weather was good and the winds right, it would be a brief voyage to scurry up the coast; perhaps they would put in overnight at one of the many safe ports they had found, though if the stars were bright and the sea calm, there was no need to halt. It was, after all, from Penobscot Bay to Cape Cod, "some 75 leagues [225 miles] by a right line distant from each other."[5]

Smith and his men had explored from the 44th to the 41st degrees north latitude, "within which bounds I haue seene at least 40. seuerall habitations vpon the Sea Coast." Smith had met, traded with, communicated with, and sometimes fought against Algonquian peoples who lived in villages along the New England coast. These villages included "Mecadacut, Segocket, Pemmaquid, Nusconcus, Kenebeck, Sagadahock, and Aumoughcawgen." Farther south, along what is today southern Maine, New Hampshire, and Massachusetts, were people who called their villages "Aucocisco, Accominticus, Passataquack, Aggawom, . . . Naemkeck, . . . Totant, Massachuset, Pocapawmet, Quonahassit, Sagoquas, Nahapassumkeck, Topeent, Seccasaw, Totheet, Nasnocomacack, Accomack, Chawmum." Smith had discovered "and sounded about 25 excellent good Harbours," as at the mouth of the rivers Penobscot, St. George, Kennebec, Saco, Piscataqua, Merrimack, and Charles; "in many whereof there is anc[h]orage for 500. sayle of ships of any burden"—so he had found at places now called Casco Bay, Marblehead, Gloucester, Newburyport, Salem, Plymouth; "in some of them for 5000"—at Massachusetts Bay, for example. On his voyage Smith had seen the mountainous backcountry of New England and had wondered about, if he did not explore, several daunting peaks, such as "them of Pennobscot; the twinkling mountaine of Aucociso; the great mountaine of Sasanou; and the high mountain of Massachusit; each of which you shall finde in the Mappe; their places, formes, and altitude." Of "Iles," he had seen "more than 200 . . . ouergrowne with good timber, of diuers sorts of wood," many of which had harbors of their own, which "requireth a longer time then I had, to be well discouered." Of these islands the "highest Ile is *Sorico*, in the Bay of *Pennobskot*." Others that served as landmarks or places to host fishing colonies included Matinnack and Metinicus, also in Penobscot Bay; Monhegan, where his voyage of discovery in America began and ended; islands at the mouth of the Kennebec; Smith's Isles; and Plum Island. These islands and harbors, and the many rivers, their mouths and falls, hosted uncountable numbers of fish.[6]

Smith and his men were leaving a region, southern New England, that was a fisher's paradise. Mullet, for example, is a bottom-feeder, a vegetarian, that will not bite at live bait so must be captured with nets or weirs. Either the fishers with Smith or Indians told Smith as much. He wrote of the abundance of mullets easily caught, "sometimes by hundreds."

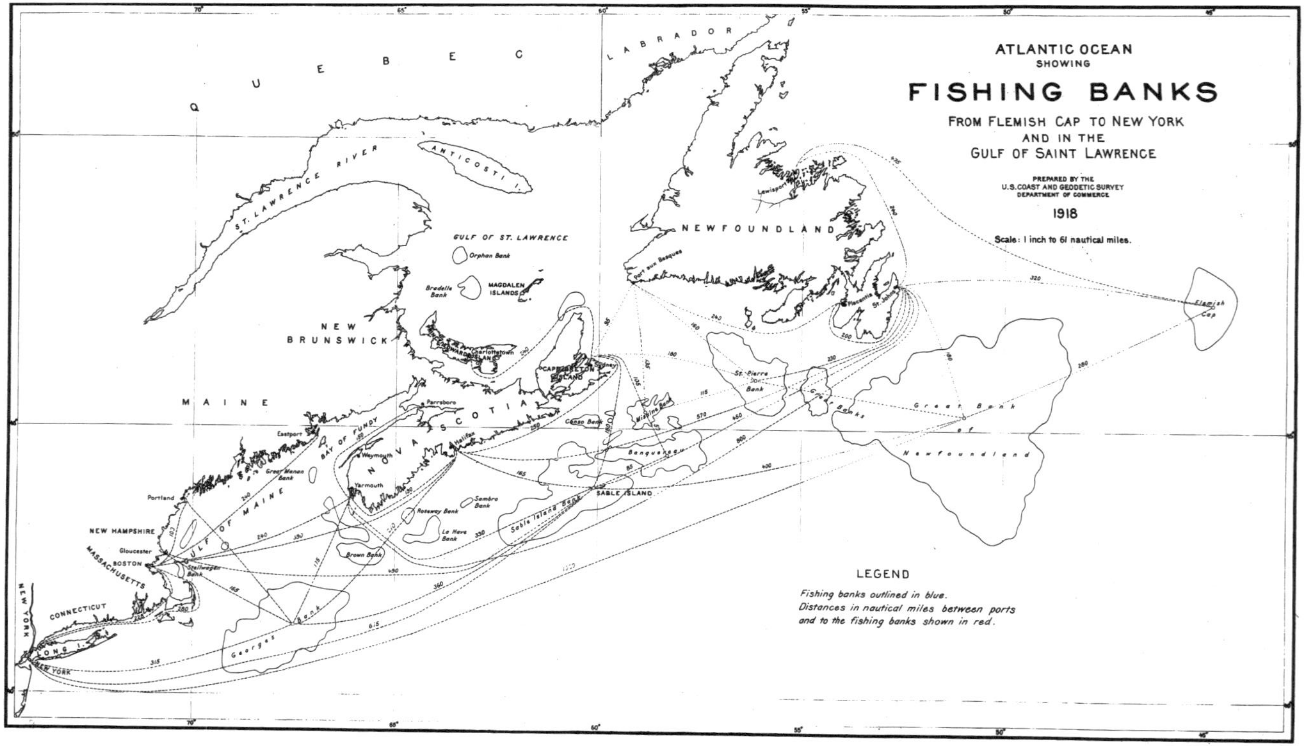

European fishers had fished the banks off the northeast American coast for a century before the arrival of John Smith. NOAA Chart 16723-05-1931.

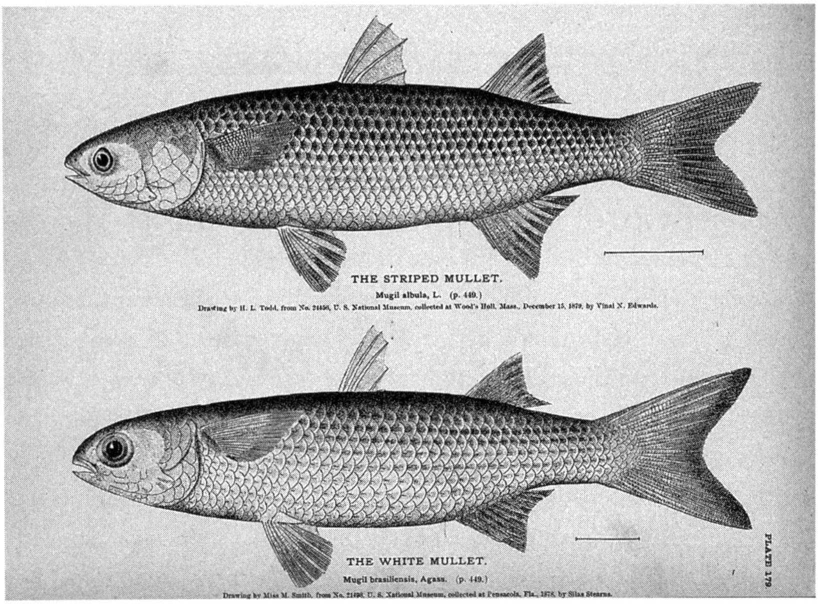

The mullet was a fish typically caught with nets or weirs.
NOAA Historic Fisheries Collection.

New England mullet was much larger—"as oft I haue measured"—two, three, even four feet long, than those he had previously seen or heard about. Smith and his men fished with nets "in diuers sandy Baies," where "a man may draw with a net great store of Mullets, Ba[s]ses, and diuers other sorts of such excellent fish, as many as his Net can drawe on shore."[7]

Over and again he was amazed because "all these and diuerse other good things do heere, for want of vse, still increase." Beachcombers gorged themselves on clams, which "growe to that abundance you shall scarce finde any Baye, shallow shore, or Coue of sand, where you may not take many." Likewise with lobsters, where "in many places lode your boat if you please." Among "Iles," there were "crabs . . . and muskles, . . . all of them for taking, at a lowe water." "In the harbors we frequented," fishers "at the ships sterne, . . . with a casting net," caught "thousands when wee pleased." All this was in addition to the fish taken with the pole and hook: "Cod, Cuske [cusk], Holybut [halibut], Mackerell, Scate [skate], or such like." And river fishers caught "plentie of Sturgion, or Salmon, or both."

Smith believed that fishing was prolific throughout the year, though, he added with a wink, "if a man will goe at Christmasse to gather Cherries in *Kent*, he may be deceiued, though there be plentie in Summer."[8]

Most adventurers and promoters of colonization looked upon fish as "a mean and a base commoditie"—of course, when there was gold and silver to be had! Yet upon this "contemptible trade of fish" depended the success of English colonization. Smith had seen clear evidence of success based on fishing many years before, during his travels in the Netherlands. Those people across the English Channel had become a first-rate power, even able to withstand the will of Spain, because of "their Myne," fish, which enabled a virtuous and hard-working people to be wealthy, independent, and strong. "The Sea" was "the source of those siluered streames of all their vertue." Smith had made a particular study of the "Hollanders," discovering that their power and wealth depended upon "Herring, Cod, and Ling." The English, Smith argued, could not only be as successful as the Hollanders but even surpass them by means of fishing colonies in New England.[9]

Smith discovered on his voyage as well that New England offered much more than fish. He dared to "boldly say" that many commodities sought by England from other countries, such as pitch, tar, masts, "Yardes," iron, rope, canvas, wine, steel, iron, oil, silk, and fruit, could be supplied, in time, by New England. The ground was fertile, "capable of producing any Grain, Fruits, or Seeds you will sow or plant," though the southern parts of New England were more prolific than northern New England. On the other hand, northern New England, because of a slightly colder climate, provided for the hunter and trapper and Indian trader thick pelts and furs. Smith, cruising the New England coast in June and July, found the climate delightful, and found little evidence either by experience or by what he understood from the indigenous people that the winters were harsh with cold. Early colonization attempts, such as at Sagadahoc, had convinced the English that this northern climate was unbearable, but Smith discounted such reports, and convinced himself (and hoped to convince others) that "both Winter and Summer hath [fish and fowl] in the one part or other all the yeare; being the meane and most indifferent temper betwixt heat and colde, of all the regions bewixt the Lyne [equator] and the [North] Pole."[10]

The latitude of New England, 41, 42, 43 degrees north, was "as good as any," "and as fruitfull as any other paralell in the world." By comparison, other thriving places were in the same northern latitude, such as Nova Albion (the Pacific coast of North America, discovered by Francis Drake), Portugal, the ancient Roman city of Valencia, and "the best and richest parts of *France*." Warming to the topic, Smith likened the potential civilization of New England to the wonders of Italy and Greece, and anticipated that it would be in time comparable to "the most pleasant and plentifull citie in *Europe, Constantinople*," which he had seen in 1603. Indeed, New England would someday be as rich as Persia and China.[11]

John Smith, like many other humanists of his time, had studied and embraced the mentality of the ancient Greeks and Romans. Smith believed in the republican ideal of early Rome and could imagine himself like a Cincinnatus or a Scipio, who used their energy and sword "for the good of the commonwealth," braving "dangers abroad" to reap benefits at home; then in time youthful ardor and patriotism gave way to "iustice and iudgement out of their experience, when they grewe aged." But the Roman Republic became a materialistic, selfish society, where "the excesse of idlenesse, the fondnesse of Parents, the want of experience in Magistrates, the admiration of their vndeserued honours, the contempt of true merit, their vniust iealo[u]sies, their politicke incredulities, their hypocriticall seeming goodnesse, and their deeds of secret lewdnesse," destroyed the virtues upon which their power had previously been built. Smith feared that England was going through the same process of youthful rise and mature decline. Some English, such as himself, felt like the youthful "Grecians, and Romanes" that sense of, "What was it they would not doe, for the good of the commonwealth, or their Mother-citie?" What dangers would adventurers such as Smith not risk for the sake of England? There were too many English, Smith believed, who chose selfish passivity and vice, rather than active, restless virtue. Some people were "temporists," living only for the present, for temporary fame and gain; Smith believed in breaking from the tyranny of the present, to use the past to anticipate the future. Colonies in America, Smith believed, would provide an outlet for England to escape the vices that destroyed Rome.[12]

As Smith sailed north along the coast of this land he had christened

New England, he was forming in his mind ideas that found their way into the *Description of New England* the following year. The adjective *New* in New England was not an arbitrary bow to custom and convention, distinguishing something newly discovered from something already known. Rather, we find in Smith's work a sense that the newness of this land meant something economically, socially, morally, and personally. He indicated as much in a marginal note made in his *Description of New England*: "A note for men that haue great spirits, and smal meanes." The note was meant for others like himself, people who had will, energy, desire, courage, and drive but few resources. "Who can desire more content, that hath small meanes; or but only his merit to aduance his fortune, then to tread, and plant that ground hee hath purchased by the hazard of his life? If he haue but the taste of virtue and magnanimitie, what to such a minde can bee more pleasant, then planting and building a foundation for his Posteritie, gotte from the rude earth, by Gods blessing and his owne industrie, without preiudice to any?" Smith, of course, was not a great thinker, not a metaphysician like Richard Hooker or a synthesizer like Francis Bacon; he was a practical, commonsense Christian humanist who combined the secular and religious concerns of himself and his time, believing that the human will subordinating itself to God's will was the best means of success. "If hee haue any graine of faith or zeale in Religion, what can hee doe lesse hurtfull to any: or more agreeable to God, then to seeke to conuert those poore Saluages to know Christ, and humanitie, whose labors with discretion will triple requite thy charge and paines?"[13]

During his voyage, Smith's mind was always on England. He saw the landmarks of the coast through English eyes, thinking of appellations to honor his homeland, and comparing the coast to places from home—for example, the New England coast reminded him of the limestone cliffs of Devonshire on the south coast of England. He anticipated the voyage home, returning to his starting place, the chalk hills of the Downs, along the English Channel south of the Thames, from which he had departed the previous March.[14]

Ultimately by mid-July Smith and his men sailed into the cold waters of the Gulf of Maine and returned to Monhegan Island, where the other three dozen men had been fishing and living since Smith's depar-

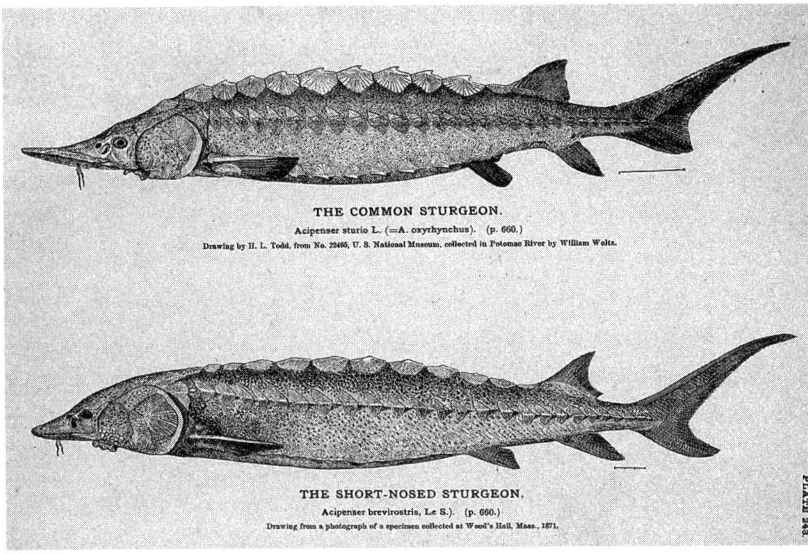

Smith and other English explorers feasted on the huge sturgeon of American coastal waters. NOAA Historic Fisheries Collection.

ture several months earlier. Smith found these men hardy and healthy, having lived off fish, "bread and vinegar," and whatever else they could contrive to eat, during his absence. They had worked "all day, laie abroade in the Iles all night, and liued on what they found, yet were not sicke." Smith and his men had similarly fared as well. Upon his return Smith found a garden of greens that he had planted upon their initial landing at Monhegan at the end April, which his companions had been using to provide themselves with "sallets," that is, salad, during the months of June and July. Smith added to the cargo of dried fish, including sixty thousand cod prepared and packed by his companions, "eleuen hundred beuer skinnes, one hundred Martins, and as many Otters" that he had acquired by trade. They made ready to go—but then well-laid plans gave way to controversy and deception.[15]

In his typically cryptic fashion, Smith records in the *Description of New England* an incident involving Captain Thomas Hunt, who was one of the adventurers on this 1614 voyage. Smith throughout his life felt himself confronted with jealous slanderers; one of the worst was Hunt. Although

Smith's narrative is very unclear, it appears that Hunt contrived to have Smith join him on a boat, perhaps a fishing shallop, after Smith's return from his explorations. Hunt "practiced to haue robbed mee of my plots [maps], and oberuations [notes], and so to leaue me alone in a desolate Ile, to the fury of famine, and all other extreamities." Where was this desolate island at which Smith was to have been marooned? He did not say, though he praised God for his deliverance: "Yet that God that always hath kept me from the worse of such practices, deliuered me from the worst of his dissimulations."[16]

Whatever happened, Smith and Hunt clearly had a falling out, as Smith determined to return to England in his bark, while Hunt (with no doubt the support of some of the gentlemen on the voyage) intended to set out south in Smith's wake to fish and trade with the natives. Smith and his men departed on July 18. The return journey east across the Atlantic featured fair winds and few storms. Whereas on the voyage out, in March, they often fought against prevailing westerlies, on the voyage in to England by the route of the Azores they had the pleasure of a following wind carrying them forward in six weeks time. Smith also truncated his voyage, determining to halt at Plymouth for a time before proceeding to London. Hence, he "arriued safe" at Plymouth "with my company the latter end of August." Not one man had been lost; rather, much had been gained.[17]

TEN

Don de Dieu

John Smith returned to England on a west wind. Having negotiated the heavy seas north of the Azores, as well as the Lizard peninsula at the southwestern extreme of England, he sailed the coast north and east along Cornwall, past Falmouth, continuing east with Devon to port; he arrived at the end of August at Plymouth Sound, where the Tamar and Plym rivers meet, mooring the bark at Plymouth Harbor east of the fort.

Plymouth was a seafaring community that had been a bastion of English defenses in the West Country. The community had several good harbors and was enclosed in a walled fort. The commander of the fort was a veteran of Elizabethan wars, for which he had been knighted. Sir Ferdinando Gorges was wealthy and ambitious; he had an adventurous mind, contemplating different schemes for achieving wealth and power, both for himself and for England. For close to ten years he had been thinking and planning about America. When in 1605 George Waymouth returned from his expedition along the Maine coast, he brought with him five Indian captives. Three of these—Skidwarres, Mannido, Sassacomoit—he presented to Gorges, with whom he was apparently friends, or at least hoped to be. Gorges entertained the three Indians, whom he regarded as savages and servants, trying to learn as much as he could from them about America and its potential for wealth. Gorges worked with Lord Chief Justice Sir John Popham to send two expeditions to the New England coast, one commanded by Martin Pring, in 1606. Although neither voyage was successful financially, Popham and Gorges and other merchants and adventurers acquired a charter from King James to settle Virginia: those from London were to establish the first colony in Southern Virginia; those in the West Country, such as

Gorges and Popham, were to establish the second colony in Northern Virginia. Inspired, Gorges and Popham then organized another, more extensive expedition in 1607, which established the short-lived colony of Sagadahoc. After the failure of the Sagadahoc colony, and the death of John Popham, Gorges scaled back his activities in pursuit of a colony in Northern Virginia. Then John Smith arrived.[1]

Whether or not Smith knew Gorges before he sailed into Plymouth Harbor, their meeting in late August or early September 1614 inaugurated a working relationship that appeared mutually advantageous. Smith later recalled that, "imparting" at Plymouth "my purposes to my honourable friend Sir *Ferdinando Gorge*" and others of the Plymouth Company, he was "assured to haue the managing [of] their authoritie in those parts, during my life, that I ingaged myselfe to vndertake it for them." Great plans were made, and dreams inspired. Gorges promised Smith that he would soon outfit a vessel for the captain to lead to America, to establish, for the first time, a successful colony in New England. Shortly thereafter, Smith sailed on to the Downs, the Thames, and London; he had concocted a plan to unite the merchants of London who had money to invest with the more modest resources of the fishers of Plymouth. He brought the bark with a modest load of fish and furs from America to the merchants who had commissioned him six months earlier. There, he met with merchants led by Michael Cooper, who offered Smith four ships to lead to America to fill their hulls with fish and furs. Smith, however, was tired of fishing trips; he wanted to begin a colony. He therefore turned down the London merchants, explaining that he "had beene verie dishonest to haue broke my promise" to Gorges. Smith's crew from the 1614 voyage joined the four ships of the London merchants, which departed in January 1615; Smith meanwhile, in December (1614), with several gentlemen supporters and £200 in funds, returned to Plymouth, expecting four ships to be outfitted ready to fulfill his plans. He unfortunately found that Gorges's promises had not reached fruition—but soon they partially did. Gorges recruited the help of a wealthy benefactor interested in America, the Anglican churchman Dr. Matthew Sutcliffe.[2]

Sutcliffe, Gorges, Smith, and his friends outfitted two ships for the expedition. Smith felt himself fortunate to be able to inaugurate his voyage from Plymouth, as "it is neere as much trouble, but much more danger, to sail from *London* to *Plimouth*, then from *Plimouth* to *New England*." One ship was two hundred tuns, the other, fifty. Smith spent the winter months of 1615 preparing for the voyage, outfitting the two ships with what he deemed essential supplies for the founding and successful operation of a fishing colony. To feed about seventy men on the two ships required "10000 weight of Bisket," "26 Tun of Beere and Sider," "2 Hogsheads of English Beefe," "2 Hogsheads of Irish Beefe," "200 Waight of Cheese," "1 Bushell of Mustard-seed," "1 Hogshead of Vinegar," "1 great Copper Kettle," "2 Small Kettles," "2 Frying-Pans," "Platters, Ladles and Cans," and "a paire of Bellowes for the Cooke." For "the 40. persons to keepe 8. fishing boats at Sea," the carpenters required "500 foot of Elme boords of an inch thicke," "2000 Nailes for the 8. Boats," another six thousand nails, "500 weight of pitch," "A barrell of Tar," "Canuas to make Boat sailes and small ropes," "12 dozen of fishing lines," "24 dozen of fishing hookes," "2000 of poore Iohn to spend," or eat, "in going," "1 Hogshead of Aquavitæ" for sailors, fishers, and adventurers alike, and rope, twine, boards, iron, wool, hatchets, and a grindstone. Whether or not Smith was able to contrive all these supplies is questionable in light of his retrospective comment in *Description of New England* that their supplies were few because of no "meanes for more," and that as captain he did not have the "authoritie, freedom, and prouision, to doe so well."[3]

The two ships set sail in March. As they made their way south from Plymouth Sound into the Atlantic waters off southern England, Smith thought of the plans he had made for a fishing colony, one that would successfully withstand the climate and other challenges of New England. Smith required sixteen men, including himself, to found this colony. These were five gentlemen, including Thomas Dermer, who commanded the smaller fifty-tun vessel; four soldiers; six men who "were to learn to be sailers"; and two boys. Their goal: "to haue staied in the Countrie, to make a more ample triall of those conclusions," that is, Smith's theories. "The maine assistance next God, I had to this small number was my acquaintance among the Saluages; especially, with Dohannida, one of their greatest Lords; who had liued long in *England*." Smith was confident that the Wawenock sachem Dohannida would embrace him as a friend and ally, which would allow Smith "quickly to haue gotte that credit with the rest of his friends and alliants, to haue had as many of them, as I desired, in any designe I intended." Smith suspected, based on his communications with the Maine Algonquians the previous summer, that the best way to befriend them was to promise them help in their wars against the "Terentynes," the Mi'kmaq to the east of the Penobscot. Smith implied that he had already met with Dohannida and his people during his 1614 voyage and that their fear of the Mi'kmaqs "did inforce them to imbrace my offer, with no small deuotion." Smith wrote, "many may thinke me more bolde then wise, in regard to their power," the Indians' "dexteritie, treacherie, and inconstancie; hauing so desperately assaulted and betraied many others." But to an old soldier such as Smith it seemed "no daunger more then ordinarie." Many people, he said slyly, knew him better than he himself. But there was a difference between those who knew him based on "the superficiall coniecture of variable relation" and what he knew of himself based on "experimentall knowledge." "Therefore, I know no reason but to beleeue my own eies before any mans imagination." At the same time, Smith respected, "with all affection, the counsell and instructions of iudiciall directions, or any other honest" advice; "so farre to obserue, as they tie mee not to the crueltie of vnknowne euents." His plans and knowledge were "the inducements that thus drew me to neglect all other imployments, and spend my time and best abilities in these aduentures."[4]

"Would God haue pleased wee had safely arriued," Smith ruefully wrote later. The small fleet quickly became separated as the larger ship, which Smith captained, soon showed itself to be hardly seaworthy. The waves and winds lashed the ship, and after a voyage of "120 leagues, shee broke all her masts; pumping each watch" of four hours "5 or 6000 strokes: onely her spret saile [spritsail] remayned to spoon before the wind till we had reaccommodated her a Iury mast, and the rest, to returne for *Plimouth*." The ship remarkably made it back to Plymouth, the jury mast "made with yards, . . . or what they can, splised or fished together." If Smith's sponsors were disillusioned, at least it did not prevent them from outfitting a replacement vessel with fourteen sailors to accompany Smith and his men. This ship, another bark, was 60 tuns; they set sail again on June 24.[5]

The Jacobean age was a time when disillusioned and unemployed sailors cast their lot with captains of heavily armed ships whose aim was gain. One such captain, known only by his surname, Fry, had acquired such a crew of ne'er-do-wells. They preyed upon the waters of the English Channel, Celtic Sea, and North Atlantic between the British Isles and the Azores. The competition with other English, French, Spanish, and Dutch pirates was heavy, and sometimes pirate battles took place to settle who would be king of the hill, or spot on the ocean as it were. There was at the same time sufficient shipping to and from Europe and the British Isles and North, Central, and South America to make piracy a lucrative profession. Fry and his men, for example, found a small bark off the coast of Devon making its way to the southwest. It flew the red cross of St. George and was lightly armed with only four cannon: doubtless a merchant vessel headed to America. Fry's bigger ship, stout and well put together, gave chase. The smaller ship was also a good sailer; it took Fry two days to finally come within range to threaten attack with a sure broadside. The smaller ship relented, and the pirates maneuvered as close as they dared in heavy seas. They demanded of the master of the English bark to tell who they were and what they had on board. We are a peaceful ship out of Plymouth on our way to New England, was the response. Fry would not have heard of New England, but he was intelligent enough to assume it was somewhere in America. He believed his suspicion that this was a merchant ship to be confirmed. He demanded to be allowed to inspect the bark for himself. Several of Smith's crewmen urged Smith to comply: "*Edmund Chambers* the Master, *Iohn Minter* [Miller] his mate, *Thomas Digby* the Pilot, and others importuned his saide Captaine to yeeld; houlding it vnpossible hee should defend himselfe." When Smith heard that his opponent was Fry the pirate, he either knew him or knew of him, and agreed to send his ship's boat to the pirate vessel to allow Fry and his companions to come aboard. But, Smith said, they must agree "not to take any thing from Captain *Smith*, that might overthrowe his voyage, nor send more Pirats into his ship then hee liked off." As the pirates boarded the bark, some professed to know and admire the captain; but Smith refused to "come out of his Caben to entertaine them." Smith, perhaps, refused to open the door to his checkered past. The pirates, however, knew him well and had "loue" for him, and would have willingly followed him or escorted him on his voyage.[6]

Half a year later, during the winter of 1615, when Smith had returned from the many adventures of the summer and autumn, he realized that what he had experienced would appear like a tall tale, so he recruited "Sir *Lewis Stukley* a worthie Knight, and Vice-admirall of Deuonshire," to hear and record the evidence of Smith's crew, so to still malicious tongues and set the record straight. Stukley (or Stucley, or Stukeley) was a favorite of King James; he would in time become the guardian of Thomas Rolfe, the son of John and Rebecca [Pocahontas] Rolfe, after her death; Stukley also gained infamy for opposing his friend Walter Raleigh, which contributed to the latter's execution. Several members of Smith's ill-fated voyage now testified before Sir Lewis; the first was "Daniel Baker, late Steward to Captaine Iohn Smith." Baker told the story of the pirate Fry and added a rather strange incident: that he had witnessed gold being passed from the pirates to the "the quarter-masters and [Master] *Chambers*." Were the pirates paying off some of Smith's crew to sabotage the voyage? Later events suggest the possibility that some nefarious plan was set in motion.[7]

Having parted amiably enough from the pirates that they were free to continue their voyage, Smith and his men sailed southwest toward the Azores; if Smith assumed that they were now free from trouble he was wrong. When they neared the island of Faial, one of the western isles of the Azores, "wee were chased by two French Pyrats, who commanded vs Amaine," that is, to yield or surrender. As before, the cowards "*Chambers, Minter, Digby* and others, importuned againe the Captaine to yeeld." They implored Smith, saying that the pirates were Turks or French who would kill them. Smith, disgusted, "vowed to fire the powder and split the ship, if they would not stand to their defence." He got his wish, as the bark ably resisted the much more powerful French pirates, especially the largest, a two-hundred-tun ship; Smith got away, "for all their [cannon and musket] shot."[8]

Meanwhile, around the same time that Smith had set sail from Plymouth on his second attempt to reach America, a well-armed French ship of 150 tuns, *Don de Dieu*, had left the port of l'Aiguillon near La Rochelle on the Bay of Biscay. Its captain, François Perret, sieur du Poiron, had

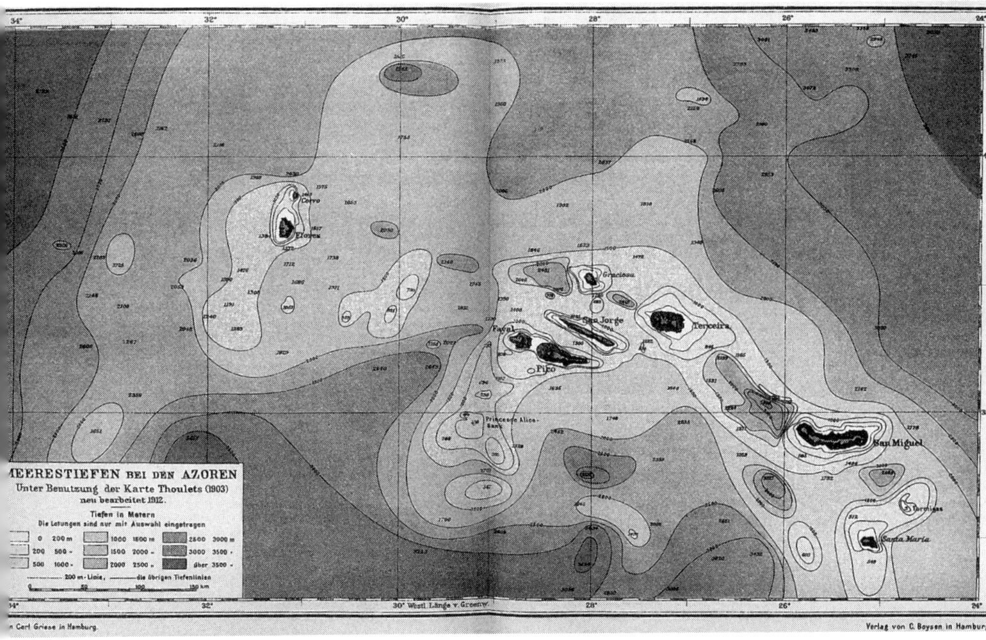

The many islands of the Azores provided the backdrop for Smith's confrontation with pirates in 1615. NOAA Central Library Historical Collection, map 00064.

a commission to trade and a penchant for piracy. He, his lieutenant, André Prevost, sieur du Pons, and about seventy-five crew members headed west for the Azores, which was a locus of piratical activities in the sixteenth and seventeenth centuries. Perret and his men arrived at the islands and continued on to the westernmost, Flores, at the same time that Smith had escaped French pirates at Faial and was making his way toward the same place. At Flores, Perret rendezvoused with other French captains and formed an agreement to stay together for the next half year to see what prizes they could capture. "At *Flowers*," testified Daniel Baker, "wee were chased by foure French men of warre; all with their close fights afore and after," that is, men in close quarters ready to fight. Outnumbered and outgunned, nevertheless Smith prepared to fight. He estimated that the lead French ship was 140 tuns, armed with thirty-six varied cannon and ninety men armed with pistols, muskets, and swords. The other three ships were of 100, 80, and 60 tuns. "Againe," the same cowards, Chambers, Minter, and Digby, "importuned him to yeeld to the fauour of those, against whom there was nothing but ruine by fighting." They requested that Smith go aboard the French vessel and parley, since Smith knew French. When Smith learned that the French "offered him such faire quarter, and vowed they were Protestants and all of" the Protestant city of "*Rochell[e],* and had the Kings commission onely to take *Spaniards, Portugales,* and Pyrats," he relented to go. The ship's boat of the admiral (the lead ship) came and ferried Smith and a few men to the *Don de Dieu*. Smith then discovered that behind Captain Perret's polite words was the duplicity of a pirate. Smith was aboard a French corsair, and there he would stay.[9]

While Smith was made, unofficially at first, a prisoner, the French boarded his bark, "tooke what they listed, and diuided the company into their seuerall ships." Perret manned Smith's bark with French sailors, who "chased with her all the shippes they saw." After "about fiue or sixe dayes" of this, however, "vpon better consideration," the French returned "the ship and victualls" back to the English, "with the most part of our prouision, but not our weapons." But although Smith's men were back on the English bark, Smith was not. Nor, he realized, was Captain Perret going to allow his freedom. Smith sent for all his personal "commodities, as powder, match, hookes, instruments, his sword and dagger, bedding, aqua vitæ, his commission, apparell, and many other things." But his belongings never arrived; Master Chambers and his "associats diuided it amongst themselves," leaving Smith with only his "wastecoast and breeches." Even so, Smith ordered his men to proceed without him on their voyage to the "*New found Land* to returne fraughted with fish, where hee would finde meanes to proceed in his plantation." Although Master Chambers and his colleagues in crime wished to make a hasty return voyage to England, the rest of the men stood with their captain and resolved either to fight (should their weapons be returned to them) or to continue their original journey per Smith's request. The smaller English boat captained by Thomas Dermer would have arrived in New England, and they could rendezvous with him and still make the expedition successful.[10]

It appears from Daniel Baker's testimony, however, that Chambers, Minter, and Digby were in command. They secretly told Perret that Smith would avenge himself on the French if they released him; he would attack French shipping at the Grand Banks or attack French settlements in America. Likewise, if he was freed Smith was liable to fire his ship to keep it out of French hands. Meanwhile they contentedly joined the French pirates in the pursuit of a prize ship until darkness overcame the chase. The next morning was stormy and the seas were high; Smith's bark briefly collided with the "French men of warre, that they split the maine sayle on the others spret sayle yard." Frightened, Chambers called to Smith to come aboard "or he would leaue him: whereupon the Captaine commanded *Chambers* to send his boate for him. *Chambers*," however, refused to send the bark's boat, and "replyed she was split (which was false), telling him hee might come if he would in the Admiralls," that is, the French, "boat. The Captaines answer was, he could not command her, nor come when hee would," continuing to be held as a prisoner. When night fell, Smith's bark drifted apart and then sailed away, leaving Smith alone, in the power of the French.[11]

Smith now found himself amid "a Fleet of eight or nine sayle" watching "for the [Spanish] *West Indies* fleet"; soon, however, *Don de Dieu* separated from the others. The French corsair hung around Faial, waiting for prey to appear. Like a rapacious hawk held at bay, Smith felt caged, silenced. He was helpless to act. At one point an English pirate named Barra, whom Smith might have known upon a time, chased them; the English pirates had "a small ship with some twelue peeces of ordinance, about thirty men, and neer all starued." Desperation drove them to challenge the much bigger French ship. Captain Perret gave them "faire promises" of relief, got the second in command Wolliston and "foure of fiue of their men aboard vs," with the intent to take the rest. Meanwhile Smith in the "gun roum" was not allowed "to speake to any of them vpon my life. Yet had *Barra* knowledge what I was," meaning that Barra smelled a trap. Perceiving French duplicity, Barra resolved to fight, for which the French had no stomach; they decided to relent and to release the men, give them some food, "vpon a small composition," or agreement of terms.[12]

Smith watched the capture of the next prize from the "great caben" of the French corsair. Peering through the ship's window he could make out in the hazy air the flag of St. George flying on the topmast of a small bark. This English merchant vessel, from Poole on the southern coast of England, was lightly armed and could not compete with the French ship. Smith watched in anger as the *Don de Dieu* threatened violence and then as its crew boarded the English bark; French sailors rifled the stores of salted fish in barrels, caught and packed in Newfoundland, and whatever personal items the English possessed. Smith could hear the shouts of men and rumbles of rolling barrels, and could see the English sailors standing by helplessly. Meanwhile Smith paced about in the cabin, lamenting his situation and God's perplexing will.[13]

The French impressed Smith not by their daring but their timidity. When they came upon a small Scottish merchant ship and began to rifle its stores of goods, Captain Perret spied in the distance the sails of four ships; the French broke away from their prize to investigate, and were content to quickly make their escape when they spied the "*English* red crosses." Next, they came upon four Spanish ships that appeared to be easy prey. They "fought with them foure or fiue houres, tore their sayles and sides"—but the French were unwilling to fight at close quarters, so sailed off. Next they found a small Brazilian caravel, lightly armed. After a fight, in which over half of the caravel's crew were wounded, the French took the prize of "370 chests of sugar." Soon after they caught up to a lumbering "*West Indies* man" loaded with Spanish treasure, "besides the pillage and rich coffers of many rich passengers." Sometimes Captain Perret required Smith on deck to manage conflicts against Spanish ships; when the St. George's cross of England was spied waving from a ship's mast, Smith was again escorted to the cabin.[14]

Smith despaired of ever returning to England. Captain Perret promised time and again to release Smith, to allow him to board one of the prizes sent to France, or at least to disembark on one of the isles of the Azores, in and about which the French corsair continued to prowl. Instead, Smith was kept aboard the *Don de Dieu* for weeks on end, waiting and watching. In his anxious boredom, Smith returned again and again to gaze upon the sea, the conduit of his dreams, the pathway of his restless search for personal justification before humans and God. The calm waters of summer days belied the desperate anger and volatile impatience that surged within him. "To keepe my perplexed thoughts from too much meditation

The Brazilian caravel loaded with sugar captured by *Don de Dieu* would have resembled this Spanish caravel. Library of Congress.

of my miserable estate," he wrote in *Description of New England*, "I writ this discourse; thinking to haue sent it you of his Maiesties Councell, by some ship or other: for I saw their purpose was to take all they could."[15]

Quill, ink, and paper provided by the often gracious French, Smith wrote: "A Description of New-England, by Captaine Iohn Smith." *New England*. Such he had decided to call that place of wild potential and mystery. *New England* was not terribly original, as Smith implied, writing that "*New England* is that part of *America* in the Ocean Sea opposite to Noua Albyon [New Albion] in the South Sea [Pacific], discouered by the most memorable Sir *Francis Drake* in his voyage about the worlde. In regarde whereto this is stiled *New England*, beeing in the same latitude. New France, off it, is Northward: Southwardes is *Virginia*, and all the adioyning Continent, with *New Granado*, *New Spain*, *New Andolosia*, and the *West Indies*." In Smith's mind this land, similar in climate to England, providing the timber, furs, fish, and minerals that England lacked, with few populous habitations waiting for the conqueror and colonist, was nothing if not a *New* England. "In the moneth of Aprill, 1614, with two Ships from *London*, of a few Marchants, I chanced to arriue in *New-England*, a parte of Ameryca."[16]

So began the discourse. Smith was, as in all things, self-taught; his writing was "plaine, or tedious in relating my knowledge for plaine mens satisfaction." Smith was to the point, often profound in his common sense, frequently humorous in his cynicism and wit. The *Description of New England* was at the same time journal, human history, natural history, promotional tract for self and England, geographical essay, and apology for colonization. Smith sometimes exaggerated without distorting the truth; he was always frank, and honest with himself. Smith was a man who had experienced every kind of fear and entertained death so often that little frightened him, hence his penchant to state what he considered to be the facts without varnish. He was equally unafraid to cast blame and risk offending those who were less forthright than himself.[17]

There was among the English still such a mistaken impression of the New World that Smith took time to describe this land between "the degrees of 30. to 45.," denoted by the English, *Virginia*, which "is no Ile (as many doe imagine) but part of the Continent adioyning to *Florida*; whose bounds may be stretched to the magnitude thereof without offence to any Christian inhabitant."[18] The land was, in short, uninhabited for all practical Christian purposes; the people were simple forest dwellers who lived in pastoral simplicity. Smith believed that God's plan, the Great Commission, aimed to bring "salvages" from their ignorant state into a civilized world, the world, that is, of the English and other Christians. God, Smith thought, first brought knowledge of His Son to the civilized Roman Empire, to the sophisticated Jews. From here, over the centuries, Christianity spread outward to less civilized peoples in northern and eastern Europe, Africa, and Asia; now, in the early seventeenth century, Christianity was spreading to the uncivilized *salvages* of America.

Yet the challenge for the English so engaged was to first discover a land that "is yet unknowne to any purpose: no, not so much as the borders of the Sea are yet certainly discouered." Still, "wee are for most part yet altogether ignorant" of "the goodness and true substances of the Land." Smith speculated that the dominions of America "doe stretch themselues into the Maine, God doth know how many thousand miles; whereof we can yet no more iudge, then a stranger that saileth betwixt *England* and *France* can describe the Harbors and dangers, by landing here or there in some Riuer or Bay, tell thereby the goodnesse and substances of *Spaine, Italy, Germany, Bohemia, Hungaria* and the rest." If any, therefore, pretend to know what America is, they are mistaken, for America could be as large as "*Terra Incognita*," for all people know. To make the unknown known requires people of the ilk of "Columbus, Cortez, Pitzara [Pizarro], [de] Soto, Magellanes," people of "incomparable merits" who "aduanced themselues from poore Souldiers to great Captaines, their posterity to great Lords, their King to be one of the greatest Potentates on earth." So, like Spain, could England be.[19]

After Smith's fitting introduction to the account of his discoveries, he describes New England: its scope, habitations, peoples, harbors, landmarks, and natural productions. Of the latter, the most significant is fish, which though not the stuff of dreams, not the aim of avarice, not worthy of pirating and conquest, is still the basis of wealth for England in America. Fish, moreover, is the means by which to alleviate the social problems of England. "So freely hath God and his Maiesty bestowed those blessings on them that will attempt to obtaine them, as here euery man may be master and owner of his owne labour and land; or the greatest part in a small time. If hee haue nothing but his hands, he may set vp this trade; and by industrie quickly grow rich; spending but halfe that time wel, which in *England* we abuse in idlenes, worse or as ill." The native inhabitants are so few and dispersed, and have such modest needs, that flora and fauna, "and diuerse other good things do heere, for want of vse, still increase, and decrease with little diminution." New England is a seafood lover's paradise: "you shall scarce finde any Baye, shallow shore, or Coue of sand, where you may not take many Clampes [clams], or Lobsters, or both at your pleasure; and in many places lode your boat if you please." Smith saw a ship's boy pass a few hours taking "cunners . . . and such delicate fish, at the ships sterne, more then sixe or tenne can eate in a daie."[20]

But Smith worried that fear, jealousy, and covetousness would overwhelm his countrymen, and allow a chance for growth and redemption to pass them by as they focused on present pleasure and temporary gain. The people of England too often, Smith felt, looked upon a future of English wealth and expansion with disdain if it did not involve the individual's

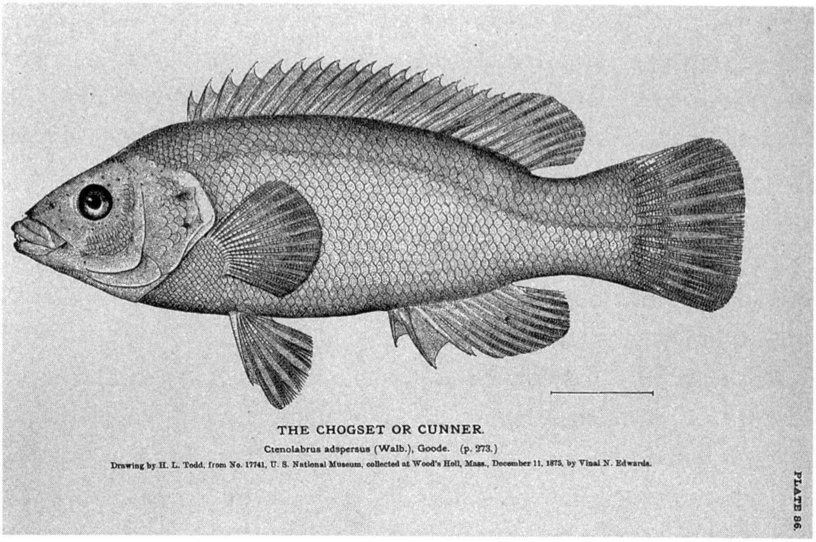

Smith and his men caught cunners along the New England coast.
NOAA Historic Fisheries Collection.

own wealth and greatness: "is our sensualities and vntowardnesse such," he asked, "and so great, that wee either ignorantly beleeue nothing, or so curiously contest to preuent wee knowe not what future euents; that wee either so neglect, or oppresse and discourage the present, as wee spoile all in the making, crop all in the blooming; and building vpon faire sand, rather then rough rockes, iudge that wee knowe not, gouerne that wee haue not, feare that which is not; and for feare some should doe too well, force such against their willes to be idle or as ill." Smith professed to have the interests of others, of the English people themselves, and not just his own, at heart. This was what drove him forward, compelled him to journey to America, to risk his life and comfort, and, now, a captive in a French corsair, to pen the truth as he saw it. The truth, based on what he had experienced in his thirty-five years, was that a love of freedom, rather than tyranny, of independence rather than slavery, of honest gain rather than illicit profit, is what drives most people, including himself. His was a political philosophy of individual merit, hard work, courage in the face of great odds: such personal characteristics, rather than inherited wealth and privilege, build the successful commonwealth. Ironically, however,

Smith lived in a land and at a time when inherited wealth and privilege were the bases of advantage and opportunity. Yet he refused to give in to that fate, that he was destined to be an obscure middleman, and so he dreamed, strove, worked, suffered, considered the past, and looked to the future. To Smith, the true calling of the Englishman was to "abound in honor, by heroycall deeds of action, iudgement, pietie, and vertue." The latter two qualities, piety and virtue, derive from "religion," which "aboue all things, should moue vs . . . if wee were religious, to shewe our faith by our workes; in conuerting those poore saluages, to the knowledge of God, seeing what paines the Spanyards take to bring them to their adulterated faith." The Spanish success in converting the Indians to Catholicism was an embarrassment to the English Anglican.[21]

"But, all men are not such as they should bee." Many profess to accomplish great deeds who have never practiced them; many profess knowledge that they have never earned by experience. "All the Romanes were not Scipioes," the conqueror of Hannibal, "nor all the Geneweses, Columbuses." History taught Smith that life was about fighting for the good, struggling against enemies to benefit one's friends and posterity. The Greeks, Goths, Romans, Spartans, and Hebrews were "industrious iron-steeled *Publicans*: They regarded more prouisions, and necessaries for their people, than iewels, riches, ease, or delight for themselues. Riches were their seruants, not their Maisters. They ruled (as Fathers, not as Tyrantes) their people as children, not as slaues; there was no disaster could discourage them." This was Smith's ideal, a free people working for the good commonwealth led by the enlightened prince. Indeed, "what haue euer beene the workes of the greatest Princes of the earth, but planting of countries, and ciuilizing barbarous and inhumane Nations to ciuilitie and humanitie?"—that is, to Christianity. The English have been shamed by the Portuguese and Spanish, whose "everliuing actions" reveal "our idlenesse, and ingratitude to all posterities, and neglect of our duties in our pietie and religion we owe our God, our King, and Countrie; and want of charity to these poore saluages, whose Countrie we challenge, vse and possesse." In return for taking and using their land, the English owe the sylvan people of America the chance to know Christ and civilization.[22]

Smith lived according to a broad perspective of time, of the continuum of past, present, and future, and he felt as obligated to his forebears as to his posterity. What is life, he thought, but action for the promotion of God and His works? "Then seeing wee are not borne for our selues, but each to helpe [the] other; and our abilities," as equal humans, "are much alike at the houre of our birth, and the minute of our death: seeing our good deedes, or our badde, by faith in Christs merits, is all wee haue to carrie our soules to heauen, or hell: Seeing honour is our liues ambition; and our ambition after death, to haue an honourable memory of our life: and seeing by noe meanes wee would bee abated of the dignities and glories of our Predecessors; let vs imitate their vertues to bee worthily their successors."[23]

ELEVEN

"Thou Art Brasse Without, but Golde Within"

The ancient city of La Rochelle on the Atlantic coast of southwest France, looking out upon the Bay of Biscay, was a seafarer's city. When Smith first saw La Rochelle as a young mercenary seeking his fortune in European wars, in 1600, he was a landsman intrigued by the sea. Smith briefly mentioned his visit to La Rochelle in his autobiography, *The True Travels*, but he did not comment on the battlements, the towers hosting artillery, the war, merchant, and fishing ships in the harbor, the city built on the sea. The Rochelais were Smith's kind of people: ambitious, independent, protective of their freedoms, aggressive, and Protestant. During the previous (sixteenth) century, Rochelais fishers had crossed the Atlantic to fish the waters off the coast of Maine and Newfoundland. They were excellent mariners, and crafty when dealing with others at sea. Smith had experienced this the summer and fall of 1615 when Captain Perret, sieur du Poiron, had detained him on the ship *Don de Dieu* for months, keeping Smith in the dark about his purposes, promising to release him then inviting him to stay.[1]

Ultimately Captain Perret relented and allowed Smith to join ship on a prize, a Brazilian caravel, that his second in command, André Prevost, sieur du Pons, was to take back to La Rochelle. As they sailed east toward the Bay of Biscay, they had a run-in with two Spanish ships but escaped with little damage, and made it to l'Aiguillon, "not far from *Rochel*," the port from which the *Don de Dieu* had departed the previous summer. Captain Prevost now revealed himself to be as duplicitous as Captain Perret. While the sailors unloaded the ship, Smith continued to be a prisoner on board the captured caravel, for "fiue or sixe daies." Although Captain Prevost had hitherto promised Smith a fantastic reward for all his troubles, he now accused Smith "to bee him that burnt their Colony in *New France*." This was not Smith, rather Samuel Argall, who in 1613 raided the French colony of Acadia, destroying a Jesuit mission at Mount Desert Island. Prevost would not listen to Smith, rather intended, Smith wrote, "to force mee giue them a discharge before the Iudge of the Admiralty, and so stand to their curtesie for satisfaction, or lie in prison, or a worse mischiefe." In short, Prevost demanded that Smith agree to set the story straight before an Admiralty judge and exonerate Perret and Prevost, which if he did satisfactorily, would win his freedom. Captain Prevost did not realize the type of man with whom he was dealing. Smith refused to be intimidated by anyone: Turk, pirate, Indian warrior, French mariner.[2]

The late autumn weather of the Bay of Biscay, the winds, high surfs, and storms, came to Smith's assistance in his endeavor to escape. Watching and waiting, he knew that if he had the chance, he could try to make it to the Isle de Ré, Rat Isle, which lay off the coast just west of La Rochelle. What Smith intended to do if he reached Isle de Ré is not clear, but that was his plan, unless fate, chance, or the will of God intervened. As the caravel lay at anchor, a fierce storm descended upon the coast, driving all the French sailors "vnder Hatches." Under cover of darkness, Smith snuck out of his quarters (perhaps the hold of the ship, perhaps the captain's cabin), quietly hurried to where the ship's boat was lashed to the side, and lowered it to the water. "I watched my opportunity to get a-shore in their boat; where-into, in the darke night, I secretly got: and with a halfe pike that lay by me, put a drift for Rat Ile." Smith had with him his only possession, sealed tightly within his doublet: the manuscript *Description of New England*. The boat was ill-equipped for escape, as it did not have oars, which would have allowed some mobility; a half pike was a weapon useful for a fight but not for navigation. Smith's hope that the boat would drift toward Rat Isle was not realized: "the Current was so strong, and the Sea so great, I went a drift to Sea." The wind and tide cradled, as it were, the helpless man and boat west beyond the strait (Perthuis Breton), which separated the Isle de Ré and l'Aiguillon, into the open sea. As the night progressed the wind changed toward the south, bringing the boat around Rat Isle "till it pleased God the winde so turned with the tide." The westerly breeze and incoming tide brought the boat east between Isle de Ré and Isle d'Oléron through the strait separating those two isles, the Perthuis d'Antioche, toward the mouth of the Charente River, south of La Rochelle.[3]

The Charente is a modest river that winds south and west over two hundred miles from inland France through Cognac and Rochefort to the sea. At its mouth the winds and currents of the Bay of Biscay create changing, oozy islands and sand banks. Shipwrecks were frequent in Smith's day all along this coast from l'Aiguillon to Charente. Such is what happened to the Brazilian caravel commanded by André Prevost. The sleepy men Smith left behind awakened to a thunderous storm that beat down upon them. There was no way for them to run before the wind except to their deaths. Smith heard later that during this night "many ships were driuen a shore, and diuerse split." Many years later, in *The True Travels*, he wrote that thirteen ships were lost in the storm, and not only the caravel commanded by Prevost, but also the *Notre Dame de Rosario*, a large Spanish ship filled with wealth that Captain Perret had captured and decided to bring back to l'Aiguillon accompanying the *Don de Dieu*; both vessels were wrecked and Captain Perret died, as did "most of his men." What of Smith? Through his resourcefulness he had escaped his death along a hazardous coast and was adrift on the ocean in the darkness of night, in "fearefull . . . gusts and raine" for "the space of 12 houres." Long ago he had learned to give himself "to the mercy of the Sea, which is said to be mercilesse, or rather to the mercy of Almighty God, whose mercy farre exceeds all his workes." Smith did his best to scull with the half pike and spent the night "bayling the water" in the boat, no doubt with his hands. He was exhausted, wet, cold, and "expected each minute" that the winds and waves "would sinke mee." Smith must have said over and over in his mind that psalm (107) he had so often heard:

> They that go down to the sea in ships, that do business in great waters;
> These see the works of the Lord, and his wonders in the deep.
> For he commandeth, and raiseth the stormy wind, which lifteth up the waves thereof.

> They mount up to the heaven, they go down again to the depths: their soul is melted because of trouble.
> They reel to and fro, and stagger like a drunken man, and are at their wits' end.
> Then they cry unto the Lord in their trouble, and he bringeth them out of their distresses.
> He maketh the storm a calm, so that the waves thereof are still.
> Then are they glad because they be quiet; so he bringeth them unto their desired haven.

The wind and waves took him nearly seven leagues away from the wrecked caravel. Such moments test faith in self, in life, in God, when human vulnerability to time and nature is more apparent than ever, when weakness, giving in and accepting, becomes a source of strength. Smith emerged from this experience with more faith, less fear, and more strength.[4]

Perhaps not at first. In the wake of the storm, guided by the faint rays of dawn, "fowlers" hunting ducks and geese in the estuarial environment at the mouth of the Charente came upon a man curled up in exhaustion, "neere drowned, and halfe dead, with water, colde, and hunger." Perhaps they had a crust of bread and a cloak to wrap around him; aroused and regaining strength and warmth, Smith asked them in French how to reach La Rochelle. They helped him pawn the ship's boat to raise funds for travel. They pointed him in the right direction, north, and Smith walked there, or hired a horse, or engaged a carriage.[5]

When he arrived, the town was buzzing with the news of the shipwrecks. Smith was not shy about his experiences, and the injustice done to him. He told whoever would listen that he had escaped his captors in a "little boate, by the mercy of God; far beyond all mens reason, or my expectation." As he put it in *The True Travels*, "God to whom all honour and praise, brought [Smith] safe on shore to all their admirations that escaped." Smith made his way to the local Admiralty Court, which had jurisdiction over the activities of privateers. He complained of the injustice done to him by the pirates Perret and Prevost, now deceased. The "Iudge of the Admiraltie" responded with "many good words and faire promises." Smith, apparently, needed to provide evidence, which he did "ere long," as he discovered those from the *Don de Dieu* and caravel who had "escaped drowning." These men marveled that Smith was still alive, when they had heard "the newes . . . of my owne death." Smith was not content to chat, but summoning the magistrate, had them arrested; "their seuerall examinations did so confirme my complaint, it was held proofe sufficient." Proof does not mean redress. The sugar, worth "36000. crowns," had been unloaded at l'Aiguillon before the storm and the caravel's breakup. Smith felt that the sugar would provide just recompense, "which I did my best to arrest." Moreover, some of the goods from the *Don de Dieu*, and perhaps even the *Notre Dame de Rosario*, were salvaged, a claim for which could have formed part of Smith's design.[6]

The shadowy "Madam Chanoyes," a wealthy Frenchwoman who is otherwise unidentified, assisted Smith in La Rochelle, perhaps with retaining lawyers or with letters of introduction. Had Smith met her in 1600 on his first visit to La Rochelle? Perhaps she wanted to see the promise of the Admiralty judge fulfilled: that Smith would see justice. Or perhaps she provided funds to help Smith on his journey in November south from La Rochelle across the Charente and Garonne rivers to Bordeaux, where he hoped to find the English ambassador to France, Sir Thomas Edmundes. This was Smith's second journey to Bordeaux; he first saw the city in 1600 on his travels through France. Smith argued that the sieur du Poiron had been granted a lawful commission to trade and, if he came upon Spanish ships, to take them as prizes, but he did not have the right to stop an English ship and detain an English captain. Smith wished to discuss the possibility of gaining recompense from the estate of the deceased privateer. The ambassador was in Bordeaux accompanying the king of France, Louis XIII, who was preparing to marry Infanta Ana de Austria, daughter of Philip III, king of Spain, in an attempt to solidify through dynastic marriage the relationship of the two countries. Smith no doubt was sufficiently resourceful and persevering to see the ambassador. He saw an old shipmate, Thomas Cramton, with whom he had voyaged to New England in 1614. Cramton helped Smith in some way or another, perhaps with funds, perhaps with lawyers; Smith indicated in his *General History* that he saw, and received assistance from, lawyers in Bordeaux. If Ambassador Edmundes also promised help, it appears to have been in vain. Smith never received anything from the French wrecks.[7]

In December, Smith traveled from France across the channel to England. In London, he reunited with friends, who encouraged him to go to Plymouth to seek redress against the mutineers on his failed 1615 voyage, and to reconnect with Ferdinando Gorges for, perhaps, another attempt at colonizing New England. Smith therefore went to Plymouth in December "to find them that had thus buried me amongst the *French*." Smith accused them (Edmund Chambers, John Minter, and Thomas Digby) of being "treacherous cowards," who covered their fears and crimes with bravado; liars, trying to destroy his reputation; deceivers, acting as though they had escaped dangerous French pirates who had stolen all of Smith's goods; and thieves, having stolen and parceled out among themselves Smith's "clothes, bookes, instruments, Armes, and what I had." Smith "laied [them] by the heales," brought them to justice (perhaps), and compelled members of the unfortunate crew to appear before Sir Lewis Stukley to confess "the truth." He was not so fortunate in convincing Gorges and other Plymouth merchants to fulfill their hitherto enthusiastic claims for colonization. Smith discovered that "all their great promises" were "nothing but air." He returned to London.[8]

Miraculously, Smith's manuscript, *Description of New England*, survived his escape from the French, night of terror in the open boat, and eventual landfall and rescue. Such fantastic events and ultimate survival might convince even the most skeptical of people that there must be a reason and purpose behind these occurrences. Smith knew that God had preserved him for one pursuit, one activity: to establish a working colony in New England. *New England* became his passion, his raison d'être. Smith began visiting and conversing with friends about publishing his work. He joined with Humphrey Lownes, a printer who had produced other noteworthy works, such as Edmund Spencer's *Fairie Queen*, and publisher Robert Clerke. Lownes and Clerke were members of London's powerful Stationers' Company; Clerke, from whose residence the book was sold, lived on Chancery Street near Lincoln's Inn in west London. Smith was also able to hire Simon van de Passe, a well-known engraver in Jacobean England, to engrave Smith's *Map of New England* from his sketches and notes.[9]

As was the custom of the time, Smith dedicated his book to the wealthy and powerful, and recruited supporters to write dedicatory verses on his behalf. Of the former, the most significant was the Prince of Wales, Charles, then fifteen years old. Charles's older brother, Henry, who had been a supporter of the Jamestown colony, had died a few years before. Smith in his dedication to Prince Charles noted that he had named two capes in Virginia for the two princes. He asked the prince to examine his *Map of New England* and change the "Barbarous names" to "English." Smith hinted broadly that he hoped the prince would support Smith's endeavors in other ways as well. He prayed "God to blesse me but from such accidents as are beyond my power and reason to preuent." Next, Smith dedicated his book "to the Right Honourable and worthy Lords, Knights, and Gentlemen, of his Maiesties Councell, for all Plantations and discoueries." Smith tried to balance the right amount of pride and humility toward these men whom circumstance and birth had made superior to him. "Reposing my selfe on your fauours," he wrote, "I present this rude discourse to the worldes construction." He provided a brief introduction of his experiences, concluding that "if I bee not able to iudge of what I haue seene, contriued, and done; it is not the fault either of my eyes, or" experiences in the "foure quarters" of the world. He relied on God's will, and the will of the council, to determine what the future held for him: "Not doubting that your goodnesse will pardon my rudenesse, and pondour errours in the balance of good will."[10]

Finally, Smith dedicated the book "to the Right Worshipfull Adventurers for the Countrey of New England in the Cities of London, Bristow, Exceter, Plimouth, Dartmouth, Bastable, Totneys, etc and in all other Cities and Ports, in the Kingdome of England." Smith felt himself more equal to these dedicatees; hence his comments were less obsequious, more frank. Smith compared human endeavors to the work of ants and bees, which are diligent and strive for the "Commonwealth"—and so should man. "Little hon[e]y has that hive, where there are more Drones then Bees: and miserable is that Land, where more are idle then well imployed." If Smith were in the place of these adventurers, he would wonder why a captain would write about what he wished to do rather than show by his deeds what he had indeed done: "I confesse it were more proper for mee, To be doing what I say, then writing what I knowe." If Smith had their support, "then would I not doubt (did God please I might safely arriue in *New England*, and safely returne) but to performe somewhat more then I haue promised, and approue my words by deeds, according to proportion." But he had faced odds far beyond his control to match. The "four [French] men of warre" that had halted Smith, and kidnapped him, would have done the same to "*Sampson*, *Hercules*, and *Alexander* the great." Smith had hoped not to make this description public, rather to have "made my returnes speake as much, as my pen now doth." He might be criticized for his emphasis on the importance of fishing, but knows the key to a successful colony: "nothing is there to bee had which fishing doth hinder, but furder vs to obtaine." West Country and London adventurers had given Smith "meanes, power, and authority . . . to plant there a Colony, and make further search, and discouery in those parts there yet vnknowne." But happenstance and God's will had brought about failure, and Smith's reputation had been abused: "I am inforced for all these respects, rather to expose my imbecillitie to contempt, by the testimonie of these rude lines, then all should condemne me for so bad a Factor, as could neither give reason nor account of my actions and designes."[11]

Eleven people wrote commendatory verses in support of John Smith and his work that, notwithstanding the point of such rhymes, which was to praise rather than criticize, still provide a glimmer of light into the shadows of the past to reveal Smith's character. Typical of the theme of these verses is the first by John Davies, a well-known Jacobean poet, who saw envy, which seeks to sap the strength of worth and wit, at work against John Smith. But the vice of others improves Smith's virtue, their hate "procure thee Loue." Davies also penned the verse that accompanied the portrait of Smith on the *Map of New England*. In it, he wrote of Smith's "Grace and Glory," and "Of Salvages, much Civilliz'd by thee." John Codrington, of the Middle Temple, Smith's "sometime souldier," recognized the truth in Smith's "Storie," which scorns "the spight Of Enuie." Envy, so much the theme of Smith's writings, was echoed in the verse by Nicholas Smith, who called himself a "Worthy friend and Cosen [cousin]": "Enuie, it selfe, will not the Truth gainesay." That envy would not invalidate the truth was echoed by Robert Gunnell, a Cambridge scholar involved with the London theater and Smith's "verie good friend," as was George Wither, an Oxford poet at Lincoln's Inn and Puritan reformer, who saw only good coming out of Smith's promotion of New

England. The verse penned by Rawly Croshaw (Raleigh Crashaw), of the Virginia Company, purported to find in Smith's *Description of New England* a pathway into "thy heart," in which Croshaw found a person not out for personal gain and fame, rather the good of England. Likewise, the verse penned by "Michael Phettiplace, William Phettiplace, and Richard Wiffing [Wiffin], Gentlemen, and Souldiers under Captain Smiths Command," commended Smith for his fearsome aspect among the salvages: "And yet a heart more milde is seldome seene." These poets, good friends to Smith, knew something about him that Smith revealed to few people. "Who saith of thee, this sauors of vaine-glorie, Mistakes both thee and us, and this true storie." These men, who had served under Smith at Jamestown, believed that Smith's aims were not for himself: "And for this paines of thine wee praise thee rather, That future Times may know who was the father Of this rare Worke (*New England*) which may bring Praise of thy God, and profit to thy King." Sergeant Edward Robinson, who had served under Smith in Transylvania, wrote of Smith's boundless energy and modesty: "And all thou yet hast done, thou dost esteeme As nothing." He believed that Smith had more to do: Smith is "yet preserued, to conuert those strangers: By God thy God; I trust it is decreed." Thomas Carlton, who also served under Smith in Europe, wrote revealingly of Smith's personal habits: "I neuer knew a Warryer yet, but thee, From wine, Tobacco, debts, dice, oaths, so free." Many captains have not done what Smith has done. The poet will continue to laud Smith, hoping "Worthies yet to come" will "liue like thine (admir'd) till day of Doome."[12]

Smith's day of doom was still fifteen years in the future. Until then, though he wrote, argued, declaimed, and pleaded; spent hours and hours at the writing desk penning works on his travels and adventures, particularly in America, and plans for colonization; and traveled about England distributing copies of his works and maps, he never returned to America. These were frustrating years, to be sure, when Smith had to sublimate his enterprising genius and assume a passive role, watching others sail down the Thames to the Downs and across the Atlantic; hear others talk of adventurers and battles in America; and converse with colonists on their way to New England, to Plymouth and Massachusetts Bay. He knew he was the right person to establish a colony. He had it all worked out, and wrote convincingly his guidelines for success. With three hundred men he could establish this colony, relying upon the Indians to feed them. He had done this before, in Virginia. "For a few trifles," the Algonquians would acquiesce, and provide sufficient corn to live on. "And if they should bee vntoward (as it is most certaine they are) thirty or forty good men will be sufficient to bring them all in subiection." Smith was realistic. The Indians had been mistreated and abused; they resented it, and sought revenge. No matter what he felt toward the Indians, Smith was a conqueror and colonist before he was a commissioner. England was fated to take this land, and Smith wanted to lead in the acquisition. He knew how to defend it, how to feed it, how to make it profitable, how to ensure its continued existence: "Prouided I haue men of ability to teach them their functions: and a company fit for Souldiers to be ready vpon an occasion, because of the abuses which haue beene offered the poore Saluages." It takes many years to grow a colony, "and who euer shall trie in these remote places the erecting of a Colony, shall finde at the ende of seauen yeares occasion enough to vse all his discretion," wisdom, and decision-making ability. Meanwhile much has to be done to help the colony "bee able to creepe, to stand, and goe, yet time enough to keepe it from running: for there is no fear it wil grow too fast, or euer to any thing; excepte libertie, profit, honor, and prosperitie there found, more binde the planters of those affaires, in deuotion to effect it; then bondage, violence, tyranny, ingratitude and such double dealing, as bindes freemen to become slaues, and honest men turne knaues: which hath euer bin the ruine of the most popular common-weales; and is verie vnlikelie euer well to begin in a new." Humans will thrive in an environment of freedom and the chance to prosper. Ultimately, colonies will reproduce in the wake of initial success. Every town founded will have to follow a prescribed order, though each will be free to produce what is needed for subsistence and trade. This will be the beginning of "new Townes in New England in memory of their olde; which freedome being confined but to the necessity of the generall good, the euent (with Gods help) might produce an honest, a noble, and profitable emulation."[13]

Smith made it sound so easy. A few opportunities presented themselves, but they never came to fruition. Smith had an on-again, off-again relationship with the merchants and adventurers of Plymouth that at least provided him with periodic hope, which he rarely found among Londoners. Merchants from both cities sent ships to America to fish and trade for furs; Smith waited for the opportunity to establish a colony. He realized that only the prospect of "gaine," rather than "Religion, Charity, and the Common good" would inspire people to invest their money or hazard their lives. Smith, unlike many promoters, not only tried to "perswade them to goe . . . but goe with them: Not leave them there; but live with them there." "I feare not want of companie sufficient," he wrote in *Description of New England*, "were it but knowne what I know of those Countries; and by the proofe of that wealth I hope yearely to returne, if God please to blesse me from such accidents, as are beyond my power in reason to preuent: For, I am not so simple to thinke, that euer any other motiue then wealth, will euer erect there a Commonweale." So he did what he could to promote the venture for fish and furs. Finally, he convinced some men of Plymouth to sponsor a voyage, part of which was to establish a colony. Smith was to lead fifteen men in this endeavor, in 1617. God decreed otherwise. The ships and men were "Windbound three moneths, as was many a hundred saile more, so that the season being past, the ships went for *Newfound land*, whereby my designe was frustrate." The Plymouth merchant-adventurers nevertheless formed big plans, which included, at first, John Smith, and he was honored with the title "Admiral of New England." Unfortunately, Smith felt "deceived" by the "Plimonthians," who "only fed me with delayes, promises, and excuses, but no performance of any thing to any purpose."[14]

The following year, 1618, Smith decided to appeal to a man who had a clear interest in America and its colonization, a man of intellect and power: Francis Bacon, Lord Chancellor of England. Smith wrote Bacon a letter calling the great man "the greatest favourer of all good designes and their Authors." Smith, the author of a design to establish a workable fishing colony in New England, provided Bacon with all the necessary details. Bacon, however, ignored Smith's petition. Meanwhile, Ferdinando Gorges and his aristocratic colleagues obtained a charter to form the Council of New England, which, according to Smith, divided "my map into twenty parts, and cast lots their shares"; Smith was largely ignored,

LEFT A flotilla of English ships flying the St. George's Cross head west toward America. RIGHT The coat of arms of New England. Both images from Smith's *Map of New England*. American Memory, Library of Congress.

even "though I had divulged to my great labour, cost, and losse, more than seven thousand Bookes and Maps"—but nobody embraced his idea. The council's plan was to tax fishing in the region under its control, which made Smith's idea of a fishing colony moot: there was no reason to establish a colony when taxing seasonal fishing yielded wealth.[15]

One opportunity arose in 1620, with "some well disposed Brownists," that is, the Pilgrims, who might have hired Smith instead of Miles Standish but did not, "saying my books and maps were much better cheape to teach them, than my self." Smith also realized that their "pride . . . and contempt of authority" would not allow them to be guided by a strong-willed, commanding person: "because they could not be equals, they would have no superiors." Relying on Standish, who knew nothing of the New England coast, the Pilgrims' initial experience in America was filled "with great losse and much miserie." Undaunted, a year later Smith proposed to the London Fishmongers, one of twelve great livery companies, or monopolies, of the city, that they support financially a fishing colony in America. They provided no encouragement. Then, after the Indian attack on the Jamestown colony in 1622 almost wiped it out, Smith proposed to the London Company that if they would outfit an expedition of "a hundred Souldiers and thirty Sailers," well supplied,

Smith would, "by Gods assistance, . . . endeuour to inforce the Saluages to leaue their Country, or bring them in that feare and subiection that euery man should follow their businesse securely." Again, he was passed by.[16]

We might wonder, as Smith wondered time and again, why the savior of Jamestown and founder of New England could never achieve the means and ways to return to America. Smith's aggressive confidence daunted the Pilgrims, and no doubt others as well. The versifiers opening his many books pointed out again and again that envy and jealousy rather than encouragement and patronage were Smith's lot; Smith would not be the first nor the last person who did the difficult initial work by which others with less effort stood for more gain. Smith had learned that England's profit from colonies would not be from gold and silver or new routes through the continent to the Orient; he had learned that *everyman*, not just the aristocrats and privileged, could thrive in America with hard work and perseverance. Such were not the qualities that brought quick returns and fame, and Smith's practical plans and egalitarian goals were easily forgotten in the waning years of King James's reign. Besides, Smith's optimistic appraisal of the mild climate of New England was not convincing in light of what the English had experienced at Sagadahoc in 1607. Indeed, it would take a greater spur to colonize America than the promise of furs, fish, and farms. Smith, of course, had argued that the English should work toward fulfilling the Great Commission in America. Religion came to be the sine qua non that led to colonization of New England—religion not as a means of converting the Indians so much as the means to create independent, self-sustaining Bible Commonwealths, at Plymouth and Massachusetts.

The Anglican John Smith remained in England. He began during these years to experience adventures in the new land, but vicariously, by means of quill, ink, and paper. He did what many an active person who is forced into inaction, a soldier who no longer experiences battle, a mariner who no longer braves the ocean, has done—Smith wrote of war, of danger, of the sea, of conquest, of colonization, of converting the Indians to Christianity. He became an apologist of England, an apologist of himself.

TWELVE

Day of Doom

John Smith was a landsman who became a seaman. He transitioned from soldier to sailor during the course of his life; if not always in reality, if he was not always at sea, in his mind and spirit he was aboard ship, directing the crew, tacking to windward, watching for shoals, seeing the safe harbor in the distance—but then he heard the timbers crack and the ship list and found himself stuck on a shelf, a warning sign to others to avoid his path. Smith became a sea mark.

During the last ten years of his life Smith turned to the quill, ink, and paper to relive his experiences of times past, to memorialize his accomplishments, to encourage others to follow in his path of conqueror, colonist, and commissioner. Of the many topics Smith wrote upon—his life, the sailor's life, Virginia, New England—it was the latter, New England, that captivated his mind and dreams and simultaneously yielded hope and despair. New England, a place of mixed success, a land that promised so much but gave way, in Smith's opinion, to greed and mismanagement, "which has bin so costly to this kingdome and so deare to me, which either to see perish or but bleed, pardon me though it passionate me beyond the bounds of modestie, to haue bin sufficiently able to foresee it, and had neither power nor meanes how to preuent it." New England, and to a lesser extent Virginia, "by that acquaintance I haue with them, I may call them my children; for they haue bin my wife, my hawks, my hounds, my cards, my dice, and in totall my best content, as indifferent to my heart as is my left hand to my right." Smith considered himself the founder, the parent, and all the discoveries and accomplishments of England's colonies in America were "but pigs of my own sowe."[1]

Such was Smith's jeremiad, as it were, in 1620 and 1622, when he wrote

Statue erected to honor Captain John Smith at the
Colonial National Historical Park at Jamestown, Virginia.
Library of Congress.

the first and second editions of *New Englands Trials*, which were updated versions of the *Description of New England*. Smith penned abbreviated accounts of what he had experienced and seen in 1614, the many profitable English voyages for fishing and furs taken after his journey, and the failure to establish what Smith had sought all along, a fishing colony. He had spent much time researching and conversing with merchants as well as "Fisher-men and Fishmongers." He was more convinced than ever of the rectitude of his plan to conquer and colonize. Indeed, God seemed to be hinting in this direction: voyages returning from New England in recent years had reported on the epidemics that had swept through the indigenous populations, killing vast numbers. "God had laid this Country open for vs," Smith wrote, "and slaine the most part of the inhabitants by cruell warres, and a mortall disease; for where I had seene 100 or 200 people, there is scarce ten to be found." Because of this the Puritans aboard the *Mayflower* had found their way to New Plymouth, and after some initial suffering had begun to thrive. But still private concerns rather than the public good drove people to America. Smith was so distraught about the passage of time and his inability to sacrifice himself on the altar of the colonization of New England that "I am neare ridden to death in a ring of despaire." Smith, who had once again dedicated his book to Prince Charles, addressed the prince and his father the king, arguing that the resources of New England could provide a shipbuilding industry to develop a Royal Navy for England while at the same time advance "Gods glorie, his Church and Gospel, and the strengthening and reliefe of a great part of Christendome, without hurt to any."[2]

Smith was so sanguine about his prospects to gain finally the interest and support of public-spirited and wealthy English benefactors that he had "two or three thousand" of his *New Englands Trials* printed; he distributed numerous copies, with maps, to "thirty of the chiefe Companies in *London* at their Halls." Doubtless he thought that his argument merging profit with patriotism, calling for worthy people of England not merely to "contend for New Englands good[s], but" work for "Englands good" as well, would garner support. He spent a year in "toile and torment," trying to show that fish rather than gold was the key to England's success in America—but he received no response or encouragement.[3]

Likewise Smith spent much time and effort trying to solicit interest in himself and his plans by means of his magnum opus, *The General History of Virginia, New England, and the Summer Isles*, which was a compilation of all his writings to date brought together between two covers. Among other groups, he approached "the Worshipfull the Master Wardens & Societie of the Cordwayners of ye Cittie of London." Smith, who was a member of the Society of Cordwainers, hence knew the art of leather work and making shoes, wrote the "Worthie Gentlemen" that along with a copy of his book he was sending his greetings and a "salute . . . with this cronologicall discourse" to the many cordwainers who had traveled to Jamestown, and the importance of their product, for without shoes an explorer in America must tie "Barkes of trees about our ffeete to keepe them from being cutt by the shelles [of clams and oysters] amongst which wee must goe or starve." Smith appealed to the Society of Cordwainers "to give" his book "lodging in your Hall freelie for it to be perused for ever, in memorie of your Noblenesse towards mee, & my Love to God, my Countrie, your Socieite, & those Plantations."[4]

By the time of the publication of the *General History*, in 1624, Smith was starting to see himself in grand historical terms, presenting his personal past in light of the human past, feeling a growing sense of aloofness from his personal goal of establishing a colony, even as his writings were gaining more readers and support. "The Illustriovs and Most Noble Princesse, the Lady Francis, Duchesse of Richmond and Lenox," for example, provided financial support for the publication of the *General History*. Smith dedicated the book to Lady Richmond, noting that she was one of several women in Smith's life—for example Pocahontas, Lady Tragabigzanda, Lady Callamatta, who helped him escape from "Tartaria" to Europe, and Madam Chanoyes, who helped Smith in La Rochelle—to have come to Smith's assistance when he was greatly in need.[5]

Smith was again able to acquire quite a number of self-professed poets to write dedicatory verses by which to launch his book. These included Samuel Purchas, the promoter of English exploration and colonization, who rhymed loosely with the blacksmith metaphor of the author's surname; Thomas Macarnesse, the Anglican churchman, who wrote, irritatingly, that Smith "loues to live at home, but look abroad"; John Donne, who wrote of "Braue Smith, that hast beat out Thy Iron thus"; and Edward Worsely, who wrote revealingly, "Like Cæsar now thou writ'st what thou hast done." This last comment Smith took to, and seemed during these last years of his life to identify himself with the great Roman general who wrote narrative accounts of his own valiant actions in a detached third-person style. In *A Sea Grammar*, published in 1627, Smith explicitly identified himself with Caesar, writing: "Julius Cæsar wrote his owne Commentaries, holding it no lesse honour to write, than fight; much hath bin writ concerning the art of war by land, yet nothing concerning the same at Sea. I have beene a miserable Practitioner in this Schoole of Warre by Sea and Land more than thirty yeeres." Rather than Caesar's sense of fate driving him, in the *General History* Smith saw himself as being an instrument of God, who watched over Smith during the many dangerous scrapes in which he found himself.[6]

A dominant theme in the *General History* is the English finding themselves in a land among a people much stranger than anything they had anticipated. The natives, the English discovered, worshiped the "Devill," called Okee: "Thus, Feare was the first their Gods begot: Till feare began, their Gods were not." The English tried their best to impart to the natives the English understanding of Christ, with mixed success. But God favored their work, and often by His will, Smith wrote, the English, and John Smith, were preserved. When the men at Jamestown were starving, "God the patron of all good indeavours, in that desperate extremitie so changed the hearts of the Salvages, that they brought such plenty of their fruits, and provision, as so many wanted." Smith ascribed his unexpected salvation through the intervention of Pocahontas to "almightie God," who "by his divine providence . . . had mollified the hearts of those sterne Barbarians with compassion." Smith informed the Indians, specifically Opechancanough, Powhatan's brother, that he had vowed to God to deal with him in peace unless he was mistreated; then he would respond in kind. "If I keepe this vow, my God will keepe me, you cannot hurt me, if I breake it, he will destroy me."[7]

Such stern, hard-bitten faith was impatient with failure, both his own and that of others. Smith watched the London Company make a mess of the Virginia colony, and believed that the Indian attack of 1622 was a recompense for error. "Where there was no honesty, nor equity, nor sanctitie, nor veritie, nor pietie, nor good civilities in such a Countrey, certainly there can bee no stabilitie." And, Smith added, "it seemes God is angry to see Virginia made a stage where nothing but murder and indiscretion contends for victory." John Smith was the solution. He offered once again, in *General History*, to pacify the Indians, unless "it be Gods pleasure I shall not liue to put in practice." Smith did well to anticipate the future. When, a few years later in *The True Travels*, he continued the story of the *General History* through 1629, he wistfully thought of what had been accomplished and what still remained to be done. When he had first traveled "to the North part of Virginia," "there was not one *Christian* in all the land." Now, a decade later, there were many, but the faithful work of planting Christian colonies among the indigenous people, which God had commissioned the English to do, had taken a wrong turn because of greed and other "mischiefes in men." Smith had seen enough of Christians in conflict with each other to know that notwithstanding the Great Commission, Christians will "persue to dispossesse the planters of the Name of Christ Iesus." Why are there religious wars in Europe, "when so much of the world is unpossessed; yea, and better land than they so much strive for." The violence and destruction of warring Protestants and Catholics is such a waste when so much of America is open, "only possessed by a few poore Savages, that more serve the Devill for feare, than God for love: whose ignorance we pretend to reforme, but couetousnesse, humours, ambition, faction, and pride, hath so many instruments, we performe very little to any purpose." Wars among Christians have neither purpose nor honor, unlike working to fulfill Christ's commission by taking possession of land and people not yet Christianized.[8]

Forgotten, too, was John Smith. Though he protested in his writings and to his friends that as he aged he grew more content with his life, and accepted what was and is as the will of God, his writings betray an angst to be active and about at sea and on land, a frustration with inactivity as the years passed and the end grew near. He kept himself busy with his pen, publishing in 1626 a manual on "the Arte of Navigation," *An Accidence or The Path-way to Experience*. Smith thanked his friend Samuel Saltonstall, customs agent for the Port of London, who "caused" the book "to bee printed." Smith addressed "the Reader; and All Generous and Noble Adventurers by Sea; and Well-Wishers to Nauigation. Especially the Masters, Wardens, and Assistance of the Trinity-House." Typically honest, Smith confessed his "imperfections," blaming them in part on his "greatest error," which "is but a desire to do good; which disease hath ever haunted mee since my child-hood; and all the miseries and ingratitudes I haue indured, cannot yet diuert me from that resolution." His many journeys to "Europe, Asia, Affrica and America," he wrote, "if all their extremities hath taught me any thing, I haue not kept it for my owne particuler." Writing was his way to impart what he knew, gained from experience, to others, which obligation he owed "To Christ and my Country" as "a true Souldier, and faithfull Servant."[9]

Smith followed up the *Accidence* a year later with a much-expanded version, *A Sea Grammar*, which he told the reader was a "rude bundle of many ages observations." *A Sea Grammar*, like the *Accidence*, has a good deal of vocabulary and detailed explanations of all things nautical. Befitting Smith's growing appreciation of his own role in England's maritime history (and consequently, America), the book has more of a sense of history, as one dedicator, Edward Ingham, realized, writing: "Reader within this little worke thou hast The view of things present, to come, and past." Another dedicator, Edward Jorden, added: "Much traveld Captaine, I have heard thy worth By Indians, in America set forth." Smith, as before, dedicated the book to "Honourable, and most generous Lords in England, especially those of his Majesties Privy Councell, and Councell of Warre," as well as "All Worthy Adventurers by Sea, and well wishers to Navigation." More informally, Smith dedicated his book to a good friend and collaborator, the recently deceased Samuel Purchas. The Reverend Purchas, a vicar and rector in the Anglican Church and successor to Richard Hakluyt in collecting narrative accounts and documents illustrative of the history of English exploration, was "a Gentleman whose person I loved," Smith wrote, "and whose memory and vertues I will ever honour." Because Purchas relied so heavily on Smith for his works and other contributions, Smith "made bold to borrow . . . from him, seeing he hath sounded such deepe waters for this our Ship to saile in." Smith's *ship*, as he called it, not only his book but his life, was nearing the last shoal.[10]

Smith's *Sea Grammar* and his *General History* were successful enough to at least gain admirers who wanted more, notably "Sir Robert Cotton, that most learned Treasurer of Antiquitie," who "having by perusall of my General History, and others, found that I had likewise undergone divers other as hard hazards in the other parts of the world, requested me to fix the whole course of my passages in a booke by it selfe: whose noble desire I could not but in part satisfie; the rather, because they have acted my fatall Tragedies upon the Stage, and racked my Relations at their pleasure. To prevent therefore all future misprisons, I have compiled this true discourse," *Notes on True Travels, Adventvres, and Observations of Captain Iohn Smith, In Europe, Asia, Affrica, and America, from Anno Domini 1593 to 1629*. Smith wrote, in his dedication, that although the book was about his experiences, he refused to allow those whom he fought with, and who died, not to have a part in this book, which he called his "tombe." Smith had by this time become something of a historian, with a clear sense of a philosophy of history, which he expressed in his soon to be published *Advertisements for the unexperienced Planters*: "history is the memory of time, the life of the dead, and the happinesse of the living." History was therefore, for Smith, something like a mausoleum, a record where anyone could go to find the life of those now buried. His *True Travels*, evoking the memory of those who once lived, hence providing for the understanding of time, or happiness, in those still living, was a cathartic activity for the cooped-up John Smith, who sought glory, indeed, but more, sought fulfillment and satisfaction in a life well lived.[11]

The many people who wrote verse dedications in *The True Travels* clearly knew Smith quite well, knew his aims and misgivings. Anthony Fereby, for example, understood that Smith's writings were, "Caesar-like, Smiths Epitaph and tombe." Edward Jorden, an English scientist who had written verse complimenting Smith for his *Accidence* and *Sea Grammar*, knowing that Smith had not received the recognition from his peers that he deserved, also knew that Smith believed, "Tis best praise-worthy to have pleased the best." Likewise the English scholar William Hawkins wrote that his friend Smith had "great patience thus to rest contented." Richard Meade agreed, recognizing the true worth of Smith's historical labors, "Which here in so few sheets doth more expresse than volumes great, this is thy happinesse." A few of the poets wrote verse comparing Smith's travels to those of Odysseus. Indeed, Smith clearly warmed to the account of his odyssey throughout Europe and parts of Africa, Asia, and America. He explained his travels as due to a "restlesse spirit, that could neuer finde content." And, Odysseus-like, he believed there was a divine impulse pushing him along; Smith's deeds were "in the defence of Christ and his Gospell." Throughout his life, Smith had discovered, "God beyond mans expectation or imagination helpeth his servants, when they least thinke of helpe, as it hapned to him."[12]

Where Smith spent most of his time during these years of the 1620s is not clear. Thomas Fuller learned from hearsay a generation after Smith's death that he "led his old age in London, where his having a prince's mind imprisoned in a poor man's purse rendered him to the contempt of such who were not ingenuous. Yet he efforted his spirits with the remembrance and relation of what he formerly had been, and what he had done." Smith also felt the burden of unaccomplished aims. He had longed not only to conquer and colonize but to spread the knowledge of Christianity to the indigenous inhabitants. Notwithstanding his critics, he continued to pursue these goals with his pen. Echoing the editors of the King James Bible, some of whom Smith knew, he recognized that those who feel "the zeal to promote the common good," who do things for the sake of religion, open themselves to criticism. Smith snubbed his critics but not his friends, with whom, as a bachelor, he stayed, enjoying their hospitality to think and write his discourses. This was certainly true about Smith's final book, *Advertisements for the unexperienced Planters of New-England, or Anywhere; or, the Pathway to Erect a Plantation*, which he penned in the autumn of 1630 at the impressive two-story home of Sir Humphrey Mildmay, whose estate was in Danbury in the county of Essex. The home was on a small hill providing a perspective of the surrounding woods, fields, and pastures. Smith sometimes compared the English countryside to what he had observed in America, dreaming wistfully of what could have been; he compared the trees of Sir Humphrey's estate with the trees he had seen in America. Sir Humphrey was a dozen years Smith's junior, heir to the Mildmay estate, knighted in 1616. He shared with Smith an introspective religious sense that led to a desire for reconciliation with God. Smith, as he aged, appears to have grown closer to the Anglican Church, feeling respect and affection for the Church's prelates. He dedicated, for example, the *Advertisements* to George Abbott, archbishop of Canterbury, and Samuel Harsnett, archbishop of York, writing: "I desire to leave testimony to the world, how highly I honour as well the Miter [bishop's hat] as the Lance." Smith requested their favor for "the worke I now prosecute, concerning the Plantation of *New-England*, for the increase of Gods Church, converting Salvages, and enlarging the Kings Dominions." These two men, "who as you are in the name of Prelacy to this Kingdome, so you are to mee in goodness both fathers and Protectors unexpectedly."[13]

Unlike Smith's other works, the *Advertisements* has no dedicatory poems from friends and admirers, rather a summary poem by Smith, *The Sea Marke*, as well as a brief note to the reader, in which Smith criticizes those who were professed experts on America although they had never traveled there. Smith's cynicism and wit were always on display in his works, perhaps never more so in his comments that such experts, in their so-called travels, "returne as wise as they went, claiming time and experience for their tutor, that can neither shift Sun nor Moone, nor say their Compasse, yet" notwithstanding their ineptness at navigation "will tell you of more than all the world" based on their travels between Westminster Abbey, St. Paul's Cathedral, and the Royal Exchange. Smith, rather, believed that "examples give a quicker impression than arguments."[14]

In *Advertisements*, Smith, remarkably, still after sixteen years, identified himself with America: "Both they [Virginia and New England] and I have beene so tossed and tortured into so many extremities, as despaire was the next wee both expected, till it pleased God now at last to stirre up some good mindes, that I hope will produce glory to God, honour to his Majesty, and profit to his Kingdomes." The good minds to which Smith referred were the Puritans who had recently voyaged to New England. Smith anticipated that "Industry her selfe [will] adventure now to make use of my aged ende[a]vours," that which "I have cherished truly, by the losse of my prime fortunes, meanes, and youth." Smith had met with men from the East Country like himself, Puritans such as John Winthrop, who were familiar with Smith's writings on New England. Winthrop and the Puritans assured Smith that they were not separatists (unlike the Brownists at Plymouth) and had Smith's three goals (God's glory, honor to king, profit to England) in mind. Smith, convinced that the leaders were "good Catholike Protestants according to the reformed Church of England" engaged in "advancing this harmlesse and pious worke," believed that they should be trusted and supported. Yet even Jesus experienced duplicity among his disciples. And indeed among the

Puritans there had been some confusion and disorder: "Some could not endure the name of a Bishop, others not the sight of a Crosse," icons of the Church, "nor Surplesse [surplice]," the vestment used by the Anglican clergy, "others by no meanes the booke of common Prayer," which was, along with the episcopacy and royal supremacy, the foundation of Anglican belief. "This absolute crue [crew], only of the Elect, holding all (but such as themselves) reprobates and cast-awaies," condemned to hell, "now make more haste to returne to *Babel* as they tearmed *England,* than stay to enjoy the land they called *Canaan:* somewhat they must say to excuse themselves." Smith knew that those who settled New England were divided: "where God hath his Church they wil[l] have a Chapel," an unnecessary extension of their own persuasion; "a mischiefe so hard to be prevented, that I have thus plainly adventured to shew my affection, through the weaknesse of my abilitie." Echoing Richard Hooker's *Laws of the Ecclesiastical Polity*, Smith argued that those who work against the Church have an "absoluteness in opinions, holding experience but the mother of fooles, which indeed is the very ground of reason." Smith believed that the conservative leaders of Massachusetts Bay have "Gods true Religion (they say) taught amongst them, the Sabbath day observed, the common Prayer (as I understand) and Sermons performed, and diligent catechizing," teaching the formal rules of belief, "with strict and carefull exercise, and commendable good orders to bring those people with whom they have to deale withall into a Christian conversation, to live well, to feare God, serve the King, and love the Country; which done, in time from both those Plantations," Massachusetts Bay and Plymouth, "may grow a good addition to the Church of *England*: but *Rome* was not built in one day, whose beginnings was once as unhopefull as theirs: and to make them as eminent shall be my humble and hearty prayers." Nevertheless, Smith admitted, the Puritans had not been clear about ecclesiastical authority, so faction had set in. Smith believed that such division led to weakness. Christians should be "constant to one God, one Christ, and one Church." The Puritans should gravitate toward the authority of the Church of England, because it will provide order. "The maintainers of good Orders and Lawes is the best preservation next God of a Kingdome." In short, if the Puritans follow such leaders as

Winthrop and do "well," it will be "a great glory and exceeding good to this Kingdome, to make good at last what all our former conclusions have disgraced."[15]

Indeed, a successful colony in New England composed of worthy people working for the king and Church would provide an outlet for the poor of England, thus reforming society. Smith proposed to the Puritans that they encourage immigration of servants and give them an acre to farm, and if they do it well reward them with more, so that people know they can thrive if they leave England for America. All of this works for the "publike good." The goal is to create a free people, because "the very name of servitude will breed much ill bloud, and become odious to God and man: but mildly temper correction with mercy, for I know well you will have occasion enough to use both; and in thus doing, doubtlesse God will blesse you, and quickly triple and multiply your numbers; the which to my utmost I will doe my best indevour."[16]

By way of contrast, Smith launched a vitriolic condemnation of the London Company and how they erred in Jamestown—solely out for wealth, ignoring the more important Great Commission. It still offended Smith that "much they blamed us for not converting the Salvages, when those they sent us were little better, if not worse." Smith still recalled that men like Justice Popham had wished that the two colonies, in Virginia and New England, would work in harmony, which "shall ever be my hearty prayers to Almighty God."[17]

Smith empathized with critics, then and hence, who condemned and would condemn the displacement of the indigenous inhabitants. He wondered "by what right wee may possesse those Countries lawfully." It was not sufficient evidence that plague and wars had decimated the tribes of New England—although God's will was certainly at work in this conclusion. But Smith still wondered, as did many other "good religious devout men" who "have made it a great question, as a matter in conscience, by what warrant they might goe to possesse those Countries, which are none of theirs, but the poore Salvages." For a Christian, the answer was obvious. "For God did make the world to be inhabited with mankind, and to have his name knowne to all Nations, and from generation to generation: as the people increased they dispersed themselves into such Countries as they found most convenient. And here in Florida, Virginia, New-England, and Cannada, is more land than all the people in Christendome can manure" and farm, "and yet more to spare than all the natives of those Countries can use and culturate. And shall we here keepe such a coyle [controversy] for land, and at such great rents and rates, when there is so much of the world uninhabited, and as much more in other places, and as good or rather better than any wee possesse, were it manured and used accordingly." In short, colonization was a providential, historical process of Christians bringing the Word and cultivating the land. Smith has no desire to destroy the natives; it is simply that the Indians are not Christian, and God wants them to be, and they are too few to use the land adequately, which is God's will as well. "*Adam* and *Eve* did first begin this innocent worke to plant the earth to remaine to posterity; but not without labour, trouble, and industry. Noah and his family began againe the second plantation," a self-sufficient agricultural enterprise, "and their seed as it still increased, hath still planted new Countries, and one Country [after] another, and so the world to that estate it is; but not without much hazard, travell, mortalities, discontents, and many disasters"—doing the work of God is fraught with the consequences of sin. Smith, willing to compare his own culture with that of the Indians through the dark lenses of the passage of time, added: "Had those worthy Fathers and their memorable offspring not beene more diligent for us now in those ages" of the distant past, "than wee are to plant that yet unplanted for after-livers," posterity; "Had the seed of Abraham, our Saviour Christ Jesus and his Apostles, exposed themselves to no more dangers to plant the gospell wee so much professe, than we, even we our selves had at this present beene as Salvages, and as miserable as the most barbarous Salvage, yet uncivilized." It is thanks to the Great Commission that the English are so advanced in society, technology, and culture. Smith's view was common to Anglicans of his time, echoed in the apology for the King James Bible with which the translators introduced the work. It was because of the translation of the Greek New Testament and Hebrew Bible into "vulgar" tongues that the "unlearned" and those who "hungered and thirsted after righteousness" came into the knowledge of "Christ." In so doing contemporary society brings forward the learning of the past to expand knowledge into the future. To colonize and convert involves "reason, liberty, and action," Smith wrote; the spread of Christianity is most rational, which God gives the English freedom to do according to His will, which spurs the English to act on behalf of king, country, God, posterity, and self.[18]

When John Smith was a young man entering adolescence, in 1592, at the same time far away in Bordeaux, France, the greatest thinker of his time, Michel de Montaigne, succumbed to old age and illness and breathed his last. Whether or not Smith knew of Montaigne and his essays is indeterminable, though many Jacobeans (such as William Shakespeare) read Montaigne by means of John Florio's English translation. Smith, of course, knew French and could have, during his many travels through France, run into a French copy of the *Essais*. Montaigne's theme in the *Essais* is that the individual knows himself best; hence personal history makes for the best historical writing. Smith purposely or circumstantially adopted Montaigne's point of view. Smith wrote autobiographically, and assuming that he was honest with himself, hence with others, his readers, as well, then we must assume that Smith knew himself best, and his writings are the best way to know him. Perhaps because Smith's writings were autobiographical, he revealed an exceptional and rare ability to contemplate the passage of time and his own experience; he was able to bridge the specific moment to see the continuum of past-present-future, and to see his role in it. The present always tyrannizes the individual; the only brief release from this tyranny is the recollection of the past and the anticipation of the future. Smith seems to have had this gift.[19]

Smith's tone in the *Advertisements* is that of a man penning his last testament. "Having beene a slave to the Turks, prisoner amongst the most barbarous Salvages," having experienced on his journeys of exploration in America "mutinies wants and miseries," including being "blowne up with gunpowder," having for several months been a "prisoner among the French Pyrats, from whom escaping in a little boat by my self, and adrift all such a stormy winter night, when their ships were split, more than a hundred thousand pound lost [which] they had taken at sea, and most of them drowned upon the Ile of *Ree*, not farre from whence I was driven on shore in my little boat"—somehow Smith survived. And he gloried in it. "There is no pleasure comparable to a generous spirit; as good imploiment in noble actions, especially amongst Turks, Heathens, and Infidels; to see daily new Countries, people, fashions, governments, stratagems; releeve the oppressed, comfort his friends, passe miseries, subdue enemies, adventure upon any feazable danger for God and his Country. It is true, it is a happy thing to be borne to strength, wealth, and honour; but that which is got by prowesse and magnanimity is the truest lustre: and those can the best distinguish content, that have escaped most honourable dangers; as if, out of every extremity he found himselfe now borne to a new life, to learne how to amend and maintaine his age."[20]

For "neere 37. yeares" Smith lived "in the midst of wars, pestilence and famine, by which many an hundred thousand have died about mee, and scarce five living of them [that] went first with me to *Virginia:* and [yet to] see the fruits of my labours thus well begin to prosper: though I have but my labour for my paines, have I not much reason both privately and publikely to acknowledge it and give God thankes, whose omnipotent power onely delivered me, to doe the utmost of my best to make his name knowne in those remote parts of the world, and his loving mercy to such a miserable sinner." Rather like a penitent seeking reconciliation, Smith confessed that notwithstanding his sins and sufferings God had ultimately blessed him, not with riches but with long life and the success of two colonies founded as well as the planting of Christianity in America, all to England's benefit. Those things that he professed to have wanted at the outset had come true—God clearly had been with him all along: "The God of Heav'n, He eas'ly can Immortalize a mortall man, With glory and with fame. The same God, ev'n as eas'ly may Afflict a mortall man, I say, With sorrow and with shame."[21]

Smith's most revealing piece of writing is the verse with which he introduced the *Advertisements. The Sea Marke* is reflective of his past and anticipatory of his future while contemplating his present. It is a poem about Smith's life, intents, errors, ruin, and salvation. Smith saw his life as a sea mark, a beacon or sign at sea, outstanding amid the waves and spray, shoal-bound and surrounded by danger, a warning to others to come no closer.

Aloofe, aloofe; and come no neare,
 the dangers doe appeare;
Which if my ruine had not beene
 you had not scene;
I onely lie upon this shelfe
 to be a marke to all
 which on the same might fall,
That none may perish but my self.

Smith thought he was in smooth waters, without shoals. He neglected to take the proper precautions in a place, the sea, that has inherent danger. Neglect and confidence, false security, a mistaken tack, caused the wreck of his ship upon the hidden shoal. Abandoned and marooned, his fate is determined, but he can at least warn others away from a like disaster.

If in or outward you be bound,
 doe not forget to sound;
Neglect of that was cause of this
 to stear amisse.
The Seas were calme, the wind was faire,
 that made me so secure,
 that now I must indure
All weathers be they foule or faire.

Time passes, and the waves and wind, heat and cold, beat upon his body, and he grows old. He knows that the end is inevitable and soon. Death approaches, but so, too, does resurrection.

The Winters cold, the Summers heat
 alternatively beat
Upon my bruised sides, that rue
 because too true
That no releefe can ever come.
 But why should I despaire
 being promised so faire
That there shall be a day of Dome.

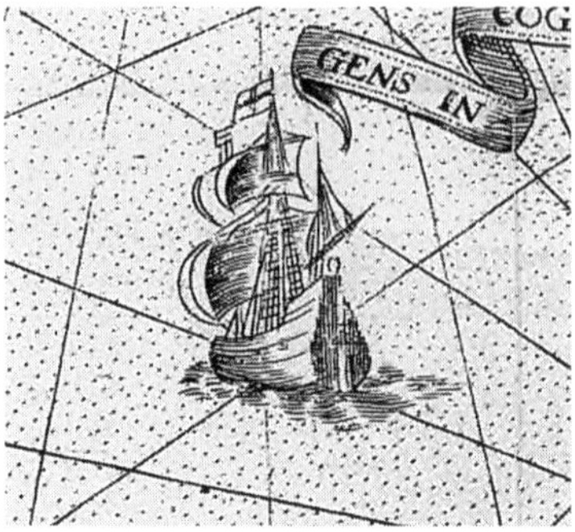

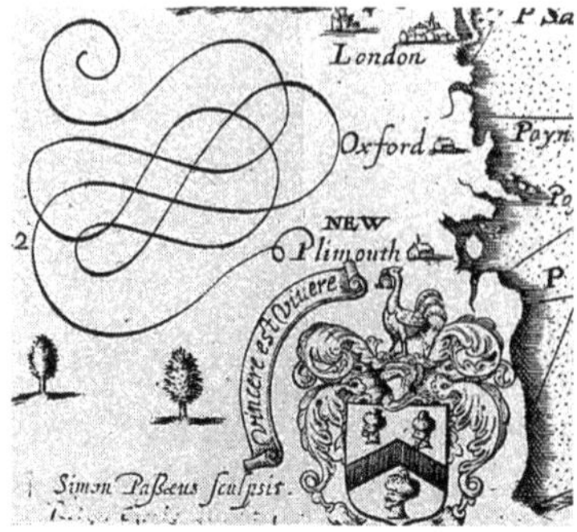

LEFT A lone bark flying the St. George's Cross approaches Cape Ann. American Memory, Library of Congress. RIGHT John Smith's coat of arms, from his *Map of New England.* American Memory, Library of Congress.

This day of doom occurred on June 21, 1631—too early for Smith, who was hard at work on a new volume, the *History of the Sea*, which was never published. In it, we can surmise from his earlier works, Smith planned to provide a natural and human history of the sea, the former speculating on its origins, dimensions, depths, and topography, the latter providing a complete naval history, which Smith argued, in *Sea Grammar*, had never been accomplished, and which he felt himself, after his many years off and on fighting and sailing upon and thinking about the sea, particularly qualified to write. The way of the sea, like the experience of life, "is tossed and turned up and downe the world with the like dangers, miseries, and extremities as a ship." Nearing port, John Smith made his last will and testament the same day he died, at the home of his friend Samuel Saltonstall, whose "house on Snow Hill" lay "under the shadow of the Church tower" of St. Sepulchre's, where Smith was soon to be buried.[22]

Who knows what a person thinks when the end is near. Perhaps Smith quickly reviewed his life, the places he had seen, the dangers he had experienced, the lessons he had learned, the actions he had taken, all for the sake of more than just himself, for the sake of that with which he most identified: England and its God—the Elect Nation. Contemplating his life, his fifty-one years, upon which he had written so much, it could have seemed like a discourse, a written life that was lived in the word "to," as he had written a few months before in the *Advertisements*, "satisfie understanding, wisdome, and honesty," both his own and that of others. Humans being what they are, he realized that many "can doe nothing but finde fault with that they neither know nor can amend." Smith knew, however, what he had done and why he had done it. He had opened up a place, New England, for others, conquering, colonizing, and commissioning for posterity. Death now brought it to a close.[23]

"So I rest."[24]

NOTES

Preface

1. John Smith, *A True Relation of such occurrences and accidents of noate as hath hapned in Virginia since the first planting of that Collony . . .* (London: John Tappe, 1608; reprint ed., *Capt. John Smith . . . Works: 1608–1631*, ed. Edward Arber, 2 vols. Birmingham, UK: By the author, 1884); hereafter cited as *A True Relation*.

2. John Smith, *A Map of Virginia. With a Description of the Covntrey, the Commodities, People, Government and Religion* (Oxford: Joseph Barnes, 1612; reprint ed., *Capt. John Smith . . . Works: 1608–1631*, ed. Edward Arber, 2 vols. Birmingham, UK: By the author, 1884); hereafter cited as *Map of Virginia*.

3. John Smith, *A Description of New England: or the Observations, and discoueries, of Captain Iohn Smith (Admirall of that Country) in the North of America, in the year of our Lord 1614 . . .* (London: Humfrey Lownes, for Robert Clerke, 1616; reprint ed., *Capt. John Smith . . . Works: 1608–1631*, ed. Edward Arber, 2 vols. Birmingham, UK: By the author, 1884), 179–80; hereafter cited as *Description of New England*.

4. John Smith, *New Englands Trials. Declaring the successe of 26. Ships Employed thither within these sixe yeares: . . . and how to builde threescore sayle of good Ships, to make a little Navie Royall* (London: William Jones, 1620; 2nd edition, 1622; reprint ed., *Capt. John Smith . . . Works: 1608–1631*, ed. Edward Arber, 2 vols. Birmingham, UK: By the author, 1884), 267; hereafter cited as *New Englands Trials*.

5. John Smith, *The generall History of Virginia, New England, and the Summer Isles . . .* (London: Michael Sparkes, 1624; reprint ed., *Capt. John Smith . . . Works: 1608–1631*, ed. Edward Arber, 2 vols. Birmingham, UK: By the author, 1884); hereafter cited as *General History*.

6. John Smith, *An Accidence or The Path-way to Experience. Necessary for all Young Seamen . . .* (London: Man and Fisher, 1626; reprint ed., *Capt. John Smith . . . Works: 1608–1631*, ed. Edward Arber, 2 vols. Birmingham, UK: By the author, 1884), 786; hereafter cited as *Accidence*. John Smith, *A Sea Grammar, with the Plaine Exposition of Smiths Accidence for young Sea-men, enlarged* (London: John Haviland, 1627; reprint ed., *The Complete Works of Captain John Smith (1580–1631)*, ed. Philip Barbour, 3 vols. Chapel Hill, NC: University of North Carolina Press, 1986), vol. 3; hereafter cited as *Sea Grammar*.

7. John Smith, *The True Travels, Adventures and Observations of Captaine Iohn Smith, In Europe, Asia, Affrica, and America, from Anno Domini 1593 to 1629* (London: Thomas Slater, 1630; reprint ed., *Capt. John Smith . . . Works: 1608–1631*, ed. Edward Arber, 2 vols. Birmingham, UK: By the author, 1884), 893; hereafter cited as *True Travels*.

8. John Smith, *Advertisements for the unexperienced Planters of New-England, or any*

where. Or the Path-way to experience to erect a Plantation (London: Iohn Haviland, 1631; reprint ed., *Capt. John Smith . . . Works: 1608–1631*, ed. Edward Arber, 2 vols. Birmingham, UK: By the author, 1884), 946; hereafter cited as *Advertisements*.

9. *The Complete Essays of Montaigne*, trans. Donald M. Frame (Stanford, CA: Stanford University Press, 1958), 304.

ONE ✦ *The Sea Mark*

1. Nathaniel Hawthorne, *Passages from the American Note-books* (Boston: Houghton, Mifflin and Company, 1900), 523, 536–37.

2. *The Society for Propagating the Gospel among the Indians and Others in North America, 1787–1887* (Boston: University Press, 1887), 42; *The Christian Register* 83 (1904): 891.

3. Smith was fifty-one, in his fifty-second year, when he died. He sailed along the Isles of Shoals in June rather than April 1614.

4. *The Christian Register* 83 (1904): 891; *Map of Virginia*, 93, 96, 167.

5. *Map of Virginia*, 96, 97, 98, 100, 101, 102, 104, 106.

6. Ibid., 109–20. For accessible maps and itineraries of Smith's Chesapeake voyages, go to www.smithtrail.net/captain-john-smith/the-voyages/.

7. *The Christian Register* 83 (1904): 891. The inscription is in part from the *General History*, 613–14, which was written in 1624 rather than 1627.

8. Thomas Hariot, *A Briefe and True Report of the New Found Land of Virginia* (London: Privately printed, 1588; reprint edited by Henry Stevens, London: Privately printed, 1900), 58. E.M.W. Tillyard writes: "There has indeed been a mistaken trend to think of the Elizabethans as specialists in things secular or religious, as if no Elizabethan explorer could be a theologian": E.M.W. Tillyard, *The Elizabethan World Picture* (New York: Random House, 1959), 23.

9. *General History*, 278.

10. *The Bible: Authorized King James Version* (Oxford: Oxford University Press, 1997), 69–70.

11. *New Englands Trials*, 244.

12. *General History*, 374; David Hackett Fischer, *Champlain's Dream* (Toronto: Vintage Canada, 2009), 143. Many of Smith's contemporaries, such as William Bradford, used the word *salvage*: William Bradford, *Of Plymouth Plantation*, ed. Harvey Wish (New York: G. P. Putnam's Sons, 1962), 62.

13. *Early English and French Voyages Chiefly from Hakluyt, 1534–1608*, ed. Henry S. Burrage (New York: Barnes and Noble, 1934), 180–81, 183, 388; *General History*, 464–65.

14. *True Travels*, 841.

15. *True Travels*, 866; Philip L. Barbour, *The Three Worlds of Captain John Smith* (Boston: Houghton Mifflin Company, 1964), 85; Mark Nicholls and Penry Williams, *Sir Walter Raleigh: In Life and Legend* (London: Continuum, 2011), 117.

16. *Harper's New Monthly Magazine* 49 (1874): 671; Winfield M. Thompson, "In the Isles of Shoals," *The Rudder* 23 (1910): 4.

17. *Dedication of a Memorial to Reverend John Tucke 1702–1773, Star Island Isles of Shoals, New Hampshire, July 29, 1914. With an Address on Captain John Smith by Justin Harvey Smith* (Concord: New Hampshire Historical Society, 1914), 55.

18. Ibid., 9–10, 62–66. For a complete list of the differing views on the Smith-Pocahontas episode, see "The Debunking of Smith and Pocahontas," The Pocahontas Archive, http://digital.lib.lehigh.edu/trial/pocahontas/debunk.php. Thomas Fuller, *History of the Worthies of England*, vol. 1 (London: 1662; reprint ed., London: Thomas Tegg, 1840), 276; Jeremy Belknap, *American Biography: or, An Historical account of Those persons who have been distinguished in America as Adventurers, Statesmen, Philosophers, Divines, Warriors, Authors And other Remarkable Characters. . .*, vol. 1 (Boston: Thomas & Andrews, 1794).

19. For an extensive discussion of the idea and method of the dialogue with the past, see Russell M. Lawson, *The American Plutarch: Jeremy Belknap and the Historian's Dialogue with the Past* (Westport, CT: Praeger, 1998). Plutarch's comment is from *Lives of the Noble Grecians and Romans*, trans. John Dryden (New York: Modern Library, 1932), 293. Petrarch's letter to Cicero is quoted in Donald J. Wilcox, *In Search of God & Self: Renaissance and Reformation Thought* (Prospect Heights, IL: Waveland Press, 1987), 63. Montaigne's comments are from *Complete Essays*, 541, 821–22.

20. *Advertisements*, 939.

21. Smith, *Address on Captain John Smith*, in *Dedication of a Memorial*, 68.

TWO ✦ *London*

1. *The Book of Common Prayer* (1604; reprint ed., London: Pickering, 1844); *A Watcher at the City's Gate for Thirty-Five Reigns: St. Sepulchre's Church over against Newgate Holborn, London, A.D. 1137–1931* (London: Williams, Lea & Co., 1931), 4, 6, 9; St. Sepulchre, London, *Commemoration Service on the Occasion of the Tercentenary of the Death of Captain John Smith, sometime Governour of Virginia and Admiral of New England, who departed this life the 21st of June, 1631* (London: Williams, Lea & Co., 1931), 2; John Rocque, *A Plan of the Cities of London and Westminster* (London, 1746), www.chethams.org.uk/treasures/treasures_rocque.html.

2. *New Englands Trials*, 256; *Description of New England*, 219; *Plan of London before the Fire,* Wenceslaus Hollar Digital Collection, University of Toronto, http://link.library.utoronto.ca/hollar/digobject.cfm?Idno=Hollar_k_2465&size=zoom&query=london&type=search; Walter H. Mayo, *The Trinity House London: Past and Present* (London: Smith, Elder, & Co., 1905); Philip L. Barbour, ed., *The Complete Works of John Smith (1580–1631),* 3 vols. (Chapel Hill: University of North Carolina Press, 1986), 1:7; hereafter cited as *Works of Smith*, ed. Barbour. Smith dedicated, in part, his *Accidence* "To the Reader; and All Generous and Noble Adventurers by Sea; and Well-Wishers to Nauigation. Especially the Masters, Wardens, and Assistance of the Trinity-House" (788). A tun was a unit of cargo, equal to about two hogsheads, or two large barrels of wine. A bark (or barque) was a small ship of a capacity of about one hundred tuns. See Samuel Eliot Morison, *The Great Explorers: The European Discovery of America* (New York: Oxford University Press, 1978), 14, 15.

3. *General History*, 696–97.

4. Ibid., 696–97, 732; *Map of Virginia*, 102. The sources on Tisquantum are scattered, vague, and secondhand. The primary source for Tisquantum is Bradford, *Of Plymouth Plantation*, 73–74, in which we learn some of the details of Tisquantum's life, such as his birthplace at Patuxet, or Plymouth, his second kidnapping at the hands of Captain Thomas Hunt during the summer of 1614, his escape to England, and his later return to America accompanying Captain Thomas Dermer, who was Bradford's source. It is easy to admit that there is no way to be certain about the relationship of Smith and Tisquantum, therefore concluding, as Philip Barbour did in his biography *The Three Worlds of Captain John Smith*, that "as to the Indian who may or may not have been with Smith at the time, he was added to the story in 1624, but it is my opinion that the addition may be dismissed as spurious" (471). Barbour changed his view, however, when he edited Smith's works. Smith had in *General History* referred to the god of the Penobscot Indians as Tantum, which Barbour concluded "must be an error for Squantum (better, Tisquantum) whom Smith put ashore at Cape Cod in 1614." See *Works of Smith*, ed. Barbour, 428, and *General History*, 747, 767. See also Karen O. Kupperman, *The Jamestown Project* (Cambridge, MA: Harvard University Press, 2009), who writes that Smith "brought an Indian man home to Cape Cod from England; Smith identified him as Tantum, and some have speculated that he might have been the Squanto (or Squantum) who lived with the later Pilgrim colony" (275).

5. *General History*, 732. The historical accounts of Dohannida are many, if confused, and few are in agreement as to who he was, where he lived, where he was captured, and when he returned to America. For a realistic appraisal of Dohannida, see Henry S. Burrage, *The Beginnings of Colonial Maine, 1602–1658* (Portland, ME: Marks Printing House, 1914). For an imaginative account of Dohannida's life, see Scott Weidensaul, *The First Frontier: The Forgotten History of Struggle, Savagery, & Endurance in Early America* (New York: Houghton Mifflin Harcourt, 2012).

6. *Advertisements*, 936; *General History*, 697.

7. In *True Travels*, 913–16, Smith wrote a brief history of pirating during the Elizabethan and Jacobean ages.

8. Such was the experience of John Winthrop's fleet at about the same time of year, fourteen years later. See *Winthrop's Journal: 'The History of New England,' 1630–1649*, ed. James K. Hosmer, vol. 1 (New York: Charles Scribner's Sons, 1908), 23–24.

9. *General History*, 547; *Sea Grammar*, 82, 85.

10. *Accidence*, 789, 790, 791.

11. Ibid., 797; *Sea Grammar*, 85–86; *The Book of Common Prayer*, 1604.

12. *Accidence*, 798–99. A good source to make out the mystifying terminology found in Smith's *Accidence* is Albert Young, *Nautical Dictionary*, 2nd ed. (London: Longman, 1863).

13. *General History*, 303–4.

14. *Accidence*, 798, 802; *Sea Grammar*, 89–90; *General History*, 396; J. W. Norie, *A Complete Set of Nautical Tables* (London: By the author, 1816), v; Robert Bud and Deborah J. Varner, eds., *Instruments of Science: An Historical Encyclopedia* (London: The Science Museum, 1998), 35–36, 159–60, 414; Albert H. Markham, ed., *The Voyages and Works of John Davis, the Navigator* (London: Hakluyt Society, 1880).

15. *Accidence*, 803–4; *Sea Grammar*, 112.

16. *Accidence*, 799–800.

17. Ibid., 799; *Advertisements*, 936.

18. *Description of New England*, 190.

19. Ibid., 191; *Capt. John Smith, of Willoughby by Alford, Lincolnshire; President of Virginia, and Admiral of New England. Works: 1608–1631*, ed. Edward Arber, 2 vols. (Birmingham, UK: By the author, 1884), 1:cxix; hereafter cited as *Capt. John Smith Works*, ed. Arber.

20. Catherine Drinker Bowen's *Francis Bacon* portrays the times in which Smith was born, grew up, and matured: *Francis Bacon: The Temper of a Man* (Boston: Little, Brown and Company, 1963). Her view goes along with the interpretation of Christopher Hill that Bacon merely expressed what was going on throughout England in the sixteenth and seventeenth centuries, in which the English embraced an attitude of exploration, of trying out ideas, of experimentation, of adopting an empirical mindset: *Intellectual Origins of the English Revolution* (Oxford: Clarendon Press, 1965).

THREE ✦ *Monhegan Isle*

1. The evidence of Norse voyages along coastal New England remains unsubstantiated.

2. *General History*, 304.

3. Samuel Eliot Morison, *The European Discovery of America: The Northern Voyages, A.D. 500–1600* (New York: Oxford University Press, 1971), 326, 329.

4. Ibid., 308–9. The narrative of Verrazzano's voyage is reproduced in *Sailors Narratives of Voyages along the New England Coast, 1524–1624* (Boston: Houghton, Mifflin & Co., 1905).

5. Morison, *European Discovery*, 233–37, 311–12. John Smith likewise called the northeast coast Norumbega until he renamed it New England.

6. Morison, *European Discovery*, 467–68; *General History*, 304. For Frobisher, see James McDermott, *Martin Frobisher: Elizabethan Privateer* (New Haven, CT: Yale University Press, 2001). "A Report of the Voyage of Sir Humfrey Gilbert, Knight, 1583," by Edward Haies, is reproduced in *Early English and French Voyages.*

7. *Description of New England*, 189; *General History*, 332–36. "Briefe and True Relation of the Discoverie of the North Part of Virginia, 1602," by John Brereton, and "A Voyage Set Out from the Citie of Bristoll, 1603," by Martin Pring, are reproduced in *Early English and French Voyages.*

8. See Samuel Eliot Morison, *Samuel de Champlain: Father of New France* (Boston: Little, Brown and Co., 1972), for an authoritative account of Champlain's New England voyage. A translation of Champlain's *Voyages* is found in W. L. Grant, ed., *Voyages of Samuel de Champlain, 1604–1618* (New York: Charles Scribner's Sons, 1907). A translation of Marc Lescarbot's *Nova Francia* is found in Charles H. Levermore, ed., *Forerunners and Competitors of the Pilgrims and Puritans*, vol. 1 (Brooklyn, NY: New England Society of Brooklyn, 1912).

9. *Description of New England*, 189. Waymouth's name is often spelled Weymouth.

10. *General History*, 337–40; *Description of New England*, 218; Burrage, *Beginnings of*

Colonial Maine, 58–60. "A True Relation of the Voyage of Captaine George Waymouth, 1605," by James Rosier, is reproduced in *Early English and French Voyages.*

11. *Description of New England*, 189.

12. "A Relation of a Voyage to Sagadahoc, 1607–1608," in *Early English and French Voyages.*

13. Ferdinando Gorges, "A Briefe Relation of the Discovery and Plantation of New England" (London: John Haviland, 1622), in James P. Baxter, ed., *Sir Ferdinando Gorges and His Province of Maine,* 2 vols. (Boston: Prince Society, 1890), 1:207; William O. Sawtelle, "Father Pierre Biard, Superior of the Mount Desert Jesuit Mission of Saint Sauveur," in *Sprague's Journal of Maine History* 10 (1922).

14. *Description of New England*, 189; *General History*, 696.

15. *Description of New England*, 206; Office of Coast Survey, National Oceanic and Atmospheric Administration, Nautical Charts & Publications, U.S. Waters, Nautical Chart On-Line Viewer, Atlantic Coast, www.charts.noaa.gov/OnLineViewer/AtlanticCoastViewerTable.shtml; hereafter cited as NOAA Chart. NOAA Chart 13288: "Monhegan Island to Cape Elizabeth." *United States Coast Pilot 1: Atlantic Coast: Eastport to Cape Cod* 43rd edition (Washington, DC: National Ocean Service, 2013), 223; hereafter cited as *Coast Pilot.*

16. *Description of New England*, 187; Robert Fotherby, *Narrative of a Voyage to Spitzbergen in the Year 1613* (Boston: John Wilson, 1860). For whale species, see the NOAA Fisheries, Office of Protected Resources, website: www.nmfs.noaa.gov/pr/species/mammals/cetaceans/.

17. *Description of New England*, 187–88; *Advertisements*, 936. Smith wrote in *Description* that "eight or nine others" accompanied him; the uncertainty was perhaps because the ninth man was the Indian guide Tisquantum (188).

18. John Josselyn, *New Englands Rarities Discovered* (London: G. Widdowes, 1672), 5. Smith wrote in *Advertisements* (937): "In this voyage I tooke the description of the coast as well by map as writing."

19. *Advertisements*, 936; *Sea Grammar*, 85.

FOUR ✦ *The Penobscot*

1. A good source for Smith's shallop, which he also used in journeying about the Chesapeake in 1608, is www.smithtrail.net/captain-john-smith/the-shallop/.

2. *Description of New England*, 190; David Y. Allen, "The So-Called Velasco Map: A Case of Forgery?" http://purl.oclc.org/coordinates/a5.htm, 2006.

3. *Accidence*, 802; *General History*, 396; *Description of New England*, 177, 232. During Smith's time there were nine different versions of the map, the last of which, published posthumously, appeared in 1634. Sources that discuss how the nine states of the map changed over time are Wilberforce Eames, *A Bibliography of Captain John Smith* (New York: 1927), 5–7, and *Capt. John Smith Works*, ed. Arber, 1:cxxxiv–cxxxv. Douglas R. McManis notes that Smith's was the most complete map made to date: "his work had details and a sense of totality and continuity absent from English reports": *European Impressions*

of the New England Coast, 1497–1620 (University of Chicago, Department of Geography, Research Paper No. 139, 1972), 112.

4. *Description of New England*, 188, 190.

5. *Sea Grammar*, 90; NOAA Chart 13288: "Monhegan Island to Cape Elizabeth"; NOAA Chart 13303: "Approaches to Penobscot Bay"; *Coast Pilot*, 221–22, 231–32.

6. *General History*, 336; *Early English and French Voyages*, 345; *Description of New England*, 203; John Gibson, *Enjoying Maine's Islands* (Camden, ME: Down East Books, 2005), 117; NOAA Chart 13302: "Penobscot Bay and Approaches"; NOAA Chart 13308: "Fox Islands Thorofare"; *Coast Pilot*, 226–27.

7. William A. Haviland, "Mi'kmaqs, Etchemins, and the Original Name of the Bagaduce River," http://williamahaviland.wordpress.com/2013/04/29/mikmaqs-etchemins-and-the-original-name-of-the-bagaduce-river/; William A. Haviland, *Canoe Indians of Downeast Maine* (Charleston, SC: History Press, 2012), 14–16; *Description of New England*, 192, 203, 206; William D. Williamson, *The History of the State of Maine*, 2 vols. (Hallowell, ME: Glazier, Masters & Smith, 1839), 1:74; Grant, ed., *Voyages of Samuel de Champlain*, 46; NOAA Chart 13303: "Approaches to Penobscot Bay"; *Coast Pilot*, 223–25.

8. *Description of New England*, 202–3.

9. George Fichter, *How to Build an Indian Canoe* (New York: McKay, 1977).

10. Fannie Hardy Eckstorm, "History of the Chadwick Survey from Fort Pownal in the District of Maine to the Province of Quebec in Canada in 1764," *Sprague's Journal of Maine History* 14 (1925); John Gyles, *Memoirs of the Odd Adventures, Strange Deliverances, &c.* (Boston: Kneeland and Green, 1736), 11; *History of Penobscot County, Maine* (Cleveland: Williams, Chase & Co., 1882), 45.

11. *Description of New England*, 203–4.

12. *General History*, 698, 700. *Works of Smith*, ed. Barbour, 1: 319; NOAA Chart 13302: "Penobscot Bay and Approaches"; NOAA Chart 13312: "Frenchman and Blue Hill Bays and Approaches."

13. *Description of New England*, 192, 203; NOAA Chart 13302: "Penobscot Bay and Approaches"; NOAA Chart 13309: "Penobscot River; Belfast Harbor."

14. NOAA Chart 13302: "Penobscot Bay and Approaches."

15. Ibid; NOAA Chart 13301: "Muscongus Bay; New Harbor; Thomaston"; *Coast Pilot*, 246.

16. "A Relation of a Voyage to Sagadahoc, 1607–1608," in *Early English and French Voyages*, 407–8.

17. NOAA Chart 13302: "Penobscot Bay and Approaches"; NOAA Chart 13301: "Muscongus Bay; New Harbor; Thomaston." See also Kerry Hardy, *Notes on a Lost Flute: A Field Guide to the Wabanaki* (Camden, ME: Down East Books, 2009).

18. *Description of New England*, 188; Cyrus Eaton, *History of Thomaston, Rockland, and South Thomaston, Maine*, 2 vols. (Hallowell, ME: Masters, Smith, and Co., 1865), 1:23; NOAA Chart 13288: "Monhegan Island to Cape Elizabeth"; NOAA Chart 13301: "Muscongus Bay; New Harbor; Thomaston"; *Coast Pilot*, 253.

19. Burrage, *Beginnings of Colonial Maine*, 126; Howard S. Russell, *Indian New England Before the Mayflower* (Hanover, NH: University Press of New England, 1980), 202; John McKeen, "Remarks on the Voyage of George Waymouth, to the Coast of Maine, in

1605," *Collections of the Maine Historical Society*, vol. 5 (Portland: Brown Thurston, 1857), 326; NOAA Chart 13288: "Monhegan Island to Cape Elizabeth."

20. NOAA Chart 13288: "Monhegan Island to Cape Elizabeth"; NOAA Chart 13293: Damariscotta, Sheepscot and Kennebec Rivers; South Bristol Harbor; Christmas Cove."

21. "A Relation of a Voyage to Sagadahoc, 1607–1608," in *Early English and French Voyages*, 409–10.

22. NOAA Chart 13293: Damariscotta, Sheepscot and Kennebec Rivers; South Bristol Harbor; Christmas Cove."

23. *Description of New England*, 193.

FIVE ✦ *Sagadahoc*

1. *General History*, 696.

2. *Description of New England*, 203, 206; NOAA Chart 13295, "Kennebec and Sheepscot River Entrances"; George A. Wheeler, *History of Brunswick, Topsham, and Harpswell, Maine* (Boston: Mudge and Son, 1878), 1. For the site of the Popham Colony and its archeology, see Peter H. Morrison, "Architecture of the Popham Colony, 1607–1608: An Archeological Portrait of English Building Practice at the Moment of Settlement" (University of Maine, master's thesis, 2002).

3. *Description of New England*, 192; Wheeler, *History*, 1; NOAA Chart 13293: "Damariscotta, Sheepscot and Kennebec Rivers; South Bristol Harbor; Christmas Cove."

4. Wheeler, *History*, 1; NOAA Chart 13297: "Kennebec River Courthouse Point to Augusta."

5. According to Patricia Roberts Clark, the Wawrigweck were the Norridgewock Indians: *Tribal Names of the Americas* (Jefferson, NC: McFarland & Co., 2009).

6. *Description of New England*, 206; "A Relation of a Voyage to Sagadahoc, 1607–1608," *Early English Voyages*, 414–17.

7. Williamson, *History of the State of Maine*, 1:42; NOAA Chart 13290: "Casco Bay."

8. *Description of New England*, 192.

9. *Description of New England*, 206–7; Russell, *Indian New England*, 128–30; Steven Foster and James A. Duke, *A Field Guide to Medicinal Plants and Herbs of Eastern and Central North America*, 2nd ed. (New York: Houghton Mifflin, 2000), 324.

10. For alkermes, see John Pory, Emmanuel Altham, and Issack de Rasieres, *Three Early Visitors to Plymouth* (Bedford, MA: Applewood Books, 1997), 26; Foster and Duke, *Field Guide to Medicinal Plants and Herbs*, 278.

11. *Description of New England*, 207; Elbert L. Little, *National Audubon Society Field Guide to North American Trees: Eastern Region* (New York: Alfred A. Knopf, 1980), 296; Foster and Duke, *Field Guide to Medicinal Plants and Herbs*, 287, 290, 292–95, 298, 313–14, 331–32; Russell, *Indian New England*, 211, 213.

12. *Description of New England*, 207.

13. Ibid., 200, 207. David E. Lantz, *The Muskrat* (Washington, DC: Government Printing Office, 1910), 21, 24.

14. *Description of New England*, 192, 203, 206; Joseph A. Conforti, ed., *Creating Portland: History and Place in Northern New England* (Hanover, NH: University Press of New England, 2005), 2; Christopher Levett, "A Voyage into New England, begun in 1623, and ended in 1624" (London: William Jones, 1628), in *Collections of the Maine Historical Society*, vol. 2 (Portland: Maine Historical Society, 1847), 84; NOAA Chart 13290: "Casco Bay." For the historical background of the naming and exploration of Mount Washington, see Russell M. Lawson, *Passaconaway's Realm: Captain John Evans and the Exploration of Mount Washington* (Hanover, NH: University Press of New England, 2002).

15. *Description of New England*, 201; *General History*, 319; Barbour, *Three Worlds*, 98, provides a convincing hypothesis that Smith knew Thomas Hariot.

16. *Description of New England*, 193; NOAA Chart 13287: "Saco Bay and Vicinity."

17. *Description of New England*, 203; John R. Swanton, *Indian Tribes of North America* (Washington, DC: Genealogical Publishing Co., 1952), 14; Grant, ed., *Voyages of Samuel de Champlain*, 62; NOAA Chart 13290: "Casco Bay"; NOAA Chart 13287: "Saco Bay and Vicinity"; John Josselyn, *Account of Two Voyages to New-England* (London: G. Widdowes, 1674), 204; Gyles, *Odd Adventures*, 27.

18. "Briefe and True Relation of the Discoverie of the North Part of Virginia, 1602," in *Early English and French Voyages.*

19. *Description of New England*, 204; NOAA Chart 13286: "Cape Elizabeth to Portsmouth; Cape Porpoise Harbor; Wells Harbor; Kennebunk River; Perkins Cove"; *Winthrop's Journal*, 48.

SIX ✣ *Smith's Isles*

1. *Description of New England*, 206; NOAA Chart 13283: "Portsmouth Harbor Cape Neddick Harbor to Isles of Shoals; Portsmouth Harbor."

2. NOAA Chart 13283: "Portsmouth Harbor Cape Neddick Harbor to Isles of Shoals; Portsmouth Harbor."

3. U.S. Coast and Geodetic Survey, *Atlantic Local Coast Pilot: Sub-Division 5: Cape Small Point to Cape Ann* (Washington, DC: Government Printing Office, 1879), 504–5; NOAA Chart 13283: "Portsmouth Harbor Cape Neddick Harbor to Isles of Shoals; Portsmouth Harbor."

4. "A Voyage Set Out from the Citie of Bristoll, 1603," in *Early English and French Voyages;* NOAA Chart 13285: "Portsmouth to Dover and Exeter." For Pring's voyage up the Piscataqua, see Russell M. Lawson, *The Piscataqua Valley in the Age of Sail: A Brief History* (Charleston, SC: History Press, 2007).

5. For more information about this region and its tribes, see Lawson, *The Piscataqua Valley in the Age of Sail.*

6. Ibid.

7. Ibid; NOAA Chart 13283: "Portsmouth Harbor Cape Neddick Harbor to Isles of Shoals; Portsmouth Harbor."

8. *Description of New England*, 206.

9. Grant, ed., *Voyages of Samuel de Champlain*, 64.

10. NOAA Chart 13283: "Portsmouth Harbor Cape Neddick Harbor to Isles of Shoals; Portsmouth Harbor." The quote is from Nicholas Burley, a dedicator of Smith's *Sea Grammar*, 50.

11. *Advertisements*, 947; NOAA Chart 13283: "Portsmouth Harbor Cape Neddick Harbor to Isles of Shoals; Portsmouth Harbor."

12. For a good description of early fishers at the Isles of Shoals see John S. Jenness, *The Isles of Shoals: An Historical Sketch* (New York: Hurd and Houghton, 1873).

13. *Description of New England,* 198. Russell M. Lawson, *The Isles of Shoals in the Age of Sail: A Brief History* (Charleston, SC: History Press, 2007).

14. *Description of New England*, 194, 196, 198, 201.

15. The name, Smith's Isles, did not survive the captain. For example, in 1630, as Winthrop sailed south on the *Arbella* toward Boston Harbor, he noted that "the Isles of Shoals were now within two leagues of us, and we saw a ship lie there at anchor." See *Winthrop's Journal*, 48–49. For the development of fishing colonies at the Isles of Shoals, see Lawson, *Isles of Shoals.*

16. For more, see Lawson, *Isles of Shoals.*

17. Joseph Dow, *History of Town of Hampton, New Hampshire*, vol. 1 (Salem, MA: Salem Press, 1893), 3–4. NOAA Chart 13278: "Portsmouth to Cape Ann; Hampton Harbor." Smith wrote that marshes were also an important source of salt: *Description of New England*, 200.

18. For an extensive description of New Hampshire coastal history, see Russell M. Lawson, *On the Road Histories: New Hampshire* (Northampton, MA: Interlink Publishing, 2005).

19. *Description of New England*, 204; *Parker River National Wildlife Refuge: Guide to the Hellcat Interpretive Trail* (Washington, DC: U.S. Fish and Wildlife Service, 2006).

20. *Map of Virginia,* 95, 155; *Description of New England*, 198, 204; Benjamin W. Labaree, *Patriots & Partisans: The Merchants of Newburyport, 1764–1815* (New York: Norton, 1975), 1; Greg T. O. LeBreton et al., *Sturgeons and Paddlefish of North America* (Dordrecht, Netherlands: Kluwer Academic Publishers, 2004), 2–3; Helen C. Roundtree, Wayne E. Clark, and Kent Mountford, *John Smith's Chesapeake Voyages, 1607–1609* (Charlottesville: University of Virginia Press, 2007), 142; R. A. Douglas-Lithgow, *Native American Place Names of Maine, New Hampshire, & Vermont* (Bedford, MA: Applewood Books, 2001), 95.

21. *Description of New England*, 192, 204.

22. Ibid., 192, 204.

SEVEN ✤ *Cape Tragabigzanda*

1. Grant, ed., *Voyages of Samuel de Champlain*, 64–65, 99; NOAA Chart 13278: "Portsmouth to Cape Ann; Hampton Harbor."

2. Grant, ed., *Voyages of Samuel de Champlain*, 65; NOAA Chart 13279: "Ipswich Bay to Gloucester Harbor; Rockport Harbor."

3. Samuel Adams Drake, *A Book of New England Legends and Folk-Lore* (Boston: Little, Brown, and Company, 1910), 245–51.

4. *True Travels*, 838–40. John Winthrop in 1630 still referred to the Turks Heads, though he mistakenly thought they were off the coast of Maine rather than Cape Ann. See *Winthrop's Journal*, 48.

5. *True Travels*, 853. When Smith met with Prince Charles to discuss naming the land New England and asking for the prince's endorsement of Smith's appellations, the prince decided to name Cape Tragabigzanda for his sister Ann. *Capt. John Smith Works*, ed. Arber, 1:cxxxvi. See also Champlain, Grant, ed., *Voyages of Samuel de Champlain*, 90–91.

6. The Puritans of the *Arbella* in June 1630, anchored near Naumkeag and exploring Cape Ann, found plentiful strawberries. See *Winthrop's Journal*, 50.

7. Grant, ed., *Voyages of Samuel de Champlain*, 65; *Description of New England*, 204.

8. *Description of New England*, 204, 206.

9. See Charles E. Beals, *Passaconaway in the White Mountains* (Boston: Richard G. Badger, 1916).

10. *Description of New England*, 204. Naumkeag is a derivative of Amoskeag, "one takes small fish" (Douglas-Lithgow, *Native American Place Names*, 67). Amoskeag Falls on the Merrimack River was a center of the Penacook tribe. NOAA Chart 13275: "Salem and Lynn Harbors; Manchester Harbor."

11. *Description of New England*, 198.

12. NOAA Chart 13275: "Salem and Lynn Harbors; Manchester Harbor"; C. H. Webber and W. H. Nevins, *Old Naumkeag: An Historical Sketch of the City of Salem* (Salem, MA: Smith & Co., 1877), 3.

13. Samuel Roads, Jr., *The History and Traditions of Marblehead* (Boston: Houghton, Mifflin and Company, 1881), 2, 7; NOAA Chart 13275: "Salem and Lynn Harbors; Manchester Harbor."

14. *General History*, 719; *Description of New England*, 192, 193, 204. NOAA Chart 13275: "Salem and Lynn Harbors; Manchester Harbor."

15. Saugus Iron Works National Historic Site, www.nps.gov/sair/index.htm.

16. See the website for the Friends of Belle Isle Marsh: www.friendsofbelleislemarsh.org/.

17. T. H. Nelson et. al., *The Birds of Yorkshire*, 2 vols. (London: A. Brown & Sons, 1907), 2:677; W. J. Kirwin et. al., *Dictionary of Newfoundland English*, 2nd ed. (Toronto: University of Toronto Press, 1990), 226; Joseph Strutt, *The Sports and Pastimes of the People of England* (London: Methuen, 1801), 21–31; *Description of New England*, 213–14.

EIGHT ✤ *"The Paradise of All Those Parts"*

1. *Description of New England*, 198, 199, 201, 213, 214.

2. Ibid., 196, 197, 198. Echoing Smith, George Hakewill argued "that nature is still bright as on creation's day": *An Apologie or Declaration of the Power and Providence of God in the Government of the World* (Oxford: William Turner, 1630), quoted in Tillyard, *Elizabethan World Picture*, 36.

3. *Description of New England*, 204; NOAA Chart 13270: "Boston Harbor." A good description of the ecological history of Boston is John Hanson Mitchell, *The Paradise of All These Parts* (Boston: Beacon Press, 2008).

4. *Description of New England*, 192; NOAA Chart 13270: "Boston Harbor"; Samuel Lambert, "A New Chart of Massachusetts Bay. And Part of the Coast of Maine," 1822, NOAA Historical Map & Chart Collection, http://historicalcharts.noaa.gov/historicals/preview/image/00-00-1847.

5. *Description of New England*, 192, 205, 214; Mitchell, *Paradise*, 19, 38, 39, 80. For the meanings of Shawmut see Darrett B. Rutman, *Winthrop's Boston: A Portrait of a Puritan Town, 1630–1649* (New York: W. W. Norton & Co., 1972), 40.

6. Mitchell, *Paradise*, 9, 10, 11, 12, 14, 19, 79; *Description of New England*, 201; Russell, *Indian New England*, 22.

7. Mitchell, *Paradise*, 19; NOAA Chart 13270: "Boston Harbor."

8. *Description of New England*, 205; NOAA Chart 13270: "Boston Harbor"; *Addresses at the Unveiling of a Memorial July 4, 1914, Commemorating the Discovery of Cohasset in 1614 by Captain John Smith* (Cohasset, MA: By the Town, 1914); E. Victor Bigelow, *A Narrative History of the Town of Cohasset Massachusetts* (Boston: Samuel Usher, 1898), chapters 5 and 6.

9. *Description of New England*, 206; Russell, *Indian New England*, 185, 189.

10. *Description of New England*, 205; Bigelow, *History of Cohasset*, 97; Russell, *Indian New England*, 190–91; NOAA Chart 13269: "Cohasset and Scituate Harbors."

11. Bradford, *Of Plymouth Plantation*, 80; Samuel Deane, *History of Scituate Massachusetts* (Boston: Loring, 1831), 19; NOAA Chart 13269: "Cohasset and Scituate Harbors."

12. William S. Perry, *The History of the American Episcopal Church*, vol. 1 (Boston: Osgood, 1885), 486; *Description of New England*, 220; *Capt. John Smith Works*, ed. Arber, 1:cxxxiv; NOAA Chart 13253: "Harbors of Plymouth, Kingston, Duxbury; Green Harbor."

13. Lincoln N. Kinnicutt, *Indian Names of Places in Plymouth, Middleborough Lakeville and Carver* (Worcester, MA: Commonwealth Press, 1909), 13, 17, 36; "The Voyage of Martin Pring, 1603," in *Early English and French Voyages*, 347–48.

14. Bradford, *Of Plymouth Plantation*, 67; *Description of New England*, 205; Champlain's "*Chart of Port Saint-Louis* [Plymouth]" is reproduced in Morison, *Champlain*, 65.

15. *Description of New England*, 205.

16. Ibid., 193–94, 205; Bradford, *Of Plymouth Plantation*, 60.

NINE ✦ *Cape James*

1. Barbour, *Three Worlds*, 86–88.

2. Champlain, Grant, ed., *Voyages of Samuel de Champlain*, 69; *Early English and French Voyages*, 332; Bradford, *Of Plymouth Plantation*, 59; *Description of New England*, 205; NOAA Chart 13246: "Cape Cod Bay."

3. *Description of New England*, 192, 205; Champlain, Grant, ed., *Voyages of Samuel de Champlain*, 72–73, 94–95; *Early English and French Voyages*, 332; NOAA Chart 13246: "Cape Cod Bay."

4. *General History*, 698–99, 732; *Description of New England*, 219; Bradford, *Of Plymouth Plantation*, 73–74.

5. *Description of New England*, 192.

6. Ibid., 192, 206.

7. Ibid., 207.

8. Ibid., 199, 207, 208.

9. Ibid., 194, 195.

10. Ibid., 197–98, 206.

11. Ibid., 196–97; *Advertisements*, 938.

12. *Description of New England*, 209.

13. Ibid., 208.

14. Ibid., 188, 193.

15. Ibid., 198, 208; *New Englands Trials*, 256; *Advertisements*, 936.

16. *Description of New England*, 219.

17. *New Englands Trials*, 256. In *Description of New England* (219), Smith wrote that he arrived at Plymouth on August 5, which if he departed New England on July 18 would be close to impossible. Assuming that he did return to Plymouth, and assuming that his comment in *New Englands Trials* that he arrived at the end of August is more accurate, Smith clearly arrived at Plymouth at the end of August 1614.

TEN ✥ Don de Dieu

1. Baxter, ed., *Ferdinando Gorges*, 2:8–17.

2. *Description of New England*, 219–20; *New Englands Trials*, 256–57; *General History*, 731, 733.

3. *General History*, 731, 778–79; *Description of New England*, 218, 221.

4. *Description of New England*, 217–19; *General History*, 732.

5. *Description of New England*, 221; *Accidence*, 794.

6. *Description of New England*, 221–22; *General History*, 734–35; Mayo, *Trinity House*, 10. Smith wrote in *True Travels* (916) of the pitiful lives of pirates, and how common seamen were in his time considered "as the scumme of the world" and had insufficient pay to make a decent living, so turned to piracy.

7. *Description of New England*, 221; Kupperman, *Jamestown Project*, 272, 275.

8. *Description of New England*, 222.

9. Ibid., 222; Philip L. Barbour, "A French Account of Captain John Smith's Adventures in the Azores, 1615," *Virginia Magazine of History and Biography* 72 (1964): 294–96.

10. *Description of New England*, 222–23; *General History*, 735.

11. *Description of New England*, 223–24.

12. Ibid., 224.

13. Ibid.

14. Ibid., 224–25.

15. Ibid.

16. Ibid., 187–88.

17. Ibid., 189.
18. Ibid.
19. Ibid., 190–91.
20. Ibid., 192–94, 196, 207.
21. Ibid., 215, 217.
22. Ibid., 228–29.
23. Ibid.

ELEVEN ✤ *"Thou Art Brasse Without, but Golde Within"*

1. *True Travels*, 825. For the history of La Rochelle, see Kevin C. Robbins, *City on the Ocean Sea: La Rochelle, 1530–1650: Urban Society, Religion, and Politics on the French Atlantic Frontier* (Leiden: Brill, 1997).

2. *Description of New England*, 225; *General History*, 738.

3. *Description of New England*, 226.

4. Ibid.; *True Travels*, 912; Barbour, "A French Account of Captain John Smith," 299; *General History*, 635–36; *Bible*, 701.

5. *Description of New England*, 226; *General History*, 739.

6. *Description of New England*, 226; *True Travels*, 912; *General History*, 739; Barbour, "A French Account of Captain John Smith," 299.

7. *Description of New England*, 226; *General History*, 739; Barbour, "A French Account of Captain John Smith," 300–301.

8. *Description of New England*, 227; *General History*, 745.

9. Barbour, *Three Worlds*, 326–27.

10. *Description of New England*, 177–78.

11. Ibid., 179–80.

12. Ibid., 181–86, 230–31; Charles Pastoor and Galen K. Johnson, *The A to Z of the Puritans* (Plymouth, UK: Scarecrow Press, 2007), 357; *Works of Smith*, ed. Barbour, 1:xxxvii. For John Davies see Alexander B. Grosart, ed., *The Complete Works of John Davies of Hereford*, 2 vols. (Privately printed, 1878).

13. *Description of New England*, 198–200, 215–16.

14. The title page of the *Description of New England* refers to Smith as "Admirall of that Country," which would imply that he received the honorary title in 1616. *Description of New England*, 212; *New Englands Trials*, 257–58; *General History*, 891; *Advertisements*, 940–41.

15. "Letter to Lord Bacon," in *Capt. John Smith Works*, ed. Arber, 1:cxxi–cxxii; *Advertisements*, 941; *General History*, 891.

16. *General History*, 588, 891–92; *Advertisements*, 941, 946; Bradford Smith, *Captain John Smith: His Life and Legend* (Philadelphia: J. B. Lippincott Company, 1953), 246–47. For the fishmongers of London, see W. Carew Hazlitt, *The Livery Companies of the City of London: Their Origin, Character, Development, and Social and Political Importance* (New York: Macmillan & Co, 1892).

TWELVE ✤ *Day of Doom*

1. *New Englands Trials*, 265.

2. Ibid., 253, 254, 259, 267, 270, 271.

3. Ibid., 271–72; *General History*, 748.

4. Smith's letter to the Society of Cordwainers is reproduced in *A Watcher at the City's Gate*, 10–11.

5. *General History*, 276–77.

6. Ibid., 282–85; *Sea Grammar*, 47. For Smith's interest in and identification with Caesar see *Works of Smith*, ed. Barbour, 3:324–25.

7. *General History*, 371, 374, 392, 401, 459.

8. Ibid., 581, 598, 600, 891, 911.

9. *Accidence*, 787–88; *True Travels*, 809.

10. *Sea Grammar*, 48, 49, 51, 95–96. Purchas published *Hakluytus Posthumus or Purchas His Pilgrimes: Contayning a History of the World in Sea Voyages and Lande Travells by Englishmen and others* (London: Henry Fetherston, 1625).

11. *True Travels*, 808–9; *Advertisements*, 948.

12. *True Travels*, 814–19, 824–25, 852, 866; Barbour, *Three Worlds*, 378, 383.

13. Fuller, *History of the Worthies*, 276; *Bible*, liii, lv; Herbert A. St. John Mildmay, *A Brief Memoir of the Mildmay Family* (London: John Lane, 1913), 78; *Advertisements*, 920, 950.

14. *Advertisements*, 921.

15. Ibid., 925–27, 954, 956–59. There are many studies of John Winthrop; one of the best is Darrett Rutman's *Winthrop's Boston*.

16. *Advertisements*, 948.

17. Ibid., 929, 932.

18. Ibid., 934–36; *Bible*, lix.

19. *The Essayes of Michael Lord of Montaigne*, trans. by John Florio (London, 1603; reprint ed., London: George Routledge and Sons, 1886). Shakespeare's *Tempest* mirrors Montaigne's ideas in *Of Cannibals* about the pastoral of America; Smith, too, shared these ideas. See John M. Robertson, *Montaigne and Shakespeare: And Other Essays on Cognate Questions* (London: A. and C. Black, 1909).

20. *Advertisements*, 945, 962–63.

21. Ibid., 945; *General History*, 409.

22. *Sea Grammar*, 47; *Advertisements*, 951; *A Watcher at the City's Gate*, 9.

23. *Advertisements*, 921.

24. *Advertisements*, 921.

WORKS CONSULTED

Published Works by John Smith

An Accidence or The Path-way to Experience. Necessary for all Young Sea-men, or those that are desirous to goe to Sea, briefly shewing the Phrases, Offices, and Words of Command, Belonging to the Building, Ridging, and Sayling, a Man of Warre; And how to manage a Fight at Sea. . . . London: Man and Fisher, 1626.

Advertisements for the unexperienced Planters of New-England, or any where. Or the Path-way to experience to erect a Plantation. London: Iohn Haviland, 1631.

A Description of New England: or the Observations, and discoueries, of Captain Iohn Smith (Admirall of that Country) in the North of America, in the year of our Lord 1614: with the successe of sixe Ships, that went the next yeare 1615; and the accidents befell him among the French men of warre: With the proofe of the present benefit this Countrey affoords: whither this present yeare, 1616, eight voluntary Ships are gone to make further tyrall. London: Humfrey Lownes, for Robert Clerke, 1616.

The generall History of Virginia, the Somer Isles, and New England, with the names of the Aduenturers, and their aduentures. Also a Catalogue of their names who were the first Treasurers heere, and planters and Gouernours there; and how they have yeerely succeeded, from their first beginning 1584, to this present 1623, with the proceedings of these seuerall Colonies, and the accidents that befell them in all their iourneys and discoueries, with the Mappes and descriptions of those countries, commodities, people, gouernment, customes, and Religion yet knowne, for the generall good of all them who belong to those Plantations and all their posterities. Discouered, obserued, or collected by Captaine In. Smith sometime Gouernour of Virginia, and Admirall of New England. London: Michael Sparkes, 1624.

A Map of Virginia, With a Description of the Covntrey, the Commodities, People, Government and Religion. Oxford: Joseph Barnes, 1612.

New Englands Trials. Declaring the successe of 26. Ships Employed thither within these sixe yeares: with the benefit of that Countrey by Sea and Land: and how to builde threescore sayle of good Ships, to make a little Navie Royall. London: William Jones, 1620; second edition, 1622.

A Sea Grammar, with the Plaine Exposition of Smiths Accidence for young Sea-men, enlarged. London: John Haviland, 1627.

A True Relation of such occurrences and accidents of noate as hath hapned in Virginia since the first planting of that Collony, which is now resident in the South part thereof, till the last returne from thence. Written by a Gentleman of the Said Collony . . . Written by Captain Smith, Coronell of the said Collony. London: John Tappe, 1608.

The True Travels, Adventures and Observations of Captaine Iohn Smith, In Europe, Asia, Affrica, and America, from Anno Domini 1593 to 1629. London: Thomas Slater, 1630.

Editions of John Smith's Collected Works

Capt. John Smith, of Willoughby by Alford, Lincolnshire; President of Virginia, and Admiral of New England. Works: 1608–1631. Edited by Edward Arber. Two volumes. Birmingham, UK: By the author, 1884.

Captain John Smith: A Select Edition of His Writings. Edited by Karen Ordahl Kupperman. Chapel Hill: University of North Carolina Press, 1988.

Captain John Smith's America: Selections from His Writings. Edited by John Lankford. New York: Harper, 1967.

The Complete Works of Captain John Smith (1580–1631). Edited by Philip Barbour. Three volumes. Chapel Hill: University of North Carolina Press, 1986.

Published Works about John Smith

Adams, Randolph G. "Notes on the Engraved Portraits of Captain John Smith." *William and Mary Quarterly*, second series, 21(1), January 1941.

Addresses at the Unveiling of a Memorial July 4, 1914, Commemorating the Discovery of Cohasset in 1614 by Captain John Smith. Cohasset, MA: By the Town, 1914.

Barbour, Philip L. "A French Account of Captain John Smith's Adventures in the Azores, 1615." *Virginia Magazine of History and Biography* 72 (1964): 294–96.

———. *The Three Worlds of Captain John Smith*. Boston: Houghton Mifflin Company, 1964.

Belknap, Jeremy. *American Biography: or, An Historical account of Those persons who have been distinguished in America as Adventurers, Statesmen, Philosophers, Divines, Warriors, Authors And other Remarkable Characters. . . .* Volume 1. Boston: Thomas & Andrews, 1794.

"The Debunking of Smith and Pocahontas." The Pocahontas Archive. http://digital.lib.lehigh.edu/trial/pocahontas/debunk.php.

Eames, Wilberforce. *A Bibliography of Captain John Smith*. New York, 1927.

Emerson, Everett H. *Captain John Smith*. New York: Twayne Publishers, 1971.

Fuller, Thomas. *History of the Worthies of England*. Volume 1. London, 1662; reprint, London: Thomas Tegg, 1840.

Hillard, George S. *Captain John Smith*. New York: Harper & Brothers Publishers, 1902.

Hutchens, Carolyn. *The Travels of John Smith's Islands: An Essay on the Enigmas of Seventeenth-Century Cartography: Questions about the Confusions Underlying the Colonization of the Atlantic Coast—and Some Answers*. Hartford, CT: Transcendental Books, 1981.

Lemay, J. A. Leo. *The American Dream of Captain John Smith*. Charlottesville: University of Virginia Press, 1991.

Olsen-Smith, Steven. "Captain John Smith." *The Oxford Handbook of Early American Literature*. Oxford: Oxford University Press, 2008, pp. 47–67.

Poindexter, Charles. *Captain John Smith and His Critics*. Richmond, VA: J. L. Hill Printing Co., 1893.

Price, David A. *Love & Hate in Jamestown: John Smith, Pocahontas, and the Start of a New Nation*. New York: Random House, 2005.

Roundtree, Helen C., Wayne E. Clark, and Kent Mountford. *John Smith's Chesapeake Voyages, 1607–1609*. Charlottesville: University of Virginia Press, 2007.

Rozwenc, Edwin C. "Captain John Smith's Image of America." In *Early American Literature: A Collection of Critical Essays*. Edited by Michael T. Gilmore. Englewood Cliffs, NJ: Prentice-Hall, 1980, pp. 11–21.

Smith, Bradford. *Captain John Smith: His Life and Legend*. Philadelphia: J. B. Lippincott Co., 1953.

Striker, Laura P., and Bradford Smith. "The Rehabilitation of Captain John Smith." *Journal of Southern History* 28 (1962): 474–81.

St. Sepulchre, London. *Commemoration Service on the Occasion of the Tercentenary of the Death of Captain John Smith, sometime Governour of Virginia and Admiral of New England, who departed this life the 21st of June, 1631*. London: Williams, Lea & Co., 1931.

Vaughan, Alden T. *American Genesis: Captain John Smith and the Founding of Virginia*. Boston: Little, Brown and Co., 1974.

"The Voyages of Captain John Smith." Captain John Smith Chesapeake National Historic Trail. www.smithtrail.net/captain-john-smith.

Warner, Charles D. *Captain John Smith*. New York: Henry Holt and Company, 1881.

Woods, Katharine P. *The True Story of Captain John Smith*. New York: Doubleday, Page & Co., 1901.

Woodward, Walter W. "Captain John Smith and the Campaign for New England: A Study in Early Modern Identity and Promotion." *New England Quarterly* 81 (2008): 91–125.

Published Contemporary Sources

Baxter, James P., ed. *Sir Ferdinando Gorges and His Province of Maine*. Two volumes. Boston: Prince Society, 1890.

The Bible: Authorized King James Version. Oxford: Oxford University Press, 1997.

The Book of Common Prayer. London, 1604; reprint edition, London: Pickering, 1844.

Bradford, William. *Of Plymouth Plantation*. Edited by Harvey Wish. New York: G. P. Putnam's Sons, 1962.

The Complete Works of William Shakespeare. New York: Crown Publishers, 1975.

Early English and French Voyages Chiefly from Hakluyt, 1534–1608. Edited by Henry S. Burrage. New York: Barnes and Noble, 1934.

Elton, G. R., ed. *The Tudor Constitution: Documents and Commentary*. Cambridge: Cambridge University Press, 1962.

The Essayes of Michael Lord of Montaigne. Translated by John Florio. London, 1603; reprint edition, London: George Routledge and Sons, 1886.

Fotherby, Robert. *Narrative of a Voyage to Spitzbergen in the Year 1613*. Boston: John Wilson, 1860.

Gorges, Thomas. "America Painted to the Life." In *Documents and Records Relating to the Province of New Hampshire, 1623–1686.* Edited by Nathaniel Bouton. Volume 1. Concord: George Jenks, 1867.

Grant, W. L., ed. *Voyages of Samuel de Champlain, 1604–1618.* New York: Charles Scribner's Sons, 1907.

Grosart, Alexander B., ed. *The Complete Works of John Davies of Hereford.* Two volumes. Edinburgh: Edinburgh University Press, 1878.

Hakewill, George. *An Apologie or Declaration of the Power and Providence of God in the Government of the World.* Oxford: William Turner, 1630.

Hakluyt, Richard. *Voyages and Discoveries: The Principal Navigations Voyages, Traffiques and Discoveries of the English Nation.* Harmondsworth, Middlesex, England: Penguin Books, 1985.

Hariot, Thomas. *A Briefe and True Report of the New Found Land of Virginia.* London, 1588; reprint edited by Henry Stevens, London: Privately printed, 1900.

Hooker, Richard. *On the Laws of the Ecclesiastical Polity.* London: George Routledge and Sons, 1888.

Josselyn, John. *Account of Two Voyages to New-England.* London: G. Widdowes, 1674.

———. *New Englands Rarities Discovered.* London: G. Widdowes, 1672.

Levermore, Charles H., ed. *Forerunners and Competitors of the Pilgrims and Puritans.* Volume 1. Brooklyn, NY: New England Society of Brooklyn, 1912.

Levett, Christopher. "A Voyage into New England, begun in 1623, and ended in 1624." London: William Jones, 1628. In *Collections of the Maine Historical Society*, volume 2. Portland: Maine Historical Society, 1847, pp. 75–109.

Markham, Albert H., ed. *The Voyages and Works of John Davis, the Navigator.* London: Hakluyt Society, 1880.

Ogilby, John. *America, Being the Most Accurate Description of the New World.* London: By the author, 1671.

Plan of London before the Fire. Wenceslaus Hollar Digital Collection, University of Toronto. http://link.library.utoronto.ca/hollar/digobject.cfm?Idno=Hollar_k_2465&size=zoom&query=london&type=search.

Pory, John, Emmanuel Altham, and Issack de Rasieres. *Three Early Visitors to Plymouth.* Bedford, MA: Applewood Books, 1997.

Purchas, Samuel. *Hakluytus Posthumus or Purchas His Pilgrimes: Contayning a History of the World in Sea Voyages and Lande Travells by Englishmen and others.* London: Henry Fetherston, 1625.

Rocque, John. *A Plan of the Cities of London and Westminster.* London, 1746. www.chethams.org.uk/treasures/treasures_rocque.html.

The Sagadahoc Colony: Comprising The Relation of a Voyage into New England. Introduction and Notes by Henry O. Thayer. Portland, ME: Gorges Society, 1892.

Sailors Narratives of Voyages along the New England Coast, 1524–1624. Boston: Houghton, Mifflin & Co., 1905.

Whitaker, Alexander. *Good News from Virginia.* London: Welby, 1613.

Winthrop's Journal: 'The History of New England,' 1630–1649. Edited by James K. Hosmer. Volume 1. New York: Charles Scribner's Sons, 1908.

Secondary Sources: Books, Articles, Reference, Internet

ENGLAND

Ashley, Maurice. *England in the Seventeenth Century*. Harmondsworth, Middlesex, England: Penguin Books, 1961.

Beer, George L. *The Origins of the British Colonial System, 1578–1660*. New York: Macmillan Co., 1908.

Bowen, Catherine Drinker. *Francis Bacon: The Temper of a Man*. Boston: Little, Brown and Company, 1963.

———. *The Lion and the Throne: The Life and Times of Sir Edward Coke, 1552–1634*. London: Hamish Hamilton, 1957.

Bridenbaugh, Carl. *Vexed and Troubled Englishmen, 1590–1642*. New York: Oxford University Press, 1968.

Fussner, F. Smith. *The Historical Revolution: English Historical Writing and Thought, 1580–1640*. New York: Columbia University Press, 1962.

Haller, William. *The Elect Nation: The Meaning and Relevance of Foxe's "Book of Martyrs."* New York: Harper & Row, 1963.

Hazlitt, W. Carew. *The Livery Companies of the City of London: Their Origin, Character, Development, and Social and Political Importance*. New York: Macmillan & Co, 1892.

Hill, Christopher. *Intellectual Origins of the English Revolution*. Oxford: Clarendon Press, 1965.

Hurstfield, Joel, and A.G.R. Smith, editors. *Elizabethan People: State and Society*. London: Arnold, 1972.

Knorr, Klaus E. *British Colonial Theories, 1570–1850*. Chicago: University of Chicago Press, 1944.

Lamont, William M. *Godly Rule: Politics and Religion, 1603–1660*. London: St. Martin's Press, 1969.

Mattingly, Garrett. *The Armada*. Boston: Houghton, Mifflin Co., 1959.

Mayo, Walter H. *The Trinity House London: Past and Present*. London: Smith, Elder, & Co., 1905.

Mills, A. D. *A Dictionary of British Place-Names*. Oxford: Oxford University Press, 2003.

Morris, Christopher. *Political Thought in England: Tyndale to Hooker*. London: Oxford University Press, 1953.

Mortimer, Ian. *The Time Traveler's Guide to Elizabethan England*. New York: Penguin Books, 2012.

Nicholls, Mark, and Penry Williams. *Sir Walter Raleigh: In Life and Legend*. London: Continuum, 2011.

Nicolson, Adam. *God's Secretaries: The Making of the King James Bibl*e. New York: HarperCollins Publishers, 2003.

Pastoor, Charles, and Galen K. Johnson. *The A to Z of the Puritans*. Plymouth, UK: Scarecrow Press, 2007.

Preston, Richard. *Gorges of Plymouth Fort*. Toronto: University of Toronto Press, 1953.

Stone, Lawrence. *The Causes of the English Revolution, 1529–1642*. New York: Harper, 1972.
Strutt, Joseph. *The Sports and Pastimes of the People of England*. London: Methuen, 1801.
Tames, Richard. *A Traveller's History of London*. Second edition. New York: Interlink Books, 1998.
Thornbury, Walter. *Old and New London*. Volume 2. 1878. www.british-history.ac.uk/report.aspx?compid=45116.
Tillyard, E. M. W. *The Elizabethan World Picture*. New York: Random House, 1959.
A Watcher at the City's Gate for Thirty-Five Reigns: St. Sepulchre's Church over against Newgate Holborn, London, A.D. 1137–1931. London: Williams, Lea & Co., 1931.

NEW ENGLAND

Babson, John J. *History of the Town of Gloucester, Cape Ann, including the Town of Rockport*. Gloucester, MA: Procter Brothers, 1860.
Bailyn, Bernard. *The New England Merchants in the Seventeenth Century*. Cambridge, MA: Harvard University Press, 1979.
Baxter, James P. *Christopher Levett, of York: The Pioneer Colonist in Casco Bay*. Portland, ME: Gorges Society, 1893.
Belknap, Jeremy. *The History of New Hampshire*. Three volumes. Philadelphia and Boston: Robert Aitken, Thomas and Andrews, Belknap and Young, 1784, 1791, 1792.
Bigelow, E. Victor. *A Narrative History of the Town of Cohasset Massachusetts*. Boston: Samuel Usher, 1898.
Burrage, Henry S. *The Beginnings of Colonial Maine: 1602–1658*. Portland, ME: Marks Printing House, 1914.
Carroll, Charles R. *The Timber Economy of Puritan New England*. Providence: Brown University Press, 1973.
Cartland, J. Henry. *Ten Years at Pemaquid: Sketches of its History and its Ruins*. Pemaquid, ME: By the author, 1899.
Clark, Charles E. *The Eastern Frontier: The Settlement of Northern New England, 1610–1763*. New York: Alfred A. Knopf, 1970.
———. *Maine: A History*. New York: W. W. Norton & Company, 1977.
Clarke, Ted. *South of Boston: Tales from the Coastal Communities of Massachusetts Bay*. Charleston, SC: History Press, 2010.
Cogswell, Jonathan. "A Topographical and Historical Sketch of Saco, County of York, District of Maine." *Collections of the Massachusetts Historical Society*. Series 2. Volume 4. Boston, 1816.
Conforti, Joseph A., ed. *Creating Portland: History and Place in Northern New England*. Hanover, NH: University Press of New England, 2005.
———. *Imagining New England: Explorations of Regional Identity from the Puritans to the Mid-Twentieth Century*. Chapel Hill: University of North Carolina Press, 2001.
Deane, Samuel. *History of Scituate Massachusetts*. Boston: Loring, 1831.
"Dedication of a Memorial to Reverend John Tucke, 1702–1773: Star Island Isles of Shoals New Hampshire, July 29, 1914. With an Address on Captain John Smith by Justin Harvey Smith." *Portsmouth Times*, July 29, 1914.

"A Description and Historical Account of the Isles of Shoals." *Collections of the Massachusetts Historical Society*. Series 1. Volume 7. Boston, 1800.

Dow, Joseph. *History of the Town of Hampton, New Hampshire*. Volume 1. Salem, MA: Salem Press, 1893.

Drake, Samuel Adams. *A Book of New England Legends and Folk-Lore*. Boston: Little, Brown, and Company, 1910.

———. *The Pine-Tree Coast*. Boston: Estes & Lauriat, 1891.

Duncan, Roger F. *Coastal Maine: A Maritime History*. Woodstock, VT: Countryman Press, 1992.

Eaton, Cyrus. *History of Thomaston, Rockland, and South Thomaston, Maine*. Two volumes. Hallowell, ME: Masters, Smith, and Co., 1865.

Eckstorm, Fannie Hardy. "History of the Chadwick Survey from Fort Pownal in the District of Maine to the Province of Quebec in Canada in 1764." *Sprague's Journal of Maine History* 14 (1925).

The Encyclopedia of New England. Edited by Burt Feintuch and David H. Watters. New Haven, CT: Yale University Press, 2005.

Freeman, Frederick. *The History of Cape Cod: The Annals of Barnstable County, and its Several Towns*. Two volumes. Boston: Rand & Avery, 1860.

Gibson, John. *Enjoying Maine's Islands*. Camden, ME: Down East Books, 2005.

Harper's New Monthly Magazine 49 (1874).

Hawthorne, Nathaniel. *Passages from the American Note-books*. Boston and New York: Houghton, Mifflin and Company, 1900.

History of Penobscot County, Maine. Cleveland: Williams, Chase & Co., 1882.

Hosmer, George L. *An Historical Sketch of the Town of Deer Isle, Maine*. Boston: Stanley and Usher, 1886.

Howe, Henry F. *Prologue to New England*. New York: Farrar & Rinehart, 1943.

Jenness, John S. *The Isles of Shoals: An Historical Sketch*. New York: Hurd and Houghton, 1873.

Jones, Capers. *The History and Future of Narragansett Bay*. Boca Raton, FL: Universal-Publishers, 2006.

Kupperman, Karen O. *The Jamestown Project*. Cambridge, MA: Harvard University Press, 2009.

Labaree, Benjamin W. *Patriots & Partisans: The Merchants of Newburyport, 1764–1815*. New York: Norton, 1975.

Lawson, Russell M. *The American Plutarch: Jeremy Belknap and the Historian's Dialogue with the Past*. Westport, CT: Praeger, 1998.

———. *The Isles of Shoals the Age of Sail: A Brief History*. Charleston, SC: History Press, 2007.

———. *On the Road Histories: New Hampshire*. Northampton, MA: Interlink Publishing, 2005.

———. *Passaconaway's Realm: Captain John Evans and the Exploration of Mount Washington*. Hanover, NH: University Press of New England, 2002.

———. *The Piscataqua Valley in the Age of Sail: A Brief History*. Charleston, SC: History Press, 2007.

———. *Portsmouth: An Old Town by the Sea*. Charleston, SC: Arcadia Publishing, 2003.
Lewis, Alonzo, and James R. Newhall. *History of Lynn, Essex County, Massachusetts: including Lynnfield, Saugus, Swampscot, and Nahant*. Boston: John L. Shorey, 1865.
Locke, John L. *Sketches of the History of the Town of Camden, Maine*. Hallowell, ME: Masters, Smith & Co., 1859.
Mitchell, John Hanson. *The Paradise of All These Parts*. Boston: Beacon Press, 2008.
Morison, Samuel E. *Builders of the Bay Colony*. Boston: Houghton Mifflin Co., 1930.
Morrison, Peter H. *Architecture of the Popham Colony, 1607–1608: An Archeological Portrait of English Building Practice at the Moment of Settlement*. University of Maine, master's thesis, 2002.
Osgood, Charles S., and Henry M. Batchelder. *Historical Sketch of Salem, 1629–1879*. Salem, MA: Essex Institute, 1879.
Parsons, Langdon B. *History of Rye, New Hampshire*. Concord, NH: Rumford Printing Co., 1905.
Peskin, Lawrence A., and Edmund F. Wehrle. *America and the World: Culture, Commerce, Conflict*. Baltimore: Johns Hopkins University Press, 2012.
Philbrick, Nathaniel. *Mayflower: A Story of Courage, Community, and War*. New York: Viking Penguin, 2006.
Roads, Samuel, Jr. *The History and Traditions of Marblehead*. Boston: Houghton, Mifflin and Company, 1881.
Rutman, Darrett B. *Winthrop's Boston: A Portrait of a Puritan Town, 1630–1649*. New York: W. W. Norton & Co., 1972.
Saltonstall, William G. *Ports of Piscataqua*. Cambridge, MA: Harvard University Press, 1941.
Saugus Iron Works National Historic Site. www.nps.gov/sair/index.htm.
Sawtelle, William O. "Father Pierre Biard, Superior of the Mount Desert Jesuit Mission of Saint Sauveur." *Sprague's Journal of Maine History* 10 (1922).
Sibley, John L. *A History of the Town of Union, in the County of Lincoln, Maine*. Boston: Benjamin Mussey, 1851.
Sullivan, James. *History of the District of Maine*. Boston: Thomas and Andrews, 1795.
Thompson, Winfield M. "In the Isles of Shoals." *The Rudder* 23 (1910).
Varney, George J. *A Gazetteer of the State of Maine*. Boston: B. B. Russell, 1886.
Waters, Thomas F. *Ipswich in the Massachusetts Bay Colony*. Salem, MA: Salem Press, 1905.
Webber, C. H., and W. H. Nevins. *Old Naumkeag: An Historical Sketch of the City of Salem*. Salem, MA: Smith & Co., 1877.
Wheeler, George A. *History of Brunswick, Topsham, and Harpswell, Maine*. Boston: Mudge and Son, 1878.
Whipple, Joseph. *The History of Acadie, Penobscot Bay and River*. Bangor, ME: Peter Edes, 1816.
Whittaker, Robert H. *Land of Lost Content: The Piscataqua River Basin and the Isles of Shoals. The People. Their Dreams. Their History.* Dover, NH: Alan Sutton, 1994.
Williamson, William D. *The History of the State of Maine*. Two Volumes. Hallowell, ME: Glazier, Masters & Smith, 1839.

Woodward, Colin. *The Lobster Coast: Rebels, Rusticators, and the Struggle for a Forgotten Frontier*. New York: Penguin Books, 2004.

EXPLORATION AND SCIENCE

Allen, David Y. "The So-Called Velasco Map: A Case of Forgery?" http://purl.oclc.org/coordinates/a5.htm, 2006.

Baker, Emerson W., et. al. *American Beginnings: Exploration, Culture, and Cartography in the Land of Norumbega*. Lincoln: University of Nebraska Press, 1995.

Bud, Robert, and Deborah J. Varner, editors. *Instruments of Science: An Historical Encyclopedia*. London: The Science Museum, 1998.

Buisseret, David. *The Mapmaker's Quest: Depicting New Worlds in Renaissance Europe*. Oxford: Oxford University Press, 2003.

Fischer, David Hackett. *Champlain's Dream*. Toronto: Vintage Canada, 2009.

Hunter, Douglas. *Half Moon: Henry Hudson and the Voyage that Redrew the Map of the World*. New York: Bloomsbury Press, 2009.

McDermott, James. *Martin Frobisher: Elizabethan Privateer*. New Haven, CT: Yale University Press, 2001.

McKeen, John. "Remarks on the Voyage of George Waymouth, to the Coast of Maine, in 1605." *Collections of the Maine Historical Society*. Volume 5. Portland: Brown Thurston, 1857.

McManis, Douglas R. *European Impressions of the New England Coast, 1497–1620*. University of Chicago, Department of Geography, Research Paper No. 139., 1972.

Morison, Samuel Eliot. *The European Discovery of America: The Northern Voyages, A.D. 500–1600*. New York: Oxford University Press, 1971.

———. *The Great Explorers: The European Discovery of America*. New York: Oxford University Press, 1978.

———. *Samuel de Champlain: Father of New France*. Boston: Little, Brown and Company, 1972.

Nicholls, Mark, and Penry Williams. *Sir Walter Raleigh: In Life and Legend*. London: Continuum, 2011.

Suárez, Thomas. *Shedding the Veil: Mapping the European Discovery of America and the World*. Singapore: World Scientific Publishing Co., 1992.

NATURAL HISTORY

Baird, Spencer F. *The Sea Fisheries of Eastern North America*. Washington, DC: Government Printing Office, 1889.

Foster, Steven, and James A. Duke. *A Field Guide to Medicinal Plants and Herbs of Eastern and Central North America*. Second edition. New York: Houghton Mifflin, 2000.

Friends of Belle Isle Marsh. www.friendsofbelleislemarsh.org.

Lantz, David E. *The Muskrat*. Washington, DC: Government Printing Office, 1910.

LeBreton, Greg T. O., et. al. *Sturgeons and Paddlefish of North America*. Dordrecht, Netherlands: Kluwer Academic Publishers, 2004.
Little, Elbert L. *National Audubon Society Field Guide to North American Trees: Eastern Region*. New York: Alfred A. Knopf, 1980.
Nelson, T. H., et. al. *The Birds of Yorkshire*. Two volumes. London: A. Brown & Sons, 1907.
NOAA Fisheries. Office of Protected Resources. www.nmfs.noaa.gov/pr/species/mammals/cetaceans.
Parker River National Wildlife Refuge: Guide to the Hellcat Interpretive Trail. Washington, DC: U.S. Fish and Wildlife Service, 2006.

SAILING

Baker, William S. *Sloops and Shallops*. Columbia, SC: University of South Carolina Press, 1988.
Blachford, M. *Sailing Directions for the Coasts and Harbours of North America*. London: R. Blachford & Co., 1836.
Norie, J. W. *A Complete Set of Nautical Tables*. London: By the author, 1816.
Office of Coast Survey. www.nauticalcharts.noaa.gov/nsd/cpdownload.htm.
Office of Coast Survey. Historical Map & Chart Collection. http://historicalcharts.noaa.gov.
Office of Coast Survey. National Oceanic and Atmospheric Administration. Nautical Charts & Publications, U.S. Waters, Nautical Chart On-Line Viewer, Atlantic Coast. www.charts.noaa.gov/OnLineViewer/AtlanticCoastViewerTable.shtml.
United States Coast Pilot 1: Atlantic Coast: Eastport to Cape Cod. 43rd edition. Washington, DC: National Ocean Service, 2013.
U.S. Coast and Geodetic Survey. *Atlantic Local Coast Pilot: Sub-Division 5: Cape Small Point to Cape Ann*. Washington, DC: Government Printing Office, 1879.
Young, Albert. *Nautical Dictionary*. Second edition. London: Longman, 1863.

AMERICAN INDIANS

Beals, Charles E. *Passaconaway in the White Mountains*. Boston: Richard G. Badger, 1916.
Calloway, Colin G. *Dawnland Encounters: Indians and Europeans in Northern New England*. Hanover, NH: University Press of New England, 1991.
Clark, Patricia Roberts. *Tribal Names of the Americas*. Jefferson, NC: McFarland & Co., 2009.
Douglas-Lithgow, R. A. *Native American Place Names of Maine, New Hampshire, & Vermont*. Bedford, MA: Applewood Books, 2001.
English, J. S. *Indian Legends of the White Mountains*. Boston: Rand Avery Supply Co., 1915.
Fichter, George. *How to Build an Indian Canoe*. New York: McKay, 1977.
Gyles, John. *Memoirs of the Odd Adventures, Strange Deliverances, &c.* Boston: Kneeland and Green, 1736.
Hardy, Kerry. *Notes on a Lost Flute: A Field Guide to the Wabanaki*. Camden, ME: Down East Books, 2009.

Haviland, William A. *Canoe Indians of Downeast Maine*. Charleston, SC: History Press, 2012.

———. "Mi'kmaqs, Etchemins, and the Original Name of the Bagaduce River." http://williamahaviland.wordpress.com/2013/04/29/mikmaqs-etchemins-and-the-original-name-of-the-bagaduce-river.

Hodge, Frederick W., ed. *Handbook of American Indians North of Mexico*. Washington, DC: Government Printing Office, 1907.

Kinnicutt, Lincoln N. *Indian Names of Places in Plymouth, Middleborough Lakeville and Carver*. Worcester, MA: Commonwealth Press, 1909.

Russell, Howard. *Indian New England Before the Mayflower*. Hanover, NH: University Press of New England, 1980.

Swanton, John R. *Indian Tribes of North America*. Washington, DC: Genealogical Publishing Co., 1952.

Weidensaul, Scott. *The First Frontier: The Forgotten History of Struggle, Savagery, & Endurance in Early America*. New York: Houghton Mifflin Harcourt, 2012.

GENERAL

Brown, Alexander. *The Genesis of the United States*. Two volumes. Boston: Houghton, Mifflin and Co., 1890.

The Christian Register 83 (1904).

The Complete Essays of Montaigne. Translated by Donald M. Frame. Stanford, CA: Stanford University Press, 1958.

Jones, Howard Mumford. *O Strange New World: American Culture: The Formative Years*. New York: Viking Press, 1962.

Kirwin, W. J., et. al. *Dictionary of Newfoundland English*. Second edition. Toronto: University of Toronto Press, 1990.

Perry, William S. *The History of the American Episcopal Church*. Volume 1. Boston: Osgood, 1885.

Plutarch. *Lives of the Noble Grecians and Romans*. Translated by John Dryden. New York: Modern Library, 1932.

Robbins, Kevin C. *City on the Ocean Sea: La Rochelle, 1530–1650: Urban Society, Religion, and Politics on the French Atlantic Frontier*. Leiden: Brill, 1997.

Robertson, John M. *Montaigne and Shakespeare: And Other Essays on Cognate Questions*. London: A. and C. Black, 1909.

The Society for Propagating the Gospel among the Indians and Others in North America, 1787–1887. Boston: University Press, 1887.

Wilcox, Donald J. *In Search of God & Self: Renaissance and Reformation Thought*. Prospect Heights, IL: Waveland Press, 1987.

INDEX

NOTE: Page numbers in *italics* refer to illustrations.